Unrepentant Radical Educator

Unrepentant Radical Educator

The writings of John Gerassi, edited and with interviews by Tony Monchinski

Tony Monchinski
John Gerassi
City University of New York, Queens College

SENSE PUBLISHERS
ROTTERDAM/BOSTON/TAIPEI

A C.I.P. record for this book is available from the Library of Congress.

ISBN: 978-90-8790-799-0 (paperback)
ISBN: 978-90-8790-800-3 (hardback)
ISBN: 978-90-8790-801-0 (e-book)

Published by: Sense Publishers,
P.O. Box 21858, 3001 AW
Rotterdam, The Netherlands
http://www.sensepublishers.com

Printed on acid-free paper

To my students, former, current, and hopefully future
– JG

TABLE OF CONTENTS

INTRODUCTION

When I started attending Queens College in 1990 I was nineteen years old and quite honestly didn't know if I had what it took to be successful in college. I came from a solid working class background in Queens, one of the five boroughs of the city of New York, though all of us who lived in Queens considered Manhattan *the city*, and though we all proudly considered ourselves middle class. My father started out as a bus driver and retired in a supervisory position from the Metropolitan Transportation Association, that august municipal institution perpetually crying fiscal crisis that would send spies in cars to sit outside the homes of its workers who had called in sick; my mother, who continues to work to the present day, was and is a secretary.

I grew up liberal in my Catholicism but conservative in my politics, though I did not recognize such at the time because I mistakenly conceived of the political as relegated to electoral politics. I believed that the United States was an unremitting force for good in the world and the only thing standing in the way of world domination by that evil empire, the Soviet Union (hadn't none other than John Rambo himself teamed up with Afghanistan's muhajadeen "holy warriors" to combat the Soviet menace?). For me, avuncular Ronnie Reagan was the face of this goodness and the epitome of the American Dream. Neither of my parents had gone to college and though I had done well in high school, university loomed before me as a mythical entity, and I wondered if and how I'd fit in, if I'd be able to scrape by.

I chose to go to Queens because it was a commuter college near my house and affordable for my parents. Though I'd no doubt they'd sacrifice to send me to a college out of state or even an Ivy League school in state if I'd wanted, I didn't feel right asking this. My dad encouraged my brother and I to take all of New York City's civil service exams—from police officer to toll booth clerk to firefighter – and we did; I did so in case "this college thing" didn't pan out. Today Jason is a cop and I'm a high school teacher.

I met John Gerassi in my first semester at Queens College. The clock on the wall indicated that the class was about to begin and the desks were filled with students shifting around, waiting for our professor. An older, short balding guy in jeans and a plaid button-down shirt swaggered into class, probably a maintenance man. What had we heard, that if a professor didn't show up within fifteen minutes of the scheduled start of a class we students had the right to get up and leave? The maintenance man approached the teacher's desk in the front of the room and put down some manila folders he carted under one arm. He introduced himself as John Gerassi. *This* was our professor? He began to discuss the course and the topic of that day. Whatever it was, I don't remember. Instead I was intrigued by this character that meandered around the room speaking extemporaneously, one hand resting on his belly, chewing on Stim-U-Dents (he had just quit smoking and kept a bowl of them in his office), answering questions and engaging us students in discussion.

In those first few days, weeks and months, Gerassi spoke of people and places I'd only heard or read about, and many I had not. These were people and places, things and events he'd *known*, he'd *experienced*, he'd *lived* through. Whether he was talking about topics I sort of recognized—Che Guevara, Jean-Paul Sartre, the Vietnam War—or altogether did not—Camilo Torres, *The Battle of Algiers*, the island nation of Palau—Gerassi spoke with such passion and conviction I felt that these were things and people I *should* know about (which is why I have attempted to include some explanatory end notes with the original interviews appearing herein; to provide end-notes for the entire book would have required a second book all its own!) At the time I studied with Gerassi, the United States fought a war against Iraq—the second Gulf War (the first having been between Iraq and Iran in the 80s, something I was largely ignorant of)—and instead of maintaining a patriotic front, Gerassi had the audacity (as I saw it then) to criticize the United States' actions, motives and intentions. He criticized the United States government's support of Columbia and Israel; he openly sympathized with those terrorist Palestinians; he attacked our country's economic system as immoral and its political system as corrupt through and through.

My parents had warned me that college could "change" me. Gerassi was obviously one of these "radical" "political" professors I'd been warned of. Gerassi would go at it with students in class, questioning their assumptions and defending his positions, always in an impassioned manner but never in a condescending or patronizing way. He had us reading people I'd never heard of, Rosa Luxemburg, Andre Malraux, and Jean Bertrand Aristide, and he didn't always agree with them and made sure we knew it. Gerassi is the guy who first got me to read Noam Chomsky, and I think it's an interesting historical aside worth mentioning that in the same February, 1967 issue of *The New York Review of Books* where Chomsky's seminal article *The Responsibility of Intellectuals* first appeared, so did Gerassi's review of a book detailing the American invasion of the Dominican Republic.

I remained guarded and cynical in Gerassi's class. I had to be safe and protect myself from brainwashing. But I also tried to keep an open mind. The things Gerassi was discussing in class, the books he had us read, the documentaries we watched and discussed, these things directly challenged a zeitgeist I took for granted at a time when I didn't know what *zeitgeist* meant (a Western European history survey class would explain that to me). But, ever so slowly, I was starting to think differently. It wasn't so much that I was accepting what Gerassi had to say hook, line and sinker; it was that I was starting to read more and pay attention to the events of the world in a different way. This was no overnight process; I studied with Gerassi all four years as an undergraduate. I was drawn to the man, to the novelty and power of his ideas but also by his personal charisma. Gerassi is an attractive figure not only for his formidable intellect but also for embodying and not trying to hide the foibles of the human condition. In class he would speak about how the United States was not an impartial broker in the Middle East and then discuss his cancer with us, why he preferred European pornography, or how he had lost a bundle down in Atlantic City the weekend before.

In Paulo Freire's language, John Gerassi engages his students in a problem posing education, centered in dialogue, aimed at helping students critically apprehend their realities and achieve *conscientization*. Tito has never been shy about espousing his particular point of view—as I think these essays and interviews make clear—but his is a "pedagogy of the question", encouraging students to critically consider the truths they take for granted. Though Gerassi never backs down from sometimes vociferously supporting his point of view, his is a humane pedagogy. Sarcasm directed towards students, denigration of an ignorance indicative of a naïve-consciousness, and a sesquipedalian vocabulary masquerading as intelligence are all absent from his pedagogy; a pedagogy through which he pursues the "inductive moment," working to bring out his particular moral and political vision, one consonant with Freire's notion of humanization.

Nearly twenty years later I am a different person than I was that first semester in Queens College, a different person than I was even upon our graduation when Queens College alum Jerry Seinfeld addressed us in our tasseled mortar-boards. Individuals and events have come and gone that have helped to shape me and that I like to think I have played my part in shaping. Along the way I enrolled in a PhD program in Political Science at the City University of New York's Graduate Center. It was there, across from the Empire State Building, that I first met Joe Kincheloe. I'd completed all my course work and was taking classes outside the department with professors I wanted to study with, whether they were known to me at the time—like Ira Shor—or not. The Urban Education Department was offering a *Critical Pedagogy* class with some guy named Joe Kincheloe. I Googled Kincheloe, read synopsis' of his books online, and got my hands on a copy of his *Critical Pedagogy Primer*. Then I registered for his class.

Which is how this book in your hands became a possibility. Thanks to Joe, I published my first academic book. And my second. And third and fourth and so on, but that's beside the point. Throughout the years I'd kept in touch with Gerassi, who I now called Tito like all his friends and comrades. This was a guy who's voice and message, I believed and believe, like Paulo Freire's, like Ira Shor's, like Joe Kincheloe's, needs to be heard. And not because they harbor some quaint, solipsistic academic theories, but because they represent—in their writing, in their activism, in their examples—the struggle for human flourishing, for social justice and democracy as a way of life. Gerassi fascinated me on a number of levels, not least of which is his ability to recount a story, and I brought my idea to Joe Kincheloe and he to *Sense* Publishers.

Gerassi's is a voice worth listening to. His life has been spent on the front lines of dissent, in the Movement and in the classroom. He adheres to no party line, is non-dogmatic, and the only absolute he embraces is his commitment to the struggle for a better tomorrow for all men and women. As we put this book together it seemed that Yale University Press came to a similar conclusion: they will be publishing Gerassi's *Conversations with Sartre* in the fall of 2009, in many ways a compliment to his Sartre biography, the only "official" biography Sartre ever authorized.

What you have here is a collection of interviews with and writings by John "Tito" Gerassi. We have chosen to separate the book into three parts. Part I: *The Political Animal*, starts with Gerassi's *Professional Autobiography*. Critical pedagogy holds that everything that occurs in our classrooms and other institutions is political, a view Tito's former boss, publishing magnate Henry Luce, would have been in agreement with. Chapter Two presents an interview between Gerassi and me where he discusses his life and the seeming six degrees of separation that connects him to historical figures from Jean-Paul Sartre to Che Guevara to Ho chi Minh. *The Political Animal* explores Gerassi's revolutionary pedigree and his contributions to the Movement and a struggle that continues today. An earlier version of this interview appeared on the *Cultural Logic* website (http://eserver.org/clogic/).

Camus, Sartre, and Tito's own father, Fernando, figure prominently in our first interview. Hence subsequent chapters focus on each of these men. Chapter Three's *Camus: Dissention or Abstention*, was originally intended as a dissenting chapter to a recent pro-Camus book. When the academic editor of the book saw that Gerassi was taking a critical stance towards Camus—at one point Tito refers to Camus as a "loser" – and questioning his revolutionary commitment, he promptly excluded the piece from his book. Gerassi posits that though Camus and Sartre both championed rebellion as an existential necessity in the face of an inevitable death, Camus' rebellion was an individual's task for the sake of rebellion, whereas Sartre favored revolution through collective strength against concrete situations and institutions of injustice. Renowned painter and anti-fascist Republican warrior in the Spanish Civil War, Fernando Gerassi never made it back to his beloved Spain after the conflict that drove his family from Europe. His son, Tito, returned after Fernando's passing and found a land in the midst of healing. In *When the War is Over...*, Tito recounts his travel to a Spain where the wounds of the war, still fresh, served to unite rather than divide those who had once faced each other across the barricades. This piece first appeared in the now defunct North American version of *Geo*.

Chapters five, six and seven all appeared in a course reader Gerassi put together for his students in 2003, titled *A Dissenter Yells in the Dark*. In *Celebrate our 50th year of life*, Tito makes the case that we may owe our own precarious existence as a species to Julius and Ethel Rosenberg. The chapter is preceded by an unpublished letter-to-the-editor of *The New York Times* penned shortly after the revelation that Ethel Rosenberg was innocent of the charges brought against her and had been wrongly executed by the American government. *Leftists you never talk to*, the sixth chapter, is more than Tito's response to an op-ed piece by *New York Times*' columnist Roger Cohen; it is a message to Americans that we must hold our country and its allies up to the same critical standards as we do other countries. How are we to view Che Guevara's popularity as a t-shirt icon in contemporary times? In *Che, where are you, now that we really need you?*, Tito does more than review Guevara's *Congo Diaries*, he testifies to the revolutionary consciousness and pedagogy of the deed of one man, the likes of which—Gerassi opines – we may very well see more of. This chapter first appeared as a review, with cuts, in the *L.A. Times* in 2002.

The second part of the book opens with the interview *Unrepentant Critical Pedagogy*. Revolutionaries are not born; they are made, and revolutionary consciousness is embraced rather than instilled from beyond. Tito discusses his own education, inside and outside of the formal institutional structure of schooling, from his days as a rowdy student at Rumsey Hall to his dissertation defense with Ralph Milliband, Eric Hobsbawm, and Christopher Hill; his friendships with important figures in critical pedagogy, from Michel Foucault to Herbert Marcuse; his own blacklisting in the late 60s and 70s and his work in universities from France to California to New York City.

What does a critical pedagogy look like on paper? Chapter nine presents Gerassi's *Ideal Syllabus* for an International Politics class, with the caveat that such is always being revised and updated. Chapter ten recounts *The Politics of Playing Poker with James Jones in Paris*, previously unpublished. The piece makes the important point that a true revolution, in the sense of a complete overhaul of a society and its institutions, stems from a vision of the future held by human beings and shared between them in dialogue. Hence, until the barricades are erected, we meet each other in deliberative democratic dialogue, learning from one another in the process of questioning and bolstering our own views and vision. To refuse to talk to someone because they differ from your particular world view is to do oneself and the world a disservice.

In Chapter Eleven, *The Second Death of Jean-Paul Sartre*, Gerassi discusses the attacks on Sartre's person and thought during his lifetime and afterwards. Tito explains the importance of Sartre's thought, which established a dialectic between the subject and object, a demand for agency, action, choice and responsibility, in a world where the relatively privileged succumb to the lure of going along to get along. "Those of us who had no power knew he fought for us and with us," Tito remarks of his close family friend and one of the twentieth century's most important philosophers. This piece first appeared in the July/August 1989 issue of *Tikkun: A Bimonthly Jewish Critique of Politics, Culture, & Society*. Although the relationship isn't explored here or in this book, Sartre and his existentialism play an important part in the history of critical pedagogy and the thought of Paulo Freire.

. Chapter 12, *The US Empire and the Death of Democracy* examines the ways in which the contempt for democracy harbored by America's ruling class plays out in the United States and abroad. In Chapter 13, Tito rebuts accusations of anti-Semitism while arguing for Palestinian rights; a battle that played out on his own Queens College campus and its student newspaper. In Chapter 14, *Will the tears ever stop?*, written the day after the the bombing of the World Trade Center, then reproduced in *A Dissenter Yells in the Dark*, Gerassi contextualizes the events of September 11, 2001. He does so not to let the perpetrators of that dark days' events off the hook, but to historicize and explain the context of their actions so we may act to avoid future 9–11s. Chapter 15, *Revolution by Lifestyle*, after the 1960s and 70s begs the question: what does revolution mean when the counter-culture itself has been commodified, when one can embrace contrarianism as a form of identity politics? *Revolution by Lifestyle* first appeared in *Counter Culture*, a collection of essays edited by Joseph Berke, in 1969. In this essay Tito draws upon what Freire labeled "revolutionary futurity", "announcing" a "possible utopian." Tito shrewdly points out that capitalism's greatest contradiction is that it just doesn't satisfy.

The third part of the book begins with the interview *The Politics of the Written Word and the World*. Gerassi discusses the politics of publishing and writing, from his creation of propaganda as a Green Beret for the United States Army in the Korean War to Putnam's putting the kibosh on his and Frank Browning's *The American Way of Crime*; from being "bumped down" to the Latin American bureau at *Time Magazine* after getting on the wrong side of Henry Luce's aesthetic preferences, to Che Guevara's role in the creation of Tito's best-selling *The Great Fear in Latin America*.

Murder Incorporated, a review of Ralph Nader's *Unsafe at Any Speed*, first appeared in *Liberation* Magazine in its January 1966 issue. It appears here in chapter seventeen, with Tito providing a brief preface where he discusses the strengths and shortcomings of Nader himself. Chapter eighteen presents Gerassi's one-act play, *The Cell*. Following the Cuban Revolution, two men find themselves together in a prison cell awaiting their execution at dawn. One is a former torturer, cop, and thug for the Batista dictatorship; the other, a university professor, supported Castro and the rebels but then turned against them. Now both men reconsider their ideals in the face of mortality. Appearing here as chapter nineteen, *Whitman and Speck Against Society* first saw print in the May 1967 issue of *Story*. Its summation that "a society deserves the madmen it breeds," stands true to this day and should serve as a caution if only we'd let it.

Chapter Twenty, *An Open Letter to Europeans*, was written in 2002. Before the escape of Osama Bin Laden, before the revelation of the full horrors of Guantanamo Bay and Abu Gahraib, of kidnappings called "rendition" and mercenaries "private contractors", Tito asked Europeans in his subtitle, *Why are you in a hurry to commit suicide?* He warned that imperial expansion and capitalist greed threatened war not only against Iraq but also, potentially, against America's allies across the Atlantic. Chapter Twenty-One, The End of Our Constitution, details how the rich and powerful do what they want, when they want, and the ways their lackeys in academia support their actions. Originally written as an introduction to his novel, The Anachronists, Tito has updated the piece following the 2008 presidential election, and thus ends with an indirect though slim hope for the future.

Despite the protestations of individuals from David Horowitz to Michael Berube and websites from *Campus Watch* to *Rate My Professor*, radical professors appear to be a dying breed as *New York Times* correspondent Patricia Cohen (08) explains that the "60s begin to fade" on university campuses. Allaying my parents' fears, professors like John Gerassi and Joe Kincheloe did not make me hate America. If anything they helped spark within me a critical inquiry of and nuanced appreciation for the country I live in and want to help make better. Today I can comprehend the difference between the American people, their capacity for good and innovation, and the crimes of the American government. I can appreciate American heroes like Dorothy Day, Vito Marcantonio, and Leonard Weinglass and remain critical of villains in high and low office. I am able to see myself as one voice in a country of many, and my country as one in a world of many. Because of professors like John Gerassi and Joe Kincheloe I can envision a better tomorrow and understand the importance of struggling for that vision—in society, in theory, and in my classroom.

PART I: THE POLITICAL ANIMAL

CHAPTER ONE

A PROFESSIONAL AUTOBIOGRAPHY

"I hear you are coming aboard," he said in his almost feminine voice. He was sitting stiffly behind a huge mahogany moon-shaped desk, staring at a black blotter. There were two equally polished wooden boxes at either end of his desk, marked "in" and "out". Both were empty.

"Yes, sir," I replied, trying to be timid.

"You should know," he went on still staring at his desk, "that we here at Time believe that objectivity is neither feasible nor desirable." Then looking up and fixing my eyes, he said as firmly as his meek voice would let him, "Any questions?"

"No sir," I replied, camouflaging my deep voice in my arrogant fear of intimidating him.

"Welcome aboard, Mr. Gerassi," he mumbled, finally smiling a bit.

Henry Luce, owner of Time, Life, Fortune and Sports Illustrated, had just made me a Time editor. After three months of writing internal kudos for Time-Life's internal house organ, FYI, and another three months manufacturing tidbits for the now-defunct Milestones and Miscellany columns, showing my prowess at Time-style, I was in, a permanent, at 24 one of the youngest editors on record.

My first slot was No. 3 art critic (called editor), and I loved it. Since my father was then a fairly well-known abstract painter, I knew many of his colleagues, and enjoyed running out (on bottomless expense accounts) to the Hamptons (Pollock, Ossorio, De Kooning) or Roxbury (Alexander Calder who had financed our family's first decade in the US) to interview the mostly odd-balls I already knew well and liked immensely (My old man, I think, or I feel guilty, resented the fact that I never did a story on him).

After a year I was informed that my salary would increase by a then-hefty $1500 and I was invited (via a printed card) to have dinner with the Luces at their home in Greenwich, Connecticut. Brash and conceited, I decided I would be modest and told no one, so I was somewhat disappointed when the limousine came to pick me up and I found two other writers, hired at about the same time as I, already comfortably ensconced with drinks in their hands.

The topic of art came up only twice during this almost formal dinner. Luce asked me what I thought of Andrew Wyeth. "Slick and sentimental" I said. And Jackson Pollock? "America's greatest painter."

When I next showed up for work, some new face scoffed at me from behind my desk. "You're in Latin America," he informed me. I barged into the senior editor's office to complain. "You schmuck," Gordon Manning shouted before I said a word. "You had dinner with Luce, right? Automatic for anyone who becomes permanent after a year. And he asked you what you thought of Wyeth, right? The only painter he likes! And then Pollock, right? The only painter he hates! Idiot. Why didn't you tell me? I would have told you what to say. Luce never reads the art column. You would have had a knock for life."

Actually, that saved my life. I was put into Latin America because I spoke Spanish. I didn't know the difference between Uruguay and Paraguay. But I read, I traveled and I learned. Boy did I.

The week at Time started with a conference, where the point of every story was spelled out – never according to facts, always according to ideology, Time's ideology, which was always conservative, always pro-business, always based on the absolute tenet that the US was the best country in the world and anyone who disagreed was either a sicko or an enemy.

I also learned that the key to any story was the lead. "Not since the battle of Agincourt..." was touted as the best example. And then the kicker, that last sentence. In between one could say almost anything, as 79 percent of Time readers, I was told, only read the first and last paragraphs.

To make that kicker "zing," I learned one could make up quotes. In fact, I soon discovered that every unattributed quote was made up. "As one official said..." "As one investigator revealed..." Or the famous one: On a story about Bolivia, the editor couldn't come up with a factual "zing." So he wrote that one US embassy official had said that Bolivia is an illogical country; it should be cut in four and given to its neighbors. The resulting anti-American riot caused scores to be mowed down by the police.

But I didn't quit. Yes, I sold out. The salary was very fat and I could save it all, as I lived off the expense account. So, like my colleagues, at least those who were liberal, I continued to lie. For a couple of years more, anyway.

Then Fidel Castro rounded up the Batista torturers and put them on trial. We had supported Castro as a nice "bourgeois reformer". But now, my senior editor, Bill Forbis, a real gentleman who always had problems with his conscience, called me to his office and told me, "We have to switch gears on Castro. We have to denounce those trials."

"But," said I, "even our correspondent, whom we know is a CIA contract agent, tells us that those being tried are scum bags who really did torture scores of people and that by making the trials a public shindig he's saving Cuba from a blood bath of vengeance."

"I know," Forbis retorted obviously in pain, "but it proves that Fidel is serious. That means he'll discover that behind Batista's corruption, repression and murders is the US, especially the big US companies, like United Fruit and IT&T. He'll expropriate them, and Washington will yell commie bastard. So we're going to yell first." (Years later I ran into Forbis' widow in Hawaii. "That was the beginning of the end," she told me, "he eventually died from his own moral corruption.")

I called Herbert Matthews who was still at the New York Times and asked if I could switch. Mathews had a long history of writing for the good guys, dating back to the Spanish Civil War of 1936–39, where he had met my old man, a commander at the battle of Guadalajara, the most magnificent victory of the anti-fascists.

Mathews had also supported Castro. And continued to do so even after Fidel conned him. Matthews had been the first US reporter to trek up the Sierra Maestra to interview him. While they talked, Camilo Cienfuegos barged in and boasted "Column 3 reporting back, all safe." Five minutes later Che Guevara showed up: "Total success comandante, but Xavier and El Gordo were wounded; they'll survive though." A few minutes later, Raul Castro interrupted the interview to report his column too had also made it back safely. Naturally, when Mathews wrote up the story, he predicted total victory for the barbudos, which is what Fidel wanted. There were no such columns at the time, just a handful of nuts who believed in Fidel.

"Don't think it'll be much better here," Mathews warned me, "but at least you won't have to make up your facts." I didn't, but my editors did.

In 1961, for example, Jack Kennedy hoped to gain Latin America's friendship by offering to help the area develop with lots of US aid. So a conference, the Alliance for Progress, was scheduled for Punta del Este, a fashionable resort three hours up the coast from Uruguay's capital of Montevideo. Every important diplomat – and correspondent – was scheduled to appear, and the New York Times sent three correspondents: Tad Szulc, then Latin America's bureau chief; Juan de Onis, top Times newshound in Brazil; and lowly little me, stationed already in Uruguay.

"You cover Che," Tad had told me, mainly because he and Juan knew that Guevara, Cuba's representative to the conference, never talked to "the imperialist press."

Che arrived late. I went to the Montevideo airport to try to meet him, but thousands of Uruguayan students were already there, and they demanded he speak at the university before he went up to Punta del Este. He accepted, and I followed.

The auditorium was so full that loudspeakers had to be set up outside and the crowds soared into the thousands. A bunch of anti-Castro Cuban exiles showed up and a fist fight erupted just as Che walked out into the esplanade. A Uruguayan policeman, who was next to Che, tried to break up the melee by firing his pistol in the air. I was on the cop's other side. I saw exactly what happened.

As I told the New York Times, filing my story through Press Wireless barely twenty minutes later, the officer's shot hit the main auditorium's overhang roof and ricocheted into one of the demonstrators, a Cuban employee of USIS (United States Information Service), killing him.

No other journalist saw what happened; they were all at Punta del Este. In my file I said (in an "fyi" aside) that I was there and that I saw the incident.

Next day, the New York Times ran a story from the Associated Press telling the world that a pro-Castro demonstrator had killed an employee of the American Embassy, a story issued by the US embassy six hours after I had sent mine. The AP version, an embassy clone, was written by a reporter who had actually asked me when I arrived at Punta del Este what had really happened. The Times knew he had not been there.

So again I quit. I wrote an article called "Alliance for Regress" which I sent to some Time buddies who were trying to launch their own magazine. The magazine failed to emerge, but my pals gave my piece to various book editors without telling me and a few weeks later I received the following telegram:

Have just read your Alliance for Regress article. Please answer by prepaid cable the following:
1. Can you write 85,000 words or more on the subject?
2. How much money do you need to visit every Latin American country and give an "I was there" feel to each?
3. Who the hell are you?

It was sent by Peter Ritner, an extremely conservative civil libertarian and Managing Editor of Macmillan, who never agreed with a single word I wrote (or said) but always defended my right to say it – including in court (with Macmillan lawyers) since we were sued for libel by three companies which did not like the fact that I reported that they systematically cheated their host Latin American countries of millions in unreported remitted income. I had the facts; we always won. Eventually the paper edition of my book, *The Great Fear in Latin America*, sold more copies (198,000) than all other books on the subject combined. (But at 5 cents a copy of royalties I never made ten grand).

Still, the Punta del Este conference changed my life, yet once again, this time into an academic. Thanks to Che. Ordered to cover him, I got nowhere, as the big boys had figured. Che just wouldn't talk to "anyone from the imperialist press". So in the dining room of the cheap hotel he (and therefore I too) had checked into, I sat alone, while he ate with a dozen Latin American newsmen, obviously mostly good friends.

Then, on the third day, Rogelio Garcia Lupo, a journalist for La Prensa of Buenos Aires and an old Che buddy (they had both been student militants in Tacuara, an anti-imperialist organization) arrived and embraced his old pal. As he turned to sit next to Che, he spotted me, and rushed over to greet me as we too were good friends. "You know this gringo," Che asked, "he works for the imperialist press." El pajarito, as we called Rogelio, laughed. "And me?" he quipped, "I work for La Prensa which is ten times worse."

From then on I always sat at Che's table. And before the conference broke up, he made the other journalists promise to show me "what gringo newsmen never see, or never want to."

They are all listed in the acknowledgement sections of *The Great Fear*. Many became good friends, including Gregorio Selser, who documented Sandino's murder by Somoza senior in a "truce" plot organized by the US ambassador Henry Bliss Lane; Rodolfo Walsh, author of the fabulous *Operacion Masacre*, who was disappeared by the Argentine fascists; Jayme Dantas and Mario Planet who got crushed by Time for being honest; Carlos Fuentes, a rich man's novelist who retains troubling ties to the US; Gabriel Marquez, who had not yet been able to find a publisher for *Hundred Years of Solitude*, which we all read in manuscript form; "El Negro" Jorquera, who became President Allende's press secretary and died with him defending democracy; and Senator Salomon Corbalan Gonzalez, head of Chile's combative Socialist Party, an absolutely adorable genuine democrat who, because of that, was doomed by Henry Kissinger's henchmen.

Once the US war on the people of Vietnam began, it became harder and harder to tell the other side's story. About anything. Gordon Manning was now at Newsweek; he hired me for the foreign news section, and encouraged me to fight to tell it as it is. But after Newsweek's owner Phil Graham, who supported us "young Turks," shot himself in his bathtub, none of us could do much, even though we knew that Kermit Lanzner, the Managing Editor, would never fire us. Instead, he offered me peace – art critic. I had done a full circle.

I then left Newsweek to teach journalism at NYU, but when I went to North Vietnam as a member of the first investigating committee of the International War Crimes Tribunal, the administration denounced me as a scofflaw. Though the department supported me and the administration finally said it would not fire me, it was too late: I had accepted a post at San Francisco State.

Not for long. I got fired there the very first semester, December 6, 1966, when I joined the students' anti-war demonstrations. Accused of being the leader (not at all true, I sided with the students whom I respected), I was arrested and jailed for "inciting civil insurrection" (which my lawyer, the great "movement" stalwart Charlie Garry got it laughed out of court). But, of course, I was blacklisted – from academia as well as journalism. My dissident days were over, at least for a few years.

I went to teach at the university of Paris, got my PhD at the London School of Economics and started writing Jean-Paul Sartre's political biography. But in 1976, the teachers' union lawyers won my case and got me reinstated, so I started it all up again, teaching first at UC Irvine, then at Queens College in New York. And ever since, I keep telling my students what Henry Luce told me when I came back from the Korean war and got my first real job. "Objectivity is neither feasible nor desirable."

"Those were the only true words I ever heard Time bosses spout," I tell my students. "No one can be totally objective. Rene Descartes wanted to clean the table, *tabula rasa*, and start fresh. *Cogito ergo sum*, 'I think, therefore I am,' he pontificated. But think a moment: how many years of living, of experiences before you can really understand the connector 'therefore'?"

"There are no clean tables in life. By the time you think, you have been bombarded by years of living. Your judgments, if you are poor in capitalist America, non-white in racist America, a female in male-dominated America, will never be the same as those of a Rockefeller, a Bushie, or even me. And the others, those who have the money, the top jobs, the great contacts, those who can snort cocaine and know they will never go to jail, those who can cheat their employees out of their retirement funds while putting millions (now it's billions) into their own coffers, those are the ones who have all the microphones."

"So don't talk to me about objectivity. Their objectivity is for them, not for you. Mine is against them. I shall never be a hypocrite and tell you on the one hand this but on the other that. You want their answer to my diatribes? Read their newspapers, the News, the Times, their magazines, Time, Newsweek, US News and World Report, whatever, or view their so- called television news. They will all say the same. So I will never give you their opinion; if you want them, listen to their loudspeakers. Any loudspeakers. We don't have any."

Ever since, still today as a decrepit old geezer of 78 who refuses to retire, I bark at those loudspeakers, I repeat *ad nausea* to my students, the only way to sleep well, to be genuinely happy, is to keep fighting, whichever way you can, in street demos, in your classes, in your confrontations with their police, yes, to keep fighting those bastards.

CHAPTER TWO

THE POLITICAL ANIMAL

INTERVIEW

John "Tito" Gerassi was born in France in July 1931, and came to the US with his father and mother in 1940. Tito has worn many hats: journalist, educator (among others at: San Francisco State; The University of Paris (XII, Vincennes), the JFK Institute of the Free University of Berlin; UC Irvine, Bard College and since 1980 the Graduate Center and Queens College of the City University of New York). He is author of such works as *The Great Fear in Latin America; The Boys of Boise, The Premature Antifascists*, the only authorized biography of Jean-Paul Sartre, *Hated Conscience of His Century*, which Sartre considered a continuation of *his* own autobiography, and *Conversation with Jean-Paul Sartre*, to be published by Yale University Press in the Fall of 2009. A raconteur, activist and father, his life personifies the personal as political and the political as personal.

Tony Monchinski: How does one go about becoming Jean-Paul Sartre's[1] "non-god son," which even he claimed you were?

John Gerassi: My father, Fernando Gerassi, an accomplished painter and a Sephardic Jew[2], and my mother, Stepha Awdykowicz, an Ukrainian writer, were Sartre and Simone de Beauvoir's[3] best friends prior to the Spanish Civil War of 1936–39. To hone his skills, Fernando had spent his youth copying Velasquez[4] painting at the Prado Museum[5], and often returned to Madrid or Barcelona, his favorite city, whenever he got depressed in Paris, and the Sartre-Beauvoir couple often visited him there. In '31, while he was running through the streets to help bring down the king and establish a Republic, my mother got pregnant. But fearing a new world war with amazing prescience, my father sent her to France for an abortion, her fourth. She had wanted a child very badly; so she took the occasion to lie to him, telling him that the doctor said it was too late.

So on July 12, 1931, Sartre, Beauvoir and practically all of Montparnasse artists and writers were waiting for my birth at the café La Closerie des Lilas, across from the Clinique Tarnier, which was then a birth clinic[6]. Every now and then my father would rush upstairs to find out if I was born, and each time would come back dejected. "Have another drink," his pals, Andre Breton or Marc Chagall or Giacometti[7] or Beauvoir, who wrote about the incident in her memoirs, would coax him, and eventually he passed out. Sartre, arriving from Le Havre where he was teaching, hence perfectly sober, told whoever was still more or less lucid that he would go up to see and when he came up I was born. So my mother called me Jean-Paul in his honor. Once sober, my father yelled "No name with a draft in the middle for my son." So Jean-Paul became Jean, Juan in Spanish, nicknamed Juanito, ergo *Tito*. Sartre was an atheist; hence my "non-god father."

Monchinski: How did your father know Sartre?

Gerassi: My mother had been placed in a convent in Llov after her father died of the Spanish flu in 1918, but she couldn't stand it, and had run away to Vienna when she was only 15, ending up a feminist writer at 16. Often arrested there, she eventually got to Germany; where she met Alban Berg[8] and they ended up living together in a house in Berlin that was only for musicians. Meanwhile my uncle, my father's brother, wanted to be a musician, and he lived in that same house. So when my father, who was studying philosophy[9] at that time with Cassirer in Berlin (then with Husserl in Freiburg), visited that house he noticed Stepha and eventually hooked up with her in Paris after she had left Alban Berg. She had registered at the Sorbonne and there had met Simone de Beauvoir. They had become very good friends to the point that she taught Beauvoir how to dress and clean her nails, "in order to pick up men," as Beauvoir admitted in her memoirs.

My father, meanwhile, was having an affair with Beauvoir's sister, Poupette[10], who introduced him to her sister and she then in turn introduced him to Sartre who had become Beauvoir's lover. My parents and the Sartre-Beauvoir couple had an affinity and stayed friends. But in 1945 Sartre came to America and immediately went to see my father who asked him if it was true that he had been a collaborationist during the war, which was then rumored in the French circle in New York. Sartre became very insulted. So their relationship was never reestablished as profoundly as it had been before the war. But it *was* between Beauvoir and my mother, which continued until Beauvoir's death (1989).

Monchinski: In *Hated Conscience of His Century* you compare your father, Fernando, and Sartre. "Fernando was intolerant, loud and proud, sure of himself and of his judgments, very angry and very loyal, flamboyant and charismatic. Sartre (in 1929) was cool and collected, equally sure and proud, but careful and calculating" (1989: 15–16). How did each man influence you and do you still feel that influence today?

Gerassi: When I was young I admired Sartre because he was a writer and I wanted to be a writer. But I couldn't read his philosophy. As a young man, say 16, I was a little bit dogmatic, a Marxist, and I couldn't reconcile his notion of the Project with Marxism. In 1954, I went to France to see Sartre and told him I was writing a dissertation on him. We started talking at length, then he quipped: "You seem to be very critical of my philosophy, why do you want to do it?" I replied that I was both an existentialist and a Marxist in my divided head, but I didn't think that he could reconcile the Project with Marxism. He was then in the process of trying to link the two, and exclaimed, *"That's exactly* my problem!" We then had a very close relationship.

My father's influence was much more as a man of action and as a moral man. The fact that my father would give up his life, his livelihood, the best part of his life when he was the most successful, because by 1936 he had really made it, he was exhibiting with Picasso, being quoted and reviewed everywhere, he was really hot, and painting like mad, when, in July 1936, Andre Malraux[11] came to the café to tell him that the Spanish Civil War had started. He was sitting at a table with Sartre and they were talking when he got up and went from the café directly to Spain, asking Sartre to take me home because he was babysitting me at the café (my mother was working).

That kind of behavior by my father always made me want his approval, which he never gave me. That is to say, my father was incapable of giving a compliment. He would criticize, and you would learn after awhile that if he didn't criticize *that* was a compliment, but he couldn't say *well done*. He also never told me he loved me. On his deathbed one day, he called me in, 1974 in Philadelphia, the last operation at the University of Philadelphia for cancer; he called me in and asked my mother to leave, that he wanted to talk to me privately. "I want to apologize for my life," he said. "I'm very sorry I never said that I loved you; I never gave you the compliments. I realize now that that was terrible."

Monchinski: "Our friendship was never easy," Sartre wrote to Camus[12] in 1952, "but I'm going to miss it." "What should I do?" mused Camus, "Go smash his face in? The guys too small." Simone de Beauvoir confides to you (1989:181) that Sartre may have been a bit jealous of Camus. Yet Olga Kosakiewicz[13] claims that Sartre broke with people like Camus because he "didn't like the way they lived or loved or whom they loved or simply the manner in which they talked" (1989:181). To what do you attribute the break between Sartre and Camus? How much of it was political and how much of it was personal?

Gerassi: The first break or cooling off was like Olga said, Sartre would judge how people behaved, especially if they did so with people he respected. And Camus was a ladies' man. He would seduce women and then dump them. Sartre didn't judge that until it was done with someone he admired very greatly, the existentialist singer Juliette Greco[14]. Camus seduced her in such a way that this woman thought that this was going to be the love of her life. Then he dumped her. That was the first real break. Sartre was a moralist, despite the fact that he hated moralists and condemned moralists. You know, he really thought it was terrible for my father to have "deflowered" Poupette in a closet; he'd make those kind of judgments.

Afterwards Camus came to be seen as a defender of imperialism, even if indirectly. He was a *pied noir*[15], came from Algeria and could not make a statement in favor of Algerian Independence. Sartre, on the other hand, was very active in helping the Algerian independence.

The big feud came out in the open with the publication of *The Rebel*. Sartre read *The Rebel* and said it was terrible, politically, but he was a friend of Camus' so he couldn't do the review for *Les Temps Modernes*. Sartre asked Francis Jeanson to review it. Jeanson read it and was very, very upset because he said it was a terrible book politically. He said to Sartre, "Look, I cannot praise this book." Sartre said "Hey, I gave it to you, you do the review the way you feel, don't worry about anything else." So Jeanson attacked *The Rebel*.

Camus responded by writing to Sartre instead of writing to Jeanson and instead of addressing him *Dear Sartre* he wrote "To the editor." Then Sartre answered a devastating attack, in which the main point is, before you can criticize the working class or the communist party, you have to know what it is to be poor and struggling all the time for just a decent living, especially in a country where there is so much divergence between the rich and the poor.

Monchinski: Did you and Sartre ever clash over morality?

Gerassi: Sartre had a great deal of difficulty agreeing with himself. When he took a particular position, something always happened to contradict it. For example, Sartre was in favor of stopping in any way possible the exploitation of poor people; on the other hand, how do you stop this? Does it mean that you resort to violence and execute people? This type of question caused Sartre to hesitate. He said "Yes, you could use violence but only in answer to violence." What happens then to the ones who exploit without the overt trappings of violence, without guns and torture? For example, the ones who carry out violence through the market. Sartre said "Yes, that's violence." Well then, do you fight that violence with violence? Do you take these greedy Wall Street bastards, line them up against the wall and shoot them? Sartre would say, "No!"

These types of conflicts led to the fact that he could not in good conscience publish a morality that was universal. The ethical books that have been published in his name since his death take a very specific incident and explores it. Take the execution of the Rosenbergs[16], for example; Sartre wrote that to execute anyone for being dedicated to the well being of the world is fascism. Well, what about intention? It would seem Mussolini genuinely thought in the beginning that he was going to set up a corporatist system that would help the poor, but he ended up a fascist. What about his methods—the brown shirts, the coup? Can you condemn the executions that the Spanish Republicans carried out against Franco's thugs?

Sartre could never find the right formula. I accept that we live in a schizophrenic society. For example, I was against the Cubans helping the Somalians fight the Eritreans. The Eritreans were a liberation front, they wanted their independence and I favored that. But at the same time Somalia was correct in combating American imperialism in Ethiopia. You have to say, "Yes, what the Cubans are doing in one place is good but what they're doing in another is bad," and be reconciled to living that sort of schizophrenic existence.

Monchinski: The US Government, although it tried, failed to devastate the Gerassi family. Attorney General Bobby Kennedy sent your family a letter apologizing "in the name of America" after it was brought to his attention that the CIA, masquerading as Immigration officials, had been harassing your family for 20 years. What were they trying to accomplish?

Gerassi: We came to the United States under fake diplomatic passports that my father had gotten from Porfirio Rubirosa. Rubirosa was the son-in-law of Rafael Trujillo[17]. My father had met him playing poker. When we were rushing out of Paris because the Germans were coming, Rubirosa made Fernando the ambassador from the Dominican Republic, gave him the official stamp. Fernando, in turn, gave 8,000 passports to Spanish Republicans, Jews, whoever he could help, before the Germans caught up, and we left.

My parents came to America as Dominican diplomats. When the US joined World War II they asked my father to join the OSS[18]. He served with the OSS in Latin America and then they sent him via submarine to Spain to set up an underground. OSS head General Bull Donovan[19] already knew the US was going to attack the Germans in North Africa and there was a possibility that Franco would allow the Germans to cross Spain to attack Gibraltar. So, my father's mission was to set up an underground in Spain and prepare to blow up all the bridges and roads. At the end of the war he got this medal and a commendation from Donovan for having made the African landing possible. But he still couldn't work because he was still not legal in the United States.

My mom and dad were limited by Immigration to a 25-mile radius around their Vermont neighborhood and the local postmaster was deputized by Immigration. To travel they needed permission. Periodically two Immigration officials would come and talk to my father, "Did you know this, did you know that?" He would never talk to them. He kept trying to schedule an immigration trial. The trials would get scheduled and then cancelled at the last minute in the name of national security. Finally Abe Fortas[20], a friend, went to immigration, which told him they did not have our family file, the CIA had it!

So that's how Fortas and then my family found out that the Postmaster and all those immigration people were really CIA agents; they were trying to blackmail my father into joining the CIA. Fortas carried the whole file to Bobby Kennedy and Kennedy had LBJ make my parents citizens by decree and Bobby apologized in the name of America.

Monchinski: How do you account for the Camelot myths which have grown up around John F. Kennedy?

Gerassi: The reason people thought Kennedy was so great, much like Reagan, was not because of his ideas, but because of his personality, his personal charm. Let's face it: Kennedy was a Hawk, basically an arch-conservative who thought the United States was the greatest country in the world and therefore had a right to impose its will on those who didn't agree with it. But Kennedy had one admirable characteristic and that was his willingness to listen to the opposition. The great French left-wing correspondent, K.S. Karol, who wrote for the Parisian magazine, *Le Nouvel Observateur*, came to Kennedy and during an interview mentioned his next stop was Cuba where he would talk with Castro. Karol served as a line of communication between Kennedy and Castro, an open exchange that Castro found very profitable. Perhaps something would have come of that if Kennedy hadn't been killed.

During the first Kennedy campaign for President he traveled by bus and had a bus for the press. I was on that press bus. When Kennedy stopped to sleep somewhere, like at a friend's house, he was ushered off to the bedrooms. We in the press could all chip in and rent hotel rooms somewhere or sleep on the floor of whatever house was hosting Kennedy. Most of the reporters were very young, which meant that our backs were sturdy, so we often slept on the floor. One time in the middle of the night when I just happened to be lying there awake, a Kennedy reporter came into the room and roused a young, attractive, female reporter. I heard him mention to her that she was invited to Kennedy's bedroom. She smiled and she went.

Monchinski: Your history in journalism includes reporting for *Time*, *Newsweek*, and *The New York Times*. When you were an editor at *Time* magazine, its owner, Henry Luce[21], told you "*We here at* Time *believe that objectivity is neither feasible nor desirable. Any questions?*" How do you feel about journalism today in this new millennium with increasing corporate hegemony of the media?

Gerassi: It was almost as bad then as it is now except that people didn't realize it as much. At *Time* magazine and *Newsweek*, every single story that we writers would write was first decided at a policy session where the angle (politically) to be taken was decided. At the *New York Times* it was even worse, because they would either edit your story to say the exact opposite of what you were saying or they would kill your story.

Here's an example. In 1961 at the Punta del Este Conference in Uruguay [from which emerged the Alliance for Progress] Cuba sent as its delegate Che Guevara[22]. *The New York Times* told me to cover Che. So I went to the airport where hundreds of students demanded he first go to the university to make a speech. I was the only American correspondent there, all the others having gone on to Punta del Este ninety miles away.

When we came out of the university there was a demonstration of anti-Castro Cubans who were trying to get close to Che. This policeman takes his gun and shoots in the air. The bullet ricochets off an overhang and hits one of the guys coming forward, a Cuban working for USIS. In my dispatch to the *New York Times*, I explained exactly what had happened and said *FYI: main witness is me, I was there*. But the article that ran was the official article USIS put out, that in a confrontation between pro-Castro and anti-Castro forces there was a fight and an employee of the US embassy was killed by a pro-Castro guy. The *New York Times* wouldn't even acknowledge that there might be two stories.

At *Newsweek* Phil Graham was trying to make it into a more liberal magazine, hiring all sorts of people that were on the left. For a while we had great freedom and wrote tremendous things. After Graham's suicide *Newsweek* became like every other newsmagazine. I was writing a favorable piece on Ralph Nader's[23] *Unsafe at any Speed.* Kermit Lansner, then managing editor, said, "we can't do that, Nader attacks General Motors by name, a company that gives us millions of dollars a year in advertisement."

So, I learned, on the job, that there is no such thing as integrity in mainstream American journalism. Where there is integrity you can't make a living. You can't make a living being a full time journalist for *The Nation* or *Z magazine.*

Monchinski: The CIA once poisoned you while you were dining with Fidel Castro. What were the circumstances behind that?

Gerassi: I learned during the Church committee hearings[24] that the CIA hired the Mafia to try to kill Castro. The mob was doing all sorts of crazy things, like giving Castro a book with very thin pages that were coated in arsenic so that he would have to lick his fingers when he went to turn the pages. But they chose the *Little Red Book of Mao TseTung* which Castro would never read anyway!

They learned that seven members of the Latin American press were going to have lunch with Fidel and one of the seven was me, from *Newsweek* (1964). The first course was shrimp salad, and as Fidel was scooping this shrimp with his fork he was talking and talking and talking and the shrimps kept falling back on his plate. He would scoop up a new forkful but keep talking until instead of eating it until, finally, the waiter showed up and Fidel saw we had all finished eating, so he let the waiter take his too though he had not touched his food.

On the ride back to where I was staying I realized I was very sick and my driver took me to a hospital. I passed out, came to a few hours later. The most beautiful woman I've ever seen in my life was standing above me: my nurse, dressed in white with a .45 above the white, and saying, "You are alive thanks to Russian medicine." In the anteroom all the six other guys were there, ill, but none of us got killed.

In the Church committee hearings it turned out that poisoning was another gimmick of the mafioso Rosselli[25] to try and kill Castro. What it did to me though is it made me allergic to shellfish from then on since my body used all its anti-bodies to fight the poison. A Movement lawyer tried to sue the CIA but the judge at the time said we cannot sue the CIA since it wasn't an official CIA policy, but we could sue the CIA officer who gave that order and of course we didn't know who that was, and Rosselli had been assassinated by then.

Monchinski: Camus wrote that he imagined Sisyphus[26] happy, even if he was never to succeed in his task, for "the struggle itself towards the heights is enough to fill a man's heart." Sartre wrote: "Will socialism, as such, ever come about? I know nothing about it. All I know is that I'm going to do everything in my power to bring it about. Beyond that, I can't count on anything" (1989: 31).

When you look at the left today, after all its been through – the hope-filled 60s, the greed dominated 80s, the apathetic 90s – do you find it easy to be pessimistic or does optimism still fuel you? Are we all engaged in "empty gestures" and should we be sated with "the struggle itself towards the heights"?

Gerassi: The gestures are not empty for individuals. Certainly in my life the happiest moments were in the Movement, even though I got arrested and bopped bopped on the head, hit hard by a cop on my lower spine, which has caused my spinal stenosis today, and exiled because I couldn't work. I was literally on a black list[27] from '67 until I won it in court in '76.

Nevertheless, that period, when we felt meaningful, was very fulfilling. It seems very hard to me today to have that attitude. Today many of us from the movement and the young as well – though *not* the ones in Seattle or Washington[28] – seem to feel we have lost. Certainly many of the older ones, the 60s generation, seem to think that nothing is going to change in our lifetime; whereas in the 60s, although it wasn't really true that all of us expected the revolution to come tomorrow, nevertheless we saw positive changes.

Abbie [Hoffman][29] and I had these discussions and he would always say, "You have to stop thinking about reaching the goal out there somewhere but concentrate on the goal of struggling with your brothers and sisters to achieve benefits here and now on the path" to the goal. The struggle is a journey, not a destination.

People have always been struck by how nice conservatives can be and how rude some leftists can be. My response to that is that people who are on the left live in a constant state of perpetual defeat and frustration. It's very hard to be nice. For conservatives it's easy to be nice because they win. I think it's much more difficult to be a leftist today, especially in a situation where you can be bought off so easily because chances are if you are educated and have a skill of some kind, which most activists do have, you can end up selling out to Silicon Valley or god knows where. It was very easy to be at *Time* and *Newsweek*. It was very hard for me to quit at the time. The status quo has its benefits.

Monchinski: You were on the front lines of the Movement as an academic. Has the academic left today entrenched itself in theory to the detriment of action?

Gerassi: Yes. The French academics have turned right wing, in great part because they're Jewish and they have allowed their support of Israel to dominate their way of thinking. I have people like Bernard-Henri Levy[30] in mind. Levy is an unbelievably terrible thinker—he's not a thinker at all; I shouldn't use that word. But he's admired by the French press. His reason for success is that he is rich and handsome and he goes off to fight the supposed good war in Yugoslavia. He writes a book about Daniel Pearl[31] without mentioning the fact that Pearl could have been a CIA asset, which, incidentally, I think he was based on all the evidence. *Axel Springer*, a right-wing magazine in Germany, showed that Pearl was in constant contact with the CIA.

Arrangements like this are not uncommon. Tad Szulz once told me a lot of his information comes from the CIA. "We do an exchange. They ask me what I know, I tell them what I think is not secret but what I know no one else knows. They tell me things which they think are not secret but no one else knows." Tad knew that could be risky if anyone ever found out about it. But Levy never mentions Pearl's contacts with the CIA because he [Levy] is so dedicated to fighting anything that is Muslim.

Monchinski: Nearly forty years after publication of *The Great Fear*, what hope do you see for oppressed people in Latin America and worldwide?

Gerassi: Little by little, the rest of the world will realize that globalization means American imperialism. Europe is beginning to react to that. Eventually Europe – after getting rid of England which is a pawn of the US – will become strong enough to rival the US. Japan (providing the technology) and China (the disciplined, not to say slave, work force) and India (the raw materials) have to form an economic unit which the tigers will join. The resulting competition will make the US unable to continue to dominate the world.

At that point, what *may* finally happen, is that US workers will come to the consciousness that they are not poor because they are schmucks as the propaganda has had them believe for so long and a new movement will start to come forth, an alliance like you saw in Seattle and Washington of the old and young, various groups putting aside differences to confront the beast head on.

Monchinski: You once described yourself as theoretically an anarcho-communist. Why not a Marxist-Leninist?

Gerassi: I have always opposed the centralization that Marxist-Leninists advocated. I believe it is the task of whoever the leaders are to convince *the people* to *take part* in the process, to realize that *they are* the process, to help instill consciousness. This will entail a certain amount of decentralization. Before we get to "*to each according to his need*" we need to get to "*to each the same amount.*" It's outrageous that today in America kids in Mississippi are allocated on average less than $5,700 a year for their education and kids in Westchester $16,350! There is no free education in this country, it's a free enterprise education, the rich get well-educated and go on to control.

One of my judgments of democracy, all economic considerations aside, is whether the best schools are available free to all. Therefore, to me there is no democracy in America. Health and education need to be centralized, the rest doesn't. Somehow or other the arrangement in the community has to be restricted to the community to the point that people feel they have an influence over the decisions that effect their lives. But every one must have access to the same medical treatment and the same educational advantages. Without good health there is no "life." Without equal education, there is no choice hence no Liberty. So how can we pursue happiness?

But for everything else, I don't want a Central Committee to decide, I want to see people have a voice and that voice must matter. Put that together with decentralization and you end up being anarcho-communist.

Every time you have had a vanguard you have had corruption. Rosa Luxemburg[32] was in favor of the mass strike, hoping that through it the masses would participate in the decision-making process that would establish egalitarian communities. In Russia, Lenin and Trotsky didn't trust the people; they nailed the lid on the coffin of the people's Revolution by crushing the Kronstadt[33] sailors.

Che Guevara said if you can't build a socialist human being, a socialist state is not worth it. I buy that to a great extent. On the other hand, there are very few examples. The anarcho-syndicalist movement in Spain[34] came very close. I am just as baffled as everyone else as to how we bring about a consciousness that will allow for societal changes through a mass movement. In the meantime we must struggle at the grassroots level together to awaken consciousness and force change where we can.

I guess the question for present and future revolutionaries is: How do you democratize a movement that is involved in the seizure of power where, by definition, power corrupts?

Monchinski: How has fatherhood changed you?

Gerassi: For me, nowhere else has the personal being political and the political personal been more palpable than through being a father. The first time I was a dad it was a disaster. I was working long hours and I was not a good father. Unfortunately that is what can happen when you marry young, are career-oriented and you want to "make it" in this system. You justify it as being the best for your family.

The second time around I did a much better job. I raised my daughter because my wife at the time was going through graduate school. My relationship with my daughter and raising her (in the Village) *also* had a political connotation. I used to take her everyday to Washington Square Park, where the pushers used to come over and say, "Hello Cutsey," in fact she still has the nickname *Cutsey*.

It left a mark on her because the people who played with her in the park were all black. Usually the police didn't bother the nickel and dime bag pushers too much unless there was an order from city hall. Even when there was that order from city hall, friendships/rapports had been formed, so we could watch the cops warn their (pusher) friends, "Hey, we're going to have a round up tomorrow at 6PM so why don't you take tomorrow afternoon off?"

How could this occur? Because the police had a relationship with these guys and they couldn't just arrest them and bop them on the head. Which makes me think of when Huey Newton[35] launched a movement in the early 70s in which he wanted the police to live in the communities. The white upper middle class movement people living there who were backing the Panthers were like, "What? We have to deal with the police, we don't want police living here." Huey and Bobby[36] would answer, "Look, if you're constantly dealing with the police day in and day out, not just as police but as neighbors, as friends, you're *both* changing, you're both interacting with one another." And you get to the point where the policeman isn't going to be able to just shoot you, and you won't be able to say he's a pig. Sure, you might call the guy who is a pig a pig, but not all policemen. And that was inbred into my daughter.

By and large the reason to become a policeman or woman these days is one of two: either because you're sadist and you like the power or you can't get any other job. It's job where one can get benefits and decent pay. It's a way for members of the working class to make it.

The fascism comes in at the corporate level where there is no equality of opportunity. We have the lowest levels here in the States of any developed country. There is no choice when it comes to education – the best schools are free in Europe – and in the US there is no national health system that everyone can benefit from. We basically have a system of corporate fascism where each corporate identity has responsibility to itself and none to the people of the country in which it profits from.

I love being a father, but I never stop being a political animal. The fact that I could take care of my daughter, raise her, walk her, made that possible, that I never separated the personal from the political.

ALBERT CAMUS IN ACTION:
DISSENTION OR ABSTENTION?

"Originally this piece was going to be published [as a chapter in a book about the Sartre/Camus feud] by the Chicago University Press," notes Gerassi. "The editor at Chicago thought that the introduction by the guy who edited it was so bad that they cancelled the whole book. Another company published it without my chapter, because Spitzer, the guy who wrote the introduction used, was pro-Camus and would not have my piece attacking Camus as an imperialist. The piece was deemed too radical, it couldn't be used."

ALBERT CAMUS IN ACTION: DISSENTION OR ABSTENTION?

Except for a few modern smart-alecs, most people and every philosopher since civilization began have tried to find, and define, the meaning of life. No one has succeeded to everyone's satisfaction. But that, said a brash young Pied-noir named Albert Camus sitting on a stifling beach in pre-World War II Algeria, is because their guide was reason. Life, he went on as he imbued the hot Mediterranean sun, is not reasonable, so why should be the quest for its meaning?

The problem, concluded Camus reasonably, is that if there is no meaning, if there is no ultimate purpose to life, hence if there is no God, then as Dostoyevsky's Stavroguin and Ivan well understood, all is permitted. But since that would be intolerable to most folks, God or purpose or some ultimate something has got to be, they say. That something can be a Buddha or a Mohammed, the promised land or nirvana, the second coming or the trinity, the thousand year Reich or the endless classless society. Otherwise, all the wise tell us, Camus lamented, life would be absurd.

And what if it was indeed absurd, "privee d'illusions et de lumieres," meaningless, futile? If so, answered Camus, man, well him, Albert Camus, for he could not talk for all men, would be alone, a total stranger in a situation where he could not even claim that his aloneness was part of the human condition, for such a statement would unite him to other men, and that unity might engender the first steps of meaning.

To illustrate the point, Camus wrote *The Stranger*, his first and by far best novel. Meursault, "the stranger", knows his life is meaningless but, said Camus, he cannot draw the conclusion that so is the human condition. Only his own. So the day after his mother dies, he saunters down to the beach, then sees a movie—a comedy— where he laughs heartily, begins a sensuous but very unconventional affair, and kills an Arab—"a cause du soliel." Condemned to die, his last hope is that many people will congregate around the scaffold to shout their hatred.

To live is to act; hence to live the most, Mersault thinks, he must act the most. But since action is meaningless in the face of death, all acts are equivalent: all is permitted. Hope is illusion. Mersaullt does not hope, but neither does he care. He perishes.

"The Stranger is not a book which explains," wrote Jean-Paul Sartre in his review of the novel at the time, "the absurd man does not explain, he describes." He is at the same time a state of facts and the lucid consciousness of certain people in place of these facts." But consciousness, as Sartre well said in *L'intentionalite de conscience chez Husserl*, is always *of* something. It is a specific act which chooses according to a specific value, which in turn must be guided by some form of reason, even if it is perceived by the rest of us as unreasonable or outright mad. For life without reason is impossible. Indeed, "to die is nothing, and I'll have the courage to face death when the time comes," Camus' own Caligula says, "but to see the meaning of life, our reason for existing, disappear, that is unbearable." And to think otherwise, as Meursault's judges insist, would be the greatest of all sins.

Meursault's concierge agrees. At his mother's wake, he tells the court, Meursault said he did not "want to see mamam. That I had smoked. That I had slept and that I drank a café-au-lait. I then felt something stirring the audience and realized for the first time that I was guilty." Concluded the prosecuting attorney: "The day after his mother died, this man went swimming, began an irregular liaison, and went to laugh at a comic film. I have nothing to add." Critic Robert de Luppe did add: "The judges condemn Meursault because he is guilty of murder, but more profoundly, because he refuses to 'play the human game'."

Thus the contradiction: only reason can explain life's unreasonability. A contradiction which will plague Camus for the rest of his life. Knowingly, he tried to confront it in his very next work: *The Myth of Sisyphus*, whose introductory inscription reads: "Oh my soul, do not aspire to immortal life, but exhaust the realm of the possible." And so Camus' Sisyphus, as much a Mediterranean sensualist as Camus himself, rejects God to remain loyal to man, in the harsh present, the unfathomable here to savor all the possible affirmations of the senses in his own immediate situation. Why? Since he suffers? Since he knows his life is absurd? Since he cannot escape his cruel condition of pushing his boulder up the mountain, without hope or respite, without purpose or meaning? Why indeed, asked Camus. "For the man who does not cheat," he wrote, "the belief in the absurdity of life orders his conduct ... to end such an incomprehensible condition."

But life and death, as Camus well knew, are not that clearly separated. The mind may decide to end the life "which is not worth its while," yet even the honest man, the one who plays "no tricks on himself," does not commit suicide. The decision to end one's life is an intellectual decision before it takes place, and an act in the past afterwards, Camus explained, but in between the two states, a certain bridge cannot be crossed, a truth we had overlooked: our bodies judge just as our minds do, and the former refuses to be destroyed. "The judgment of the body is well worth that of the spirit and the body shirks from its destruction. We acquire the habit of living before that of thinking." We exist before we think.

Twisted, inverted, amended or reformulated, Descartes *cogito* always remains an integral part of the French philosopher's lexicon. But Camus did not want to be a rationalist. On the contrary, he insisted that his starting point was the meaninglessness of life, the irrational absurdity of it all. And understanding its absurdity, Camus claimed is not giving it meaning: "To understand the world for a man is to render it human." I can feel my own heart and declare that it exists, wrote Camus, I can touch the world and judge that it too exists. But I can never define either. Thus Camus' subjectivism forced him to conclude that on the one hand "between this certitude that I have of my own existence and the content which I try to ascribe to this certitude a gulf will never be bridged. I shall always be a stranger to myself." And on the other that "to live is to give life to the absurd. To give it life is to face it, hence to be outraged by it. Hence, the only coherent philosophical position is revolt, the permanent confrontation of man against his own absurdity."

To rebel is to hope. To hope is to believe in a meaning or a purpose, which is the same thing. So in his desperate attempt to define the human condition so as to affirm a morality for all men, but without God, Camus traveled from suicide to its very opposite, the affirmation of life. Suicide, he now wrote, resolves the absurd. It ends it. It is, therefore, acceptance and resignation. The rebel, however, revolts precisely against this limitation of his understanding which he maintains: "the opposite of suicide is precisely the condemned man." Man is condemned to death and therefore he must live.

And so Camus returned to his Sisyphus, condemned, like us all, to live his absurd existence which he neither chose nor can alter. "If he becomes the effort which he is," Camus pontificated, "if he knows only his moment, his very existence, then he is the master of it. He is his own creator. He is free...The struggle itself toward the summit suffices to fill a man's heart. We must imagine Sisyphus happy." The question, however, is whether Sisyphus knows he is happy when his only child, whom he loves and for whom he is responsible, and who, side by side with his dad, was helping him push the boulder, died on his way to the summit.

No one asked. A resistance hero with impeccable literary credentials, Camus got away with it, even from his existentialist colleague-critics who began to feel uncomfortable. For, as Francis Jeanson said in his later review of *The Rebel*, the stranger discovered his place in this senseless world as a "concrete subjectivity" existing "among other concrete subjectivities" and the *Myth of Sisyphus* simply "furnished the logic for the stranger's behavior." (See below).

But it did more. It posited a universal. By using Sisyphus, who precisely because he is a myth is also a universal, and not Meursault, to describe happiness in the effort of the moment, it defined *the* human condition, not *a* human condition. Like the self-appointed preachers of Alcoholic Anonymous it told the whole world: "One day at a time." Like Andre Malraux's *Man's Fate*, it claimed that life was like trying to swim across a turbulent river knowing one can never reach the other side, yet trying anyway. Except that if Malraux believed it as a universal, he never said so; only his hero believed it, and he perished.

Clearly, Sisyphus is a slave, a slave of God. And his rebellion has absolutely nothing to do with the devastating injustices of everyday existence; it is a rebellion against God. In his motivation, ordinary folks, you, me, his own son (of whom only

I have ever talked about), count for naught. Unlike Abraham's rebellion whose refusal to sacrifice his son Isaac is done in the name of mortal justice. No matter what may be God's purpose, said Kierkegaard whom Camus so admired, no one can be sacrificed without an acceptable reason. Acceptable to mortals, not gods. That's what Luppe meant by "playing the human game." Thus Jeanson's criticism of Camus' rebel already clearly applied to Camus' Sisyphus: "A strange slave who only wants 'to conquer his own being and maintain it in the face of God,' a pure metaphorical conflict in which there is no role for men and their history."

In the cries of the children who are burned alive in Sierra Leone, of the pregnant women buried alive by American soldiers in mass graves in Panama, of the tortured and raped in Bosnian ethic cleansing houses, Sisyphus' rebellion against God is a sham. And so was Camus' attempt to give it human meaning. Still, Jeanson, Sartre and the other existentialist critics gave Camus the benefit of the doubt: Sisyphus was simply telling God to go to hell for having created an absurd world in which He did not even exist. The book appealed to everyone who was outraged by the fact that we are all condemned to die.

But was Camus' real intent to cope with his rage, your rage, my rage? Did he really feel violated by the death of this or that particular innocent, or rather by the fact of Death? The difference is enormous. Individuals die for all sorts of reasons, most of them man-made. Mankind dies because God or nature or What-you-call-it wills it. The difference became crystal clear in Camus' next work: *The Plague*.

Written after the war and much influenced by Camus' own heroic resistance to German domination, *The Plague* had two goals: to test in living, horrifying situations Oran's rebellion against the absurd and to find common ground for a collective revolt against dignity and honesty. The jump was from the subjectivism of *The Stranger* to the objectivism of a general plague, from a particular experience to a universal law.

The story of the plague was simple. One day, without warning, striking with devastating force, the plague invades Oran. Though no one knows why it struck and all are certain that nothing can be done to defeat it, some folks nevertheless fight it with their full intensity. This action serves no purpose and they know it. Then, one day, for no apparent reason, the plague disappears. Camus' clear message: we are all in the same prison, therefore we must all accept our roles as co-prisoners, which means unity. That makes each of us responsible for all, whatever the consequence. All very nice, but why? Because it will make us feel good? What about the corporation executive who feels good only when he successfully cheats his customers? What about the fanatical anti-abortionist who feels good when the media dubs him "pro-life" instead of mass murderer because he refuses to guarantee the ongoing life of the embryo he saved?

Fact is, Camus does not deal with ordinary mortals, only archetypes. The plague itself, as a symbol of German occupation, is wrong: it did not strike out of nowhere nor did it disappear mysteriously; it was the consequence of the greed of the allies, especially the French, of the Versailles treaty, of capitalist competition, of colonialism, of unequal distribution of wealth, and so on, and it disappeared because it was beaten, by human not unexplainable effort. But already in his much-heralded but actually outrageous "Letters to a German friend," Camus complained that "for so many years now, you tried to make me enter into History" and "we entered History. And for five years, it no longer possible to enjoy the birds singing." Sartre was correctly shocked that "you fought, as you ... Camus wrote, 'to save the idea of man,'" not to save men. At what point does one "enter History" and stop enjoying birds singing? Did it start when the rich decided to get richer by conquering colonies, then sending millions to their death for the sake of future profits? Did it start earlier, with the East Indies company? Or with the crusades? Have the Mayan peasants of Guatemala stopped hearing birds sing since 1502?

Sartre and Jeanson were perfectly correct: "*The Plague* was already a transcendental chronicle... [it] recounted events as seen from on high, by a non-situated subjectivity who didn't live them and was limited to contemplating them." *The Plague* thus turns out to be nothing more than a non-existing, unjust God whom Camus wants us to fight. And History with a capital "H" is simply that same vindictive, cruel non-existing God. "As courageous as you were during World War II," wrote Sartre, "you allowed you to conceal from yourself the fact that man's struggle against Nature is at the same time the cause and effect of another struggle, equally old and pitiless, the struggle of man against man."

By choosing the rats of God instead of the price of butter, Camus could choose all injustice without being unjust himself. And that is precisely what, as a moralist in the best Christian tradition, Camus the atheist tried to do next in *The Rebel*. He could have mimicked Gandhi or foreshadowed Martin Luther King. He could have condemned violence and made man an end in himself. Or he could have praised good old Confucius and told us all not to do what we don't want done to us. But Camus was an absolutist (like all moralists). He had to ground his morality into some eternal tablets handed down to him by a non-existing deity. And so he reified rebellion into a moral imperative in an absurd godless world.

In the face of an unjust and incomprehensible condition, Camus wrote, man revolts. What's more, *The Rebel* not only describes, it prescribes. As Georges Bataille said: "This study constitutes in fact a 'discourse on the method' of revolt." After having destroyed all our traditional mores (he thought), Camus sought to show us the universal application of the human values he discovered through the lives of his heroes in *The Plague*, namely the unity, hence solidarity, that is our salvation, in revolt. He was "trying to lay the foundation for a secular humanism, to base it on an act ... the act of limited revolt."

"What is a rebel?" Camus asked. His answer: "A man who says no. But in refusing he does not renounce: he is also a man who says yes, right from the start. A slave, who received orders all his life, suddenly judges a new command unacceptable ... Rebellion does not proceed without the feeling of being right." Continued Camus: "In experiencing the absurd, suffering is individual. But in the move to rebel, suffering becomes conscious of being collective, the adventure of us all ... This evidence pulls the individual out of his solitude. It is a bond which links all men in their first value. I rebel, therefore we are."

(Ah, remember the good old days when a genuine fighter for the rights of men, not Man, men, could say with such simplicity and power, as Paul Nizan said before he was killed at Dunkirk: "The revolutionary is he who has conquered his solitude").

Camus' rebel is no revolutionary. He takes a stand against his whole condition, but offers no replacement, no solution. He refuses the contradiction of an ordered unity as a substitute for the City of God." The rebellion is hence a metaphysical construct. Indeed, said Camus, "it is metaphysical because it puts into question the goals of men and of all creation."

Having thus set his rebellion into the ethereal sphere, unattached to and unimpeded by human frailty in day-to-day existence, Camus could keep it pure: "Whereas the history, even a collective one, of a movement in revolt is ... merely an obscure contest which commits neither systems nor reasons, a revolution is an attempt to model the act on the idea, to mold the world into a theoretical frame. That's why the revolt may kill men but the revolution destroys at the same time men and principles." Hence, insisted Camus, revolutionary governments cannot themselves be revolutionary, only revolutionary towards other governments. They become war governments: 1789 and 1917 led to war, as will any new revolution to come. "Most revolutions take their shape and their originality in murder ... The revolutionary spirit, wanting then to affirm the separation of earth from sky, begins by discarding divinity by killing its representatives on earth. In 1793, in a way, the era of revolt ended and the revolutionary era began, on the scaffold."

Not only is this reactionary hogwash masquerading as ethical non-violence—which explains why Camus became so popular in the McCarthyite West—but it is plain historical and empirical nonsense to boot. What Camus wants to affirm is that revolts fail because they are pure, while revolutions may succeed because they resort to terror. In the first place, revolutions, even against Camus' non-existent God, occurred long before 1789. Spartacus' revolt, to name one, was a genuine revolution in so far as it opposed the dominant and then-world-wide system of power based on slavery, and it excluded God from its strictly human struggle (not to mention that the real terror was endemic to the power structures, not the revolutionaries). The French peasant wars of the Middle Ages were waged by revolutionaries against unfair taxation, that is, again, against a system, and once again it was the system that practiced terror. The English glorious revolution, had it succeeded, would have happily executed a dozen divine kings, but not because they were divine but in order to establish bourgeois rule. Tupac Amaru rebelled not only against Spain's goon squads but also against their fearsome, spiteful and terror-prone God. And what about that very conservative revolution, sponsored by greedy millionaire gun and spice smugglers who wanted to keep it all for themselves and not share it with England, or anyone else for that matter? Of course, the American revolution did lead to war with England, but was that America's doing? Louis XVI was executed not because he was divine but because the population deemed him a traitor when he tried to flee. And if the Girondins, before they were all beheaded, sought war against England, wasn't it because of trade, competition and profits on and by the high seas, in other words, good old-fashioned human greed? As for "Lenin-Trotsky's war of the worlds," which Camus disdains the most, did not fourteen capitalist countries ship their "volunteers" into Russia to crush the idea that ordinary men and women could rule themselves long before a paranoid torturer saw more such volunteers behind every dacha?

Camus was wrong. People do not rebel because they are afraid of death. They dread the inevitable. They try to cheat it by all means possible, by writing novels in which a beginning, a middle and an end rivals God's creation. Or by painting the meaning of a sunset which God cannot see. Or by having children and reveling joyously when a friend quips that he/she "looks just like you." Or indeed by affirming reincarnation or kneeling piously at Lourdes or reverently toward Mecca. But no one rebels against what is not man-made.

People rebel because they are hungry, because they are repressed, dominated, exploited, tormented, alienated. If they can organize in sufficient number folks who suffer similarly, they can mount a revolution. Sometimes, such revolutions succeed, frightening the world's repressors, dominators, exploiters, tormentors and alienators, that is, the privileged few who monopolize power, wealth and loud-speakers. "You rebelled against death," Sartre told his former friend, Albert Camus, "but in the industrial belts which surround cities, other men rebelled against social conditions that raise the mortality rates. When a child died, you blamed the absurdity of the world and this deaf and blind God that you created in order to be able to spit in his face. But the child's father, if he were unemployed or an unskilled laborer, blamed men. He knew very well that the absurdity of our condition is not the same in [upper class] Passy as in [working class] Billancourt."

Haughty, arrogant, elitist, always shunning "the Plebe", unable to address an unemployed worker or any poor person normally, Albert Camus became the idol of the uncommitted intelligentsia of the world because he preached verbal dissent, that is inaction, in other words defeat. "You have chosen defeat and given it style," wrote Jeanson. "You maintain that revolution can only remain worthwhile, that is rebellious, at the cost of total and almost immediate failure (for example, the Commune)." In fact, Camus could not tolerate victory because no one could defeat God and we are all doomed anyway. "God interests you infinitely more than men," complained Jeanson. "I understand perfectly well that you claim God does not exist. But you are so insistent about it. You reproach him so regularly, and seem so concerned not to be taken in by him, that it could be said at the same time that you resent him for being dead and are afraid that he is some living Devil ... You experience a rather exceptional need for justice; but it is directed against God, and only he seems worthy of your interest."

And since God does not side with the poor, the colonized, or the wretched, neither did Camus. He refused to take sides in the Cold War even when Sartre convinced him that the U.S. was capable of launching a first nuclear strike while the USSR was not (and he was right: President Truman toyed with dropping one in Korea). He refused to support the Algerian independentists even after Frantz Fanon convinced him that French support for their government's violent domination was racist as well as economic. He refused to condemn the violent US overthrow of Guatemala's legitimate elected government even after Nobel Laureate Guatemalan novelist Miguel Angel Asturias convinced him that the invasion was to maintain United Fruit's profits. Yet in the two self-serving replies to the criticism of *The Rebel*, Camus could only plead for us to like him on the grounds that he always opposes violence. (see below).

In the first of these articles, published in Sartre's magazine *Les temps modernes*, Camus tried to obliterate Jeanson by pretending that he was only Sartre's mouthpiece, then tried to denigrate Sartre, who had been his close friend since the 1930s, by referring to him only as the magazine's editor. In the second, which he shrewdly did not publish, his defense relied on such mumbo-jumbo as "nihilism is defined less by the negation than the affirmation of a privileged negation that rejects any other kind of negation. It is at the place of the most extreme tension, on the contrary, at the precise frontier where nihilism is turned against itself, and upon which my study [*The Rebel*] is focused, that the contradiction becomes fruitful and makes progress possible." (Was Camus trying to legitimize the logical positivists' concern with the language of philosophy?).

Camus also had the effrontery of disparaging every rebel, every exploited Mayan Indian, every cop-harassed unemployed ghetto black, every tortured East Timor resistance fighter by claiming that "the aggression that pits one against the other is only the wicked hatred that each of us bears for a part of himself." Do not hate, Camus said, accept. Even if they kill your children, or bomb your church, or you will be as guilty as they. Except that Gandhi sat with his followers in front of English bayonets and Martin Luther King marched with his downtrodden flock into the jaws of the hellish Bull Connors. Where was Camus? In his ivory tower or St. Germain nightclubs. Which is why he remains today so admired by those who do nothing to fight injustices because, they say, nothing makes any difference anyway. Losers all, like Camus.

Outrageous, responded Jeanson. Hunted by the French police, condemned to die by the vindictive Organization of the Secret Army (which planted bombs in the apartments of Sartre, Yves Montand, Brigitte Bardot, etc. for supporting Algerian independence), organizer of the Committee of 21 which upheld sedition, treason by French law, Jeanson smuggled money, medicine and arms to the Algerian rebels when most French Communists and Socialists (and of course conservatives) were still shouting that Algeria was a French province. Jeanson saw Camus as a "prisoner of yourself, desperately concerned about your dignity, your grandeur, your honor, your *public bearing*. Alone, walled in by your spite, full of resentment, irritated by all those who do not want to despair ... *you*, who perhaps don't want to despair at all, and who insist on distinguishing between misfortune of being born mortal and that of being oppressed."

And indeed, once the world was embroiled in the Cold War, Camus never took a position on the struggles of his time. He had condemned Franco's destruction of the Spanish Republic, but that had taken place in the late Thirties (to be fair, at the time of his criticism, right after World War II, the US officially loved Spain's fascist dictator and signed a slew of treaties with him). Otherwise Camus made no statement, supported no movements, praised no living activists. Thus, he made no mistake, and the world loved him.

Sartre, meanwhile, made plenty of mistakes. In the third volume of his trilogy, *The Roads to Freedom*, he revealed the class structure of the army and showed that the little guy always gets killed while the office eats pate de foie gras. When Korea exploded, he chose the side who would not use the atomic bomb. When Rousset documented the existence of the gulags, he ordered his "pro-communist" magazine to publish the facts, the first to do so. He courted jail by denouncing France's war in Vietnam. He joined Jeanson's pro-Algerian front and even lugged suitcases full of contraband to the fedayeen. Though he once stupidly (and, to be fair, in sickness) claimed that the USSR was the freest of all dominant powers, he denounced it for invading Czechoslovakia while still supporting the French communist party (which heaped filth on him anyway) because it did represent most exploited French workers. And though he systematically opposed all colonial oppression, from Vietnam to Madagascar, from Brazil to the Philippines, he never forgot that we live in a schizophrenic world where ethical issues must be re-evaluated with each incident. Thus he doggedly supported the State of Israel while demanding the same right for Palestine. He condemned the massacre at Lod as sheer butchery, but defended the desperate Palestinian action at Munich and almost alone, at the time, documented the fact that all the dead, the Israeli gymnast-soldiers as well as the Palestinian "terrorists," had been killed by the German police. He praised Cuba's help to Ethiopia against imperialist Somalia, but condemned Cuba's support of Ethiopia's colonial war on Eritrea. He hailed Cuba's defense of Angola against the US puppet, the gangster Zavimbi, and his South African allies, but damned Cuba for jailing its non-conformist intellectuals (the Padilla affair). He despised America's genocidal war on the Vietnamese but helped the pro-American Vietnamese boat-people refugees settle in France. Thus Sartre was hated by almost everyone. He still is—to his immense credit.

CHAPTER FOUR

WHEN THE WAR IS OVER...

My father loved Barcelona above all other places on earth. In a way, this was only natural; he had sought to defend the city during the Spanish Civil War and had been its last Republican military commander. But in another way it was strange, for Barcelona was not his native town: he was born of a Sephardic family in Constantinople and was educated in Germany. He went to Barcelona only in 1922, when he was 23; and after he fled Spain in 1939, he lived most of the rest of his life in the foothills of Vermont's Green Mountains.

Nonetheless, Barcelona was always first in his heart. It had inspired much of his best painting-he was an artist who paid homage in his work to both Cezanne and Velazquez-and during his two-year losing battle against cancer in the mid-1970s, he often reminisced about the city. He liked to recall its Barrio Chino, an infamously rough part of town; Montjuich Park, where a typical house from each of Spain's regions was built for the 1929 World's Fair; and the romance of the *sardana*, the traditional Catalan dance performed on holidays in the workers' district of La Ciudadela. From time to time, my father would say he wanted to die in Barcelona; the trouble was that he refused to return to Spain so long as Francisco Franco was there.

By the time my father died in December 1974-a year before Franco -I had come to know, through him, the Barcelona of my earliest years as well as I knew the Manhattan of my adolescence. And when I decided to go back to Barcelona for the first time since 1934, I knew I would see the city through my father's eyes and that it would be a painful experience. For one thing, I knew I would relive the civil war. What would be worse, I realized, was that I would surely have to come to grips with the love-hate relationship I had had with my father, a man fictionalized by both Hemingway and Sartre, a man of courage and conceit, beauty and bitterness, terror and tenderness-a true Barcelonan.

Before I even got to Barcelona, I met two men who reminded me powerfully of my father. The Iberia flight from Paris being delayed as usual, we passengers huddled in the lounge at Orly Airport. A fat, balding, red-faced little man sitting on a sofa to my left and sweating heavily asked permission to remove his jacket; when he did, he revealed both a pair of wide, black suspenders and a hand-stitched leather belt. To my right sat a tall, thin, elegant figure in a Levi's suit. His hair was silvery white, his shirt open, his tanned neck protected by an inch-long golden Virgin of Montserrat. Both men were evidently in their sixties. The fat one, Costa by name, was tense and irritated; he obviously hated to fly, and the waiting was stretching his nerves. As if to soothe him, Pedro, the thin man, a fashion illustrator, began to talk. Within an hour, each of us had told his story.

Costa had been caught in Burgos, Franco's wartime capital, in 1936 and therefore had had to fight with Franco. After the war he continued his studies, and he now owned an art gallery. His father, an anarchist, had been executed in 1939 by the victorious fascists. Only when Franco died had Costa dared to talk to his mother again, and then they had cried together for a whole night.

Pedro had joined Barcelona's anarcho-syndicalist militia, was wounded at the first battle of the Ebro in 1937, then spent 17 months in a concentration camp, where he taught himself to draw. He had done no other work since. All his family except a sister had died during the bombings of the city. He lived with her until she, too, died last year in a car accident.

At first, obviously, I loved Pedro and hated Costa, though both of them kept telling me to forget the past, just as they had. Enjoy modern Barcelona for its art, they said, for its Gothic treasures, its classical palaces, Antonio Gaudi's architectural "monstrosities." But the more they insisted on the present, the more they seemed to be drawn into the past, and I began to feel a mounting animosity between them.

"After all," Costa suddenly exclaimed, "it wasn't my fault that I was in Burgos, was it?" Costa was a genuine Catalan. His eyes were sad, almost as if he had felt guilty for the last 40 years. "Anyway," he added with a sigh, "at least we can speak Catalan now." (The language was forbidden in Spain during the Franco years.) I suggested a drink at the bar.

Costa and Pedro both started to rise, then fell back heavily into their sofas, as if they were thinking the same thought: only one of them could accompany me. Finally, Pedro got up while Costa kept his seat, obviously feeling out of place. "Come with us," I said to him, and before he could refuse, I added: "After all, we're all three Catalans." Beaming as if I had given him absolution, Costa leaped to his feet.

By the time we reached Barcelona, five hours behind schedule, Pedro and Costa had refought the battles of the Ebro half a dozen times, had insulted each other at least as often, and after each insult had squeezed each other's arms in gestures of friendship. "Let this be a warning," Pedro said to me as we parted in front of the air terminal's multicolored mosaic mural. "Don't talk politics in Spain, especially with strangers." He turned toward Costa. They embraced and promised to keep in touch. As I watched them go in different directions, I realized I liked them both-and equally.

There is one subject all Barcelonans are eager to talk about: Catalonian independence. "When I first went to Barcelona from Madrid," my mother had told me, "I felt I was in a foreign country. Very few uneducated people spoke Spanish, and they all referred to themselves as Catalans, not Spaniards." Today, all Catalans know how to speak Spanish, but they prefer not to. Whether they support the Communists, the Socialists, the Democratic Center, or even the extreme right wing, Barcelonans want to be autonomous, and they do not hesitate to say so-in rallies, demonstrations, and riots. Even the Paseo de Gracia, the most aristocratic of Barcelona's streets, is covered with handbills and graffiti demanding some sort of independence from Madrid.

It was along the Paseo de Gracia, a wide, tree-lined boulevard divided by a grassy island, that my mother often took me strolling before the war. Whenever we passed by the two weird buildings at number 43 and number 92, Mother would say, "They look like stone witches." Designed by Gaudi long before the civil war and seemingly poured in hot wax, the buildings are forbidding, their iron and concrete balconies, set against fading mosaics, resembling the open mouths of attacking sharks. In 1938, number 43, at the corner of Aragon Street, became the Republican general-staff headquarters. Now, as I stared at the third-floor balcony, I could well imagine my father standing there and slapping his hunting boots with a riding crop, shouting orders to militiamen in the same cutting tone he would later use to tell me to clean up my room.

At the southern end of the paseo, where it flows into the Plaza de Cataluiia, the city's main square, there used to be a whole flock of sidewalk cafes. A few have survived, surrounded by snack oars, kiosks, peddlers' stands, and street-corner hustlers of every type. But along the eastern flank of the square now rises the nine-story department store El Corte Ingles, which is crammed with French shirts, English sweaters, and American toys. From the terrace of its top-floor restaurant, one sees the plaza's full glory: the grandiose star of black, beige, white, and red tiles set into the pavement and surrounded by lush semitropical trees and fountains. To the left, the southeast, the hill of Montjuich with its palace and fortress frames the city; to the right, at the city's northern extremity, rises the mountain of Tibidabo. (That means "I will give it to you" in Latin, and local legend says the mountain is where Satan took Jesus to tempt him, offering him all the glories of Cataluiia that he could see if he would renounce the Lord.) What struck me most, however, was the sight of the thousands of pigeons on the plaza, unconcerned by the crowds of tourists strolling through. "During the bombings of 1936-38," my mother once said, "the pigeons disappeared, and no one knew where they went."

Beyond the plaza is the Barrio Gotico, the old town, built during the Middle Ages. on a Roman site. Here the streets narrow, traffic piles up, and tempers flare. The cathedral, with its two octagonal towers, was erected during the thirteenth, fourteenth, and fifteenth centuries on the site of an ancient Visigothic basilica and is Gothic at its most romantic. Coming down its long brick steps onto the quaint Plaza del Cristo Rey, I could not help remembering the last time my mother had walked there. It was late in 1938, and Barcelona was encircled by the Francoist forces. Somehow, as Mother told it, she had managed to find a few fresh vegetables in one of the market stalls behind the cathedral. Just then, a squadron of German Junkers unleashed a load of bombs on the center of town. Rushing back toward the Plaza de Catalufia, clutching her groceries in her string bag, Mother suddenly found herself staring at a woman about her age hugging a bundle of her own. "I, too, have my package," the woman shrieked as they crossed. My mother looked at what the woman was carrying-and fainted. It was a headless child. The next day, my father sent my mother to Paris (where I had been sent earlier), but for the next three decades, she occasionally dreamt about that scene. Now what I saw there were scores of tourists, wearing shorts and T-shirts, photographing the cathedral with Instamatic cameras.

Not that Barcelona is totally free of the memory of the civil war. On many walls appear the yoke and crossed arrows of the Falangists and the word *renace*, a rallying call for the fascist movement. While I was in Barcelona, a group calling itself Black Falange issued a proclamation saying it planned to assassinate every *rojo*-i.e., Communist or Socialist-mayor in Spain, because "to kill a *rojo* is not a sin." And the day after the local television station broadcast *Holocaust*, posters went up all over town calling it a lie, and neatly painted swastikas appeared on almost every public building. But few Barcelonans take the extremists seriously.

People are frightened, however, by the new violence in the city. As in New York, police sirens now howl throughout most nights in Barcelona, and muggings, fistfights, knifings, gunplay, and bombs shatter the peace of the Ramblas. A long, wide thoroughfare running from the port to the Plaza de Catalufia, the Ramblas was once frequented by Christopher Columbus, who haunted its many palaces in a search for funds to finance his visionary voyage to the Indies. The cafes in the center strip of the Ramblas are still there. So are the kiosks, flower stands, and bohemians (today called beatniks or hippies). But the palaces, bourgeois and aristocratic alike, have been turned into cheap cabarets and clip joints, the revelers no longer linger leisurely over Jerez and *bocadillos* (sherry and snacks), and the talk is no longer of art but of survival. Indeed, middle-class couples now seem to stay home at night to watch American television programs. Of the people who do float up and down the Ramblas, a great many seem to be drug addicts and cops.

"Barcelona is now very much like New York," a police lieutenant explained. "There's heroin, hence muggings; there's unemployment, hence muggings; there's anger and frustration, hence muggings. The Ramblas used to be filled with *gente buena* [nice folk]. Now look at it. Sure, there are a lot of tourists. After all, we get our share of the thirty-eight million who visit Spain every year, and they have to go somewhere at night. But look at the others, look ..."

When I looked, the people I saw were mostly members of motorcycle gangs, pimps, and prostitutes. There were, however, still enough of us ordinary onlookers to give the Ramblas a festive air-and the transvestites along the way were full of laughter, almost enough to drown out the wailing of the sirens.

But not when the right-wing terrorists strike. In Barcelona, as in so many places, the extremists claim to stand for purity, morality, and tradition-meaning they are anti-gay, anti-weirdo, anti-new. Every now and then they sweep down on the Ramblas and beat up the whores and transvestites with iron bars. Mostly the frustrated sons-or daughters-of the old fascist bourgeoisie, these youngsters are members of such militant groups as Fuerza Nueva, Union Nacional, or Falange Negra; they make easy prey of the harmless transvestites.

The angry young fascists, however, carefully stay away from the Barrio Chino. Situated to the west of the Ramblas, the barrio has always been the preserve of the poor, the aged, the abandoned, the unemployed, and the marginal. For a woman tourist to walk through its maze of narrow streets, which smell of fried oil, flowery perfume, urine, and sweat, has always been risky. Even the police have traditionally tried to avoid the area. But today it has become an open war zone. The quaint cabarets are gone, replaced by scroungy bars. The friendly prostitute who used to talk as well as play is now bitter and angry. Her pimp is no longer a spirited con man but a hood dependent on a hit for survival. When the cops do go into the barrio nowadays, they travel in groups, with guns at the ready. And occasionally one of them gets picked off. The poor of the barrio view all authority as the enemy.

"We are all responsible for the poverty," King Juan Carlos never fails to say. Though he was carefully trained by Franco to perpetuate the repressive ultra-moralism of the Falangist credo, the king, who sometimes sports a beard and is often seen in jeans, has repudiated all that and instead is helping to guide Spain toward an open, democratic society. Today, no sensible politician, right or left, wants him out. Yet neither the king nor the politicians offer a workable solution to Spain's mounting economic problems. In Barcelona itself, factories are closing, strikes multiplying, and city hall is so broke it must constantly beg Madrid for bail-out funds. Sometimes the workers close down the port completely when their demands are not met: sometimes it closes because the employers cannot meet the payrolls. Sometimes the whole city is paralyzed by victorious footballers on a spree, by the gay community, on a march, or by the military making a show of force, which no one takes very seriously. Still, the streets are jammed with cars, the stores crammed with imports, and the dangerously polluted beaches are packed with swimmers.

Yet for its devotees, Barcelona, somewhat like New York, remains an enchanted city, full of verve, vitality, and humor and populated by a people in search of a meaning to life-a search that, while never resolved, gives life a meaning nonetheless. True, those who flock to the ornate blue- and white-tile-faced bullring are older and less exuberant than those described by my father or by Hemingway. But they still admire the sensuousness, even eroticism, of the matador who caresses his carnal enemy in a loving duel that must be resolved by a graceful, ritualistic, almost mystical danse macabre. Barcelonans are fascinated with sex, God, and death.

In the same spirit, Barcelonans gape at Gaudi's baroque Church of the Holy Family, with its helicoidal and hyperbolic towers, begun in 1882 and still unfinished. In the old town, they revere the warmth and simplicity of one of the purest of Gothic churches, Santa Maria del Mar, built between 1329 and 1383, partly bombed out in 1936 and restored after the civil war, its nave rising 120 feet. They swarm to the gaudy Church of the Sacred Heart on the top of Mount Tibidabo, with its huge copper Christ flanked by two anachronistic Byzantine towers. But rarely do they pray in these churches. To Barcelonans, death and religion are fascinating, sacred-but private.

Visiting the Fortress of Montjuich, which guards the port, I could not help remembering my parents' story about the first ship to run the fascist blockade of 1938 and bring food into the city. The people of Barcelona had gone hungry for nearly six months before a Russian freighter finally broke through. Looking down from Montjuich's stark ramparts, now equipped with U.S.-made 75-mm howitzers dated 1944, and acutely conscious of a bronze Franco on horseback looking over my shoulders, I could almost see the scene that followed the arrival of the food ship: militiamen dancing the *sardana.* women embracing the Russian sailors, anarcho-syndicalist workers, soon to be executed or jailed by Communist troops, raising clenched fists in salute to their Soviet saviors. But that, of course, was 40 years in the past; what I really saw were huge modern cranes and skyscraper-high lifts, some loading ships, others dredging the harbor, and still others unloading Hondas from Japan.

With a French journalist friend, I stopped for lunch at a restaurant called Flash-Flash just off Tuset Street, Barcelona's center for advertising and model agencies. Filling the white vinyl booths were models, politicians, poets, jazz musicians, con men, and journalists. My friend knew them all, so we table-hopped and chatted with one guest after another. No one, not even those over 60, wanted to talk about the civil war. It was the present that was on everyone's mind. All seemed to think that the more Barcelona adopted American habits the better. "Even American violence?" I asked sarcastically. "That's the price of modernism," one politician-turned poet replied. "Sooner or later we will gain autonomous status in Catalufia. Then all of Spain will join the European Common Market. The poor will become poorer, as in England; the rich, richer. Eventually, like the ancient Greeks and Egyptians, and Franks, for that matter, we will use the poor to build the temples and pyramids and cathedrals of the twenty-first century. They died by the thousands then, but look at the civilization they left us!"

I reminded him that almost a million Spaniards had died during the civil war without noticeable progress in the march of civilization. He frowned. "Let's not talk of the past," he said. "Let me say this: for generations and generations, we Spaniards have been afraid of sex. So we invented *machismo*. We were afraid of God, so we blasphemed and flagellated ourselves. We were afraid of death, so we constantly risked it. But now we are changing. At least we are finally learning to stop being political. Black or red, except for a few madmen, we are becoming technocrats, even in the arts. Look at Carrillo [the leader of the Spanish Communist party]! Even that old Stalinist is no longer political. Neither is Suarez [the prime minister]. Nor Juan Carlos. We're all more and more like you Americans. That's the future. Those who can't hack it, as you say, have had it. We are finally understanding that life is just like business. Who needs gods or bullfighters to run a modern state? If you can't sell it, fold up."

I left the restaurant and resumed my wandering. I passed the building that once housed the avant-garde Galeria Layetana, where my father used to exhibit his paintings. It was now a snack bar. I stopped in bookstores, where books on everything from Trotsky to Sorel could be found, a psychoanalysis of Franco lying alongside a condemnation of King Juan Carlos. Mostly, however, the stalls were filled with pornography and crime stories.

On the Plaza Calvo Sotelo, named for a champion of Spanish fascism, I heard two students praising the courage of the Basque terrorists. I took a bus down the eight lane A venida Generalisimo Franco, which even the young bus driver called La Diagonal-which was its name before the civil war. I ambled into the tiny Calle Moncada and in a mansion there saw the new Museo Picasso, dedicated to Franco's best-known enemy. I stood in the center of the Plaza San Jaime and stared at the city hall's neoclassical, lacelike stonework; inside, a Socialist mayor was attempting to put all the city's unemployed on some form of guaranteed income. Across the square, in the Gothic building with a Renaissance facade that houses the provincial parliament, Catalans of all political complexions were trying to establish statutes of self-rule acceptable to Madrid.

Suddenly sirens dissipated the breeze and frightened the pigeons: a federal policeman, a "gray" as Barcelonans and Spaniards say-a species of cop hated even more than the members of the semi mythical Guardia Civil-had just been gunned down in a tough little street called Escudilers, near the Plaza Real, one of Barcelona's most picturesque squares of eighteenth-century neoclassical homes.

To try to escape the whirlwind of contradictions in my head, I decided the next day to journey northeast along the Mediterranean coast to the small resort of Tossa de Mar. The town sits on a promontory that juts into the azure sea. There in the summers of 1932, 1933, and 1934, my father, my mother, and I shared a house at times with Marc Chagall and his family, at other times with the French poet Henri Michaux and the Italian futurist painter Luigi Russolo. In a café on the main square, facing the church, an old man told me where to find Chagall's house. "You'll be disappointed," he said. "It's now the bar Lolita, next to the pharmacy." And so it was.

In the renovated home of the fourteenth-century governor of Tossa, the town council maintains a small but beautiful museum. It was started in 1934 by, among others, Chagall and his friend the Czech painter Georges Kars, and it is graced by a 1934 Chagall oil of a flying violinist. In the museum, I met Sebastia Coris i Mestres, a sad but friendly white-haired gentlemen of 60-odd years who was Tossa's mayor from 1970 to 1975. A Franco adherent for reasons of class and family, Coris had fought against the Republic, made a small fortune running a bar-restaurant and hotel, then dedicated himself to the welfare of his town. Thanks to his cool headedness, the town has been spared the high-rise tourist condominiums that have so disfigured most of the rest of the Costa Brava.

It was in 1972 that Mayor Coris first learned that Tossa owned a Chagall and that he was one of contemporary art's most famous painters. "You must understand," Coris explained in a gentle, semi-apologetic voice, "that I was a businessman. I had never heard of Chagall. Then, when I realized how illustrious he was, I suggested we stage a special homage to the man, not so much because I cared about Chagall, but because I thought it might bring some fame or prestige to Tossa. So I wrote him. He said no thanks. I wrote him again, offering him a choice of dates. He kept refusing. Finally he gave me a reason. Franco. I couldn't understand that. After all, Chagall wasn't Spanish and he wasn't a red. So I decided to go see him in Vence, in southern France, where he was living. We talked and talked and talked, and I began to understand."

One of the stories Chagall told Coris that helped the mayor understand was about Chagall's friend Georges Kars. A Jew and a Republican, Kars abandoned Tossa in 1939 and took refuge in southern France. When the Germans occupied the area in November 1942. Kars rushed back to the Spanish frontier, But Franco's police turned him away. There on the border, Kars took out a pistol and shot himself. As it turned out the suicide attempt failed, and Kars eventually escaped to Geneva where he died in February 1945. But for Chagall, the decisive act was the one at the border. "I can never return to Spain. as long as Franco is alive," he told Coris.

Coris staged the homage to Chagall anyway, in June 1974. And he explained in public why the mister would not be present. That eventually cost Coris his job-and a lot of supposed friends. But he continued to work behind the scenes for better housing for the poor fishermen, for more services, for a more open society. In 1978, his assistant, supported by Coris and the Socialist party, became the first freely elected mayor of Tossa, and together he and Coris have done more than their share to keep the town manageable and attractive despite the fact that the population, which is barely 3,500 in the winter, soars to 60,000 every summer. Today, Coris collects everything on Chagall he can find—books, reproductions, memorabilia, and original letters, plus some stunning drawings by the master and the other painters who lived and worked in the area.

During the afternoon, Coris took me to his brother's café for a drink, and he invited an old man, a sculptor he helps to support to sit with us. "Oh, yes, I remember the summers of '33 and '34 very well," the old man began, after Coris had introduced us and told of my childhood visits to the town. "Chagall and his friends used to sit every evening at the Café Biel, over there." I stared at the name and stared at the terrace of the café next door. How often I had heard my father and mother mention that cafe. "Yes, yes, that was it, right there. It's called the Café Ysadora now, but they haven't changed it. It's just like it used to be."

"Didn't they used to dance in the Café Biel?" I asked carefully. The old man looked at me strangely. "How did you know?" he asked, then went on, "Yes, there was a platform there between the two sets of rows of chairs, and people danced there sometimes. Now they've stopped. I guess they can't compete with that rock music coming from the beach. Chagall and his friends used to enjoy looking at the dancers, especially the children." My heart was pounding. "Do you by any chance remember," I asked, "a short, stocky painter, prematurely bald, with a thick black mustache, who was with Chagall; a man with deep, black, peering eyes but a wide, open smile; a man ..."

The old man interrupted me. "Of course, I remember him very well, because I met him later during the collapse of Valencia. He was a general then, and he was in charge of the rear guard-the retreat, you know. Yes, yes, he was a friend of Chagall, and he had a lovely blond wife, and he used to come to the Café Biel all the time with the French poet Michaux, and sometimes with Calder and Miro. He had a son, two or three years old, who used to dance all the time over there with the small daughter of the sculptor Casanova. You know Casanova? He was one of the founders of our museum. Well, yes, that painter, I wonder what ever happened to him. His name was ..." I got up and embraced the old man. I wanted to cry. "He was *my* father." I said softly, "and I was the kid."

Two days later in Barcelona. I could no longer restrain the tears. I had finally gone to see the house where we had lived in 1934 at the corner of Diputacion and Lauria streets. My mother had said that we could see the Ritz from all five of our balconies. and that eliminated all but one of the six apartments. The Ritz, a white seven-story luxury hotel, its marble entrance lined with iron grilles and graced by a marble statue, was exactly as she had described it-except that the wide divided avenue in front was no longer called Cortes (Parliament) but Avenida de Jose Antonio Primo de Rivera, after the founder of Spanish fascism.

I must have stared at 301 Diputacion a bit too long. A gray-uniformed policeman approached me. "Something wrong?" he asked warily. I tried to dry my tears, but they kept flowing. So I explained that there, on the fifth floor, my father, mother, and I had lived for the first three years of my life. And now my father was dead before he could see it again.

"My father, too, is dead," the cop said curtly, "killed during the war." He paused. looked at me squarely, and added: "By your father's side." Then suddenly, smiling sadly, he patted me on the shoulder and invited me to have a glass with him. I'm still not sure what impulse made me accept, but I did. And as we sat at a terrace table of a cafe a block away, he told me that he had only one job in his life-being a cop. He knew he was hated. he said, that he remained a symbol of the past, yet what else could he do? He was exactly two months older than I and had never traveled farther than Madrid; and that, only for two tough months of military schooling. He talked more and more freely, about his fears of being shot from behind, not seeing "the bullet coming," about his children, who are ashamed of him. I, too, talked, about my father and the pain he suffered for two years, his lack of hope that his flaming, fiery paintings would ever be recognized. The cop told me how his father had died from a mortar shell in the stomach. And then, with the most natural grace, he too began to cry. "Spain killed your father," he said, trying to smile, "and yours killed mine."

He rose, wiped his eyes, and said he had better be back to his beat. We started to reach out our hands, then stopped. We both hesitated for a moment, then suddenly embraced each other so tightly our tears mixed along our cheeks. And I thought, with both happiness and pain, that the civil war was really over.

"Be careful," the policeman shouted back at me as he crossed the street. "Barcelona is dangerous now! Just like New York!"

CHAPTER FIVE

CELEBRATE OUR FIFTIETH YEAR OF LIFE!

Below is the text of a letter Tito sent off to the *New York Times* in September, 2008, following Morton Sobell's revelation that though Julius Rosenberg had, indeed, been spying for the Soviet Union, Julius' wife, Ethel, had not. Julius and Ethel Rosenberg met their end in the electric chair in 1953. *The New York Times*, of course, did not publish Tito's letter. Following the letter is the text of a talk Tito often gives in class, the subject of which—thank you Julius and Ethel for saving all of us in the world from nuclear obliteration—seems counter-intuitive at first.

TO THE EDITOR

In his "A Spy Confesses" (Week in Review 9/21), Sam Roberts claims that folks "fiercely loyal to the far left, believed that the Rosenbergs were not guilty ... " I am and have always been, since my stint as a correspondent and editor in Latin America for Time and Newsweek, a "far leftist," and I have never claimed the Rosenbergs were not guilty. Nor have any of my "far leftist" friends. What we always said, and what I repeat to my students every semester, is that "if they were guilty, they are this planet's great heroes." My explanation is quite simple: The US had a first-strike policy, the USSR did not (until Gorbachev). In 1952, the US military, and various intelligence services, calculated that a first strike on all Soviet silos would wipe out all but 6% of Russian atomic missiles (and, we now know, create enough radiation to kill us all). But those six percent would automatically be fired at US cities. The military then calculated what would happen if one made a direct hit on Denver (why they chose Denver and not New York or Washington was never explained). Their finding: 200,000 would die immediately, two million within a month. They concluded that it was not worth it. In other words, I tell my students, you were born and I am alive because the USSR had a deterrent against our "preventive" attack, not the other way around. And if it is true that the Rosenbergs helped the Soviets get that deterrent, they end up among the planet's saviors.

CELEBRATE OUR 50th YEAR OF LIFE (written June, 2003)

What a way to come of age! On June 19, 1953, I was 21, about to graduate from Columbia and face the draft. To go fight in Korea, divided by the cold war and led, on both sides of the demarcation line, by bloody tyrants. I was supposed to go help a vicious fascist named Sygman Rhee because my government liked him. Why?

Because a couple of brothers, rich powerful lawyers whose clients, before they joined President Eisenhower's government, were America's elite and wanted no country in Asia (except defeated hence dependent Japan) to develop into an economically viable state.

These two nail-polished brothers hated the poor. That's why they were Republicans. Not that Democrats didn't also hate the poor, but they tried to make voters believe otherwise. Like President Truman who campaigned against that ridiculous fop, New York Governor Thomas Dewey, by claiming that the playboy was merely a machinist for the country's Brahmin turbines.

Truman was right, of course, but he himself was no better than an oiler for those Brahmin engines, and once re-elected proceeded to grease the wheels all the way to Korea.

In 1953, however, the engineer was Eisenhower. And since he didn't know which way the coils were meant to push, he called in the brothers, John Foster Dulles as Secretary of State and Allen Dulles as head of the CIA. Brahmins themselves, veterans of Sullivan and Crowell, Washington's most powerful and most amoral law firm in hell or heaven, the Dulleses knew very well what had to be done: scare all dissenters by killing a couple of ordinary ones.

The Dulleses didn't invent that tactic. It's an old Brahmin ploy. It was used just after World War I, when too many Italians flocked to the US to find a decent job. After all, the Italians felt they were our allies, since they had fought on our side against Germany and the Austro-Hungarian empire. But they had strange ideas, these Italians. They believed they had a right to work and a right to eat, that their children had a right to go to school and a right to be healthy, in other words, a right to participate in the American dream.

Absolutely subversive! That's what the Brahmins said. But then the Brahmins were always nativists, that is, hating any American settler who did not come from England or the Low Countries. In New Orleans in February 1891, for example, 19 innocent Italians were lynched by a frenzied mob of WASPS (White Anglo-Saxon Protestants) because the Italians got along with the other poor folk who worked in the sugar and lumber mills – the blacks. The New York Times, top nativist mouthpiece, congratulated the lynch mob who had now made "life and property safer."

So when the State of Massachusetts arrested a poor unemployed Italian and his fish-peddler friend as thieves and murderers, the Times – and most of the press – applauded again.

"All over the country, alien or foreign-born agitators are carrying on in many languages," the Times complained, and demanded that "these enthusiasts of destruction … [with] their campaign of murders" be stopped. (04/25/19;05/01/19; 07/04/19; 10/17/19; 11/08/19; etc).

They were. Sacco and Vanzetti were executed, but not for the crime they did not commit, for their ideas. They were anarchists. The object was to scare all other Italians who came to the US believing in the American dream and who then realized that the dream was manufactured by the Brahmins. Sacco and Vanzetti said so. So they were killed. As criminals. The US always criminalizes dissent.

Now it was the turn of communists. Not party leaders; everyone expects leaders to be vulnerable. If chief Gus Hall had to be executed, every rank-and-file communist would have taken it in stride. It had to be commoners, like two poor, hard-working ordinary communists who sold the Daily Worker every Saturday at the corner of 14th Street and Second Avenue because they hoped for a better world, one that guaranteed life and liberty and the pursuit of happiness, not only to the Brahmins and the New York Times' nativist coterie but for each of us, to you and me.

Oh yes, they also had to be Jewish. No less than 60 percent of the communist party's rank-and-file were Jews. Most had fled pogroms in Europe with their parents, and had learned that all ruling classes hated the poor. That had made them cosmopolitanists. That's why Stalin executed them. That's why the US wanted to execute them.

So they arrested the Rosenbergs. We now know that they knew that Ethel was innocent. But maybe if she is threatened to die, husband Julius will admit he was guilty. He didn't. So they executed them both. For passing atomic secrets to the Russians. In 1947 when the war was over. But on the wartime espionage act. Of course, they weren't executed for being communists. Oh no! For being traitors.

No one much cared about the contradiction. Either they were traitors because they spied for the Russians during the Cold War – in which case they should not be tried under the wartime espionage act. Or they spied during the war, when Russia was our ally, then they were not traitors. Ah, who cares about logic. To that despicable hangman, "judge" Kaufman, chosen as a Jewish Judas (who illegally checked all his "judicial" moves with the FBI) logic was irrelevant.

The Dulles brothers, and their mild-mannered henchmen, Attorney General Howard Brownell, who did not want the Rosenbergs killed but worried that the Republicans might be labeled soft-on-communism, agreed on one undisputed fact: We Americans are brilliant. No other countrymen are as smart. Hence, no one but us Americans could possibly develop the formula and create the atomic bomb. (Ignoring that Oppenheimer was a German Jew, as was Einstein, Fermi was Italian, Niels Borg was Danish, etc.). Therefore, since Russia got it, some son-of-a-bitch spy must have given them the secret.

Russia of course put a man in space, Lt. Gargarin, before the US. And the Russians developed and tested the Hydrogen bomb before the US. So what? Jean-Paul Sartre, Europe's most important intellectual, described us as "Mad Beasts" in an editorial reprinted the world over (Liberation 6/22/53). So what? Americans are brilliant, no one else is.

OK, lets go with it. We had the bomb, Russia did not. And another point, so often overlooked. We had a first strike policy. Russia did not.

The Rosenbergs ruined it. That's right, the Dulleses, who also wanted to drop the A-bomb on the Vietnamese when they clobbered the French at Dien bien Phu, and SAC (Strategic Air Command) bigwigs seriously contemplated (a bit early) Bush II's doctrine of pre-emptive war. They wanted to wipe out Russia with A-bombs without warning, one stormy night, just like that, a rainfall of A-bombs all over Russia, killing some 100 million dirty reds.

Why not? We would be masters of the world. The radiation would dissipate into the atmosphere and a year or two later we'd take over the Russian steppes, their gold and, most importantly, their oil. One hundred million Russians would have been evaporated to make a better world.

Ah shucks, the Rosenbergs ruined it all. By the time our brass was ready, the Russians had set up their defense silos. So the experts sat down to figure out if our first strike policy could still be functional. What they concluded was that six percent of Russia's missiles would escape our attack, and some would hit us hard. They studied one city – Denver. One Russian missile could incinerate 100,000 people immediately and within a month cause the death of two million more Americans.

What they didn't realize then was that the radiation would not dissipate into the atmosphere. Nothing dissipates. It's additive. That's why dentists today leave the room and put on leather frocks to boot each time they give you x-rays. Those tiny measly x-rays add up and never go away. In other words, none of us would be alive today if the US had launched its pre-emptive first strike. The radiation would have wiped out everything on this planet by now.

Conclusion: the Rosenbergs, if guilty as charged, are humanity's greatest heroes. They saved us all! Today is the 50th anniversary of my life – and yours! Thanks to two ordinary Jewish communists.

CHAPTER SIX

LEFTISTS YOU NEVER TALK TO

In his October 11 column "Where Europe's Leftists Fear to Tread: Saddam", Roger Cohen asked why has "the left lost their voice?" Why is there no self-analysis? and Why has anti-Bushism "replaced reflection?" But there is a voice and analysis, a lot of it, it just does not get printed in the mainstream media.

Cohen begins by telling his readers that the left was in favor of NATO's intervention in Yugoslavia. Maybe *his* left, but certainly not the left I know or support. We believed right from the start that all sides were guilty of horrendous crimes, not just the Serbians. As we now know for sure, especially after that carefully researched 4-hour BBC 4 documentary (which I show my students), ethnic cleansing began with the Croates, who as soon as they became independent adopted their parents' Nazi flag, praised their Ustashi Nazi collaborators, and weeded out anyone who opposed total subjugation to the interests of imperial Europe, specifically their old ally, Germany. We also quickly realized that NATO, and then the US with its massive indiscriminate saturation bombing of Serbia, wanted to destroy the Serbian government because Milosevic refused to privatize his country's utilities and its state companies which furnished its main source of income. We now know that Europe and the US wanted to break up Yugoslavia, to render all its components totally dependent on Europe and the US. What's more, we have always been opposed to a NATO dominated by the US; like General de Gaulle, we want the US out of NATO and all US bases closed. De Gaulle was not very left, was he, but he knew, as he said: "Any country that allows a foreign base on its territory is not free."

Never did we claim that Milosevic was innocent of the charges of ethnic cleansing, concentration camps and executions of prisoners. But we always believed, and now we know we were right, that Bosnia-Herzegovina, Kosovo, and mostly Croatia were just as guilty, if not more so.

Obviously, that's not the left that Roger Cohen knows or talks to.

And now Iraq. Cohen claims that "Milosevic pales besides Saddam Hussein." True. But we also know that he was a US ally, indeed a CIA asset when he was chief of intelligence under the African nationalist revolutionary leader Karim Kassem, and that when the US began to worry about Nasser's United Arab Republic, which Kassem joined (as did Libya), it ordered their stooge, Saddam, to murder Kassem. The US also backed Saddam in his war against Ayatollah Khomeini's Iranian regime, giving him weapons and, more important, battlefield information. It also furnished him the poison gas he used at Hablaja, which he used in a battle against Iranians, who used poison gas first, as reported in the New York Times by the CIA's area chief at that time (NYTIMES 01/31/03), as much as against the Kurds.

But that's not the only reasons we opposed the neocons' "fraudulent" (Cohen's word) war on Iraq. We know that all the administration and media talk of freedom and democracy is just that, talk, propaganda. If the US really cared about democracy it would not have overthrown every independent leader in Latin America, ending with Chile's Allende. Nor murder the Congo's great leader, Patrice Lumumba (which the Belgiums have publicly admitted doing with the CIA), nor currently try to overthrown Venezuela's Chavez. It would say, ok we lost in Iran but they had a fair election, so let's try to deal honestly with its government.

And even more so in Palestine, where everyone admits HAMAS won fairly. We on the left are not impressed by the neocon's babble to justify preemptive wars. But more important we see the real reasons for the war on Iraq. Why not a war on Saudi Arabia which has a vicious dictatorship that does not even recognize women as human beings (whereas in Saddam's Iraq, they could drive, teach, practice medicine, etc, none of which they are allowed to do in Saudi Arabia, Kuwait, or Pakistan for that matter, another great US dictator and ally). So why Iraq? The neocon's New American Century Project has said it very clearly: the US must control the Middle East so it can control its oil and gas (control, not own, since the US does not need it). That way, the US can decide who get what energy, hence who develops.

Ideally, the neocons wrote as early as 1992, we should invade Iran. But the Iranians are religious fanatics and will keep fighting us after we have defeated their army. So let's invade Iraq, a secular country, where, once beaten, the people will hail us as liberators and let us run their affairs. Convinced, Bush, as the world knows, put both his feet (and the rest of him) in his mouth and shrieked that the war was over – just as it really started. His "mission accomplished" has now caused more than 4000 American and 600,000 Iraqi lives, as compared to a total toll of 30,000 over a 20-year reign by Saddam, still of course inexcusable. Over two million Iraqis have fled their country just in the last year. And Halliburton has reaped billions of dollars in profits without giving Iraqis clean water, electricity or security, which was what our taxes were meant to pay. Mr Cohen can call our opposition "Smug", but it is as principled and as honorable as was our struggle to stop the war in Vietnam. I for one, and most of the "leftists" Cohen tries to ridicule, opposed that war as early as 1963, when JFK was still claiming he was sending only "advisers". I was fired as an editor of Newsweek in 1965 and from teaching at San Francisco State College in 1966 for my opposition to that war. I went to jail and I was blacklisted (until teachers union lawyers won my appeal and broke that blacklist almost 10 years later). But, I was lucky since I spoke fluent French, I taught at the University of Paris (Vincennes) and worked with Sartre helping many Frenchmen, if not Mr. Cohen, understand the scope and viciousness of US imperialism. I am proud to have been and to be one of those Leftists that Mr. Cohen chastises for not having his point of view.

CHAPTER SEVEN

CHE WHERE ARE YOU?

When asked if there could there ever be another Che Guevara, Gerassi replies, "Will there be another one? Of course! The next Che may very well be Panamanian, a kid who was born during the disgusting American invasion of Panama. Maybe he'll be from El Chorillo, the slum where the US wiped out five thousand innocent people. The US attacked Chorillo because the presidential palace was behind it and ostensibly America wanted to get Noriega. But that wasn't true because the papal nuncio had called the American government and said that Noriega was holed up with him and wanted to surrender. The Americans knew all along Noriega wasn't in the palace, but they wanted to destroy Chorillo precisely because it was a hotbed of nationalism. So may be the next Che will come from Panama. I've long expected the next Che to be from Africa.

"In a strange way, if you remember that Che in the beginning was hated by everyone in the industrialized world, then Osama bin Laden can be seen as a Che Guevara-like figure. Like Che, bin Laden is basically a revolutionary nationalist. Whatever the motive—whether it is to bring a reactionary and ultimately terrible vision to the Middle East, as is bin Laden's plan—the impetus has been American intervention. Che was in Guatemala when the US overthrew the Arbenz government in 1954; bin Laden and his followers view American military bases set up in Saudi Arabia after the Persian Gulf War as a violation of their religious code."

CHE WHERE ARE YOU? (December, 2002)

To the world's romantic and idealistic youths, no icon is more cherished than Ernesto Guevara. His beautiful beret-topped, bearded face hangs in dorms from Oshkosh to Oxford, covers T-shirted chests from Peoria to Paris, and is used as encouragement whenever they fight the police-protected profit-minded business-men trying to set global terms of trade. From Seattle to Quebec to Genoa, flags bearing Guevara's portrait have flown in the midst of the tear-gas, with no expla-nation, since none were needed.

Known as Che, which is the Argentine equivalent to "hey" (and is usually accompanied by "vos", Hey You!), born to a fading oligarchical Argentine family in 1928, and trained as a doctor who wanted to be a writer, Guevara, who was seriously plagued by asthma from the age of 4, lost most of the battles he waged, yet remains, perhaps precisely because he lost them, the most admired revolu-tionary of the century.

After motorcycling from Argentina and Chile up the Pacific Coast to Colombia and Venezuela, he decided, as he wrote in his first memoir, *The Motorcycle Diaries*, that he would spend his life trying to fight the "poverty, racism and injustice," caused by the exploitation of foreign, mostly US, companies. "The Third World is very rich," he said, "it contains 75 percent of the raw materials, which the First World needs. Yet we rot while they flourish, because they take all our goodies, and give us 'loans' in payment."

Guevara arrived in Guatemala in 1954, just as a popularly elected president decided to put 180,000 landless peasant families on fallow land and pay the owner its full book value (as declared by the owner for tax purposes) – an agrarian reform that every academic commentator deemed fair and just (see Columbia University Professor Albert O. Hirshman's article in *Latin American Issues*).

But Secretary of State John Foster Dulles and his brother, Allen, head of the CIA, both of whom had worked for the United Fruit Company which owned the untilled land, called the reform pure communism and ordered the CIA to train an army to overthrow the Guatemalan government.

Guevara volunteered to help resist the CIA army, whose victory led to the immediate execution of 30,000 peasants and a civil war lasting until 1998 costing more than 300,000 lives. That US intervention convinced Guevara, as it did most liberal Latin American students and intellectuals, that the US must be confronted with violence, a conviction still strong in Latin America today.

Guevara fled to Mexico where he joined Fidel Castro's *barbudos* in 1956 and became economic tsar of the revolutionary government after they chased out Dictator Fulgencia Batista and his IT&T allies in 1959. (It is said that Guevara asked Fidel why he had appointed him as minister of the economy when he designated his first cabinet. "I asked who was an economist," Fidel explained, "and you said me." "Oh, I thought you asked who is a communist," Guevara smiled.)

Desperate to help the development of "The New Man" who would be dedicated to his fellow human beings and motivated by moral not material incentives, Guevara labored long hours at the Central Bank (signing the new paper currency "Che"), and also chalked up hours of volunteer work everyday, cutting cane, building houses, planning new revolutions.

The first one, a guerrilla operation in the north of Argentina, was to be led by a close friend, the Argentine journalist Jorge Masetti who had created Prensa Latina, Cuba's still flourishing news service. But after Masetti's group was wiped out by the Argentine army, Guevara decided he had to go himself on the next one. "No longer subject to silence, diplomacy and protocol," wrote then the Mexican mystery writer Paco Ignacio Taibo in one of the best of the many Guevara biographies to appear after his death (*Guevara: Also Known as Che*), "he was Ernesto on a motorbike again, not knowing what the future would bring." It brought disasters.

In 1965, Guevara and some of his top aides, veterans of the Sierra Maestra war against Batista, journeyed to the Congo to help remnants of the nationalist movement of Prime Minister Patrice Lumumba who had been murdered by Belgians and CIA effectives. (See the recent careful docu-drama "Lumumba" and Ludo De Witte's *The Assassination of Lumumba*, based on Belgian government

documents). Then, and finally, in September 1967, after Belgian and US puppet armies forced the Cubans back across Lake Tanganyika into Tanzania, Guevara, with only 16 men, launched a guerrilla war in Bolivia, which he hoped would unleash anti-US wars of liberation throughout the Latin America continent.

Yankee imperialism is like an octopus, he explained; its tentacles reach across the globe. Our task is to keep trying to cut them off, he told revolutionaries, "Create two, three, many Vietnams!"

Defeated by 1,800 CIA-trained and led Bolivian Rangers, Guevara was caught wounded but alive in October and was summarily shot in the heart by a Cuban veteran of the Bay of Pigs who had become a CIA officer. He was then displayed bare-chested (neatly patched up so as not to show torture marks) in the hope that no more such nonsensical attempts would ever again be initiated.

Instead, Guevara became a quasi religious symbol of justice and liberation to the poor and exploited all over the world, and to the socially-conscious new generations, then and today. "Be like Che," Fidel boomed to Habaneros on the day he announced his death. "May our children be like Che," he still says today.

Most reviewers scoff at such ludicrous but dangerous slogans. Jon Lee Anderson who has written the longest (814 pages) and most fact-laden of the spate of recent biographies (*Che Guevara: A Revolutionary Life*) views the Castro-US rivalry as a tit-for-tat game and, while admiring Guevara, cannot take US domination of the Third World seriously, which makes Guevara's commitment appear somewhat absurd.

Alma Guillermoprieto (in the New Yorker), a very courageous Washington Post correspondent in Salvador during its worst military repressive days, sees Guevara only as a fanatic: "He found it unbearably humiliating ever to lose face, back down, admit defeat."

Jorge Castaneda uses his acute analytic powers (*Companero: The Life and Death of Che Guevara*) to try to destroy the Che legend, mainly because his own Mexican middle class wants peace and tranquility.

Tad Szulc, once the New York Times' most perspicacious correspondent in Latin America, feels that Guevara failed because he ignored Castro (*Fidel: A Critical Portrait*), though he does admit, as he wrote in the Los Angeles Times in 1997, that Latin America is still as Guevara complained: "torn asunder by hunger, poverty, disease, injustice and hatred. In this sense, Guevara's offering may be found in the lessons of his short life."

During each of his ventures, or shortly thereafter, Guevara wrote and Cuba published a detailed memoir about their goals, tactics, risks and achievements. Brutally honest about his own character, he inevitably gave his reviewers plenty of ammunition with which to condemn his temper, his arrogance and his misplaced self-confidence.

In his *Reminiscences of the Cuban Revolutionary War*, he gave ammunition to his arm-chair critics for calling "the need to live" a revolutionary weakness. In his *Bolivian Diary*, they focused on his lament that he did not really feel at home – or wanted – in Cuba, abandoning wife, children and happiness for meaningless bravado.

But Guevara abandoned his Cuban life before his hapless trek through the Bolivian jungles. As I reported in the 1967 introduction to *Venceremos*, a compilation of Guevara's speeches and writings that my students and I put together when we learned he had been killed, he had gone to help the Congolese revolutiona-ries in 1965. When we had discussed the Congo a few months before he left Cuba, Guevara had explained that it was the most advanced revolutionary state of black Africa.

"If the Congo can liberate itself from the imperialists," I remember him saying, "the revolutionary wave can keep moving South until, perhaps years later, it will be strong enough to assault South Africa. The imperialist will never survive a united revolutionary black Africa." In 1967, not wanting to break any off-record understanding but convinced he had gone to Congo, I asked the Cuban UN Ambassador to check if it was okay to say so. He said yes.

In 1964, I was Newsweek Latin American editor. As I was about to board a Cubana Airline plane at the Mexico City airport one day in 1964, an airline employee asked me to carry a box to Havana. Once on the plane, I nervously started wondering what if the woman did not work for Cubana, what if the box contained a bomb. I told the stewardess who told the captain who finally opened the box, signing his name as responsible.

The box contained 24 cans of Off anti-mosquito spray. It was for Guevara. Three days later, when he came to an Algerian Independence Day Party and was besieged by the press, he refused to talk "to the imperialist press." But he saw me (I had met him before, in Uruguay) and said, "you're the one who brought the box, right? Alright come on," and we talked through the night, off-record.

But when I asked him how a brave fighter such as he could worry about mosquitoes, he fired back: "I am very allergic to them. 'Off' helps. Why shouldn't I use it? Sacrifice for the sake of sacrifice is not bravery, it's stupidity."

The African Dream: The Diaries of the Revolutionary War in the Congo, as it is called by its western publishers, reveals many of the sacrifices Che and his men had to endure. None were done out of stupidity, but genuine care for the fate of the hapless, exploited Congolese.

Guevara's newly published memoir was kept secret for 35 years because it documented that Cuba's main hope in the Congo, Laurent Kabila, the second vice-president of Lumumba's Supreme Council of the Revolution and the Soviet-chosen leader against the US-Belgian puppet forces of Mobutu and Tshombe (who had actually carried out Lumumba's assassination), was no more than a lazy drunk and womanizer living high on the hog off Soviet largesse. As we now know, Kabila remained unchanged when his troops finally put him on the Congolese throne in 1997, probably the reason he was killed three years later.

But with only one rather useless map of the whole contested area, and none showing the deployment of forces, this memoir has little historical or military value. The battle plans are confusing, the camp sites hard to locate or even imagine, the confrontations inexplicable. Even the list of names offered as an "explanation" fails to explain who was where and did what.

Those details, however, are clearly included in Richard Gott's first-rate 32-page introduction, which gives a crystal-clear overview of the Congo's bloody history from its 1961 independence from Belgium to the present, and a step-by-step account of Guevara's 160-strong Cuban militants come to help curtail the Belgian-US lust for the Congo's vast mineral wealth.

Longtime Latin American correspondent for England's The Guardian, Gott never underestimates the problems facing Guevara and his men, nor, unlike most US observers, does he pooh-pooh the CIA's vicious methods used to capture that wealth. Gott's objective account cannot help back up Guevara's warning that neo-colonialism "is the most redoubtable form of imperialism – most redoubtable because of the disguises and deceits that it involves, and the long experience that the imperialist powers have in this type of exploitation."

Guevara's Congo diaries, however, are extremely valuable for what they tell about the man, his Cuban contingent, and revolution in the Third World. Committed to the very core of his being to creating a just society by "rebuilding men's souls," his conviction that revolutionary soldiers "cannot be formed in an academy but only in warfare," is bound to win the hearts of the young, disillusioned with the corruption of their elders, but alienated his allied leaders who obviously felt that their sacrifice deserved some recompense. Which is why Kabila and the other Congolese revolutionary leaders seemed to have helped the Cubans only in order to get their own expenses covered.

Guevara had no illusions. His very first line says it clearly: "This is the history of a failure." And while he does write that the People's Liberation Army "was a parasitic army; it did not work, did not train, did not fight, and demanded provisions and labour from the population, sometimes with extreme harshness," he partly blamed himself and his fellow Cubans for their haughtiness, coldness and aloofness. "Our primary function is to educate people for combat, and if there is no real coming together this will not happen."

But do citizens of one country want to be educated by strangers from another? And do their leaders want to be led by such a stranger? Certainly Kabila did not. And although Guevara could easily have passed him off as a charlatan and opportunist, which he was, he also drew the wrong conclusion: since the others, wherever or whoever they are, do not initiate the revolution, I, Guevara, will do so, and be the chief.

In Bolivia, that cost the Cubans dearly, for it convinced Mario Monje, head of the Bolivian communist party, to stay clear. As a result, Guevara received no logistic support and very few recruits from the cities. In the Congo, the Cubans were just across Lake Tanganyika from Tanzania, a friendly nation. In Bolivia, they were boxed in, with no escape route. But even in the Congo, to insist on being top dog risked alienating all the small cats. Egypt's Colonel Nasser certainly thought so. Be careful, he warned Guevara, don't become "another Tarzan, a white man among black men, leading them and protecting them … It can't be done."

The Cubans never did win the support of Congolese peasants, nor did Guevara forget to stress how crucial was such a loss. But he blamed neither the Congolese organizers who have had no experience mounting revolutionary war, nor his own folk, who couldn't speak Swahili, much less the local dialects. He himself took lessons and tried hard, but there was never enough time. Actually, he repeatedly complained that everyone had misjudged how much time it would take to start making headway.

Back in Havana, he wailed, they thought in terms of months. He himself estimated at least five years. In reality, it took 30. But even then, Kabila did not win, temporarily, with the support of Congolese peasants, but with Rwandan soldiers who had been politicized by the first wave of Tutsi-Hutu massacres stimulated by the French.

As it turned out, the lack of peasant support doomed Guevara's efforts in Bolivia as well. And he should have known better, since he himself had stressed in his *Reminiscences* the crucial support that Cuban peasants, organized by a squatter chief named Crescencio Perez and a 26-of-July militant named Celia Sanchez (who later became Fidel's lover) gave the *barbudos*.

True, in Bolivia, the peasants were much more politicized; they had gone through the nationalist revolution of 1952. Yet they were reluctant to risk their lives for results not at all guaranteed, and when it looked as if the Rangers would prevail, they tried to assure their own survival by cooperating with the army. On April 30, 1967 Guevara complained to his diary that "the peasant base is still not being formed" and on September 30, nine days before being caught, that "the mass of peasants does not help us at all and have become informers."

Whether in the Congo or in Bolivia, the Cubans failed to unleash people's war against the US not because of their personal weaknesses or lack of effort. On the contrary, the most striking conclusion that Guevara's diaries makes absolutely clear is that these were totally committed, dedicated revolutionaries.

Most of his aides and many of his soldiers were veterans of the Sierra Maestra. They fought under unbelievably adverse conditions in the Congo, often going without food for days at a time, ravaged by malaria, mosquitoes, scorpions, snakes and hysterical extremely superstitious allies (whose cult forbade them to touch a dead man).

Sixteen of the Cuban survivors then joined Guevara in his equally arduous attempt to generate a continental guerrilla in Bolivia. Like Guevara, they sometimes got depressed, sometimes lost their cool, sometimes wanted to quit, sometimes lost their lives. But they stuck it out, because, like Guevara, they believed that human beings deserve a better world, and it is clear from reading these Congo diaries, that most would do it again. And so would their sons, especially against an invader backed by the US.

PART II: UNREPENTANT CRITICAL PEDAGOGY

UNREPENTANT CRITICAL PEDAGOGY

Monchinski: What is an unrepentant critical pedagogy and what does that term mean to you?

Gerassi: I've been in academia ever since I got burned as a member of the mainstream press. I was too active against the war in Vietnam and eventually I sort of got fired from *Newsweek*. Not really "fired"; the managing editor was a good friend of mine. He said to me, "Under what circumstances can you leave *Newsweek* in such a way that you can never publicly claim you got fired for political reasons?" [laughs]. I laid out my conditions, "I keep my job, I keep my researcher, and I keep my salary until I get another job." He said, "Well, how long could that be?" I couldn't tell him. "Come on! That could be in ten years" he said and I had to agree, "Yeah, could be." He laughed and said "okay."

Monchinski: So you did that?

Gerassi: Yeah, but then I decided to research and write the *Boys of Boise*. It was about a homosexual witch hunt that took place in Boise, Idaho. A lot of people got arrested. My researcher and I went there and it wasn't long after we arrived that I realized this was a hot potato. It wasn't at all just a salacious story about homosexuals. It was an attempt by a bunch of urban renewalists—who happened to be headed by a homosexual—to change the configuration of Boise, Idaho. They were going to bring all sorts of new things and new ideas to Boise and that was a threat to the elite of Idaho because the consequence was that blacks and unions would surely come with the projects. The elite tried to stop that. They met at a club called the Arid Club and while they were there they were mulling over what they could do, one of them said, "There must be some way to stop these goddamn faggots" and someone immediately asked "Are you just calling them that or do you know something?" The loud-mouth replied: "No, the banker is as queer as a three dollar bill." So they started a witch hunt in order to stop them and it got out of hand.

Monchinski: How so?

Gerassi: They arrested a few people and threw them in jail for crimes against humanity. When they arrested the banker he hired a lawyer to fight back. It turned out that the good guys were the bad guys. What I mean by that is that the people who fought against the witch-hunters included Carver, who was Eisenhower's Secretary of the Interior, and Glen Smiley, who had been a Republican governor of Idaho. In other words, these so-called conservative guys were also civil libertarians and their attitude was, "It's none of our business what these guys are doing in their private lives." The so-called liberals, like Frank Church and his father, were on the wrong side. They wanted to kick these people out. The witch hunt got completely out of control. They brought in McCarthy's investigator from the State Department to carry out the witch-hunt.

Well, I ended up writing the book in such a way that it got great reviews and was considered very seriously. The sociologist at Harvard, Becker praised it. When I saw the praise in *Book Week* I called up my editor all excited, saying, "Boy, we got a great review!" And he said, "Yeah, your book is dead." I said, "What do you mean it's dead?" He said, "Yeah, dead. You get great reviews from academics, [which means] your book doesn't sell." It did eventually sell well, in part, because several years later CBS did a whole special on homosexuals in America and they included the *Boys of Boise* in one segment.

As a result of all that, I was sort of out of journalism, period. I did kind of keep my hand in it by being a correspondent for the Inter-American Press Association. It was a Christian news service all over the world, sort of left wing. I was their Paris correspondent for awhile.

But I was burned. So I started in academia. I was hired at NYU[37] and started teaching journalism. I discovered that in academia the same things happen that happen in journalism. You have to be careful; you can't say this, you can't say that; if you don't have tenure … And this continues to this day.

Monchinski: More and more teaching at the undergraduate and graduate level is done by graduates students who don't have their PhDs, lack benefits, and are not on tenure tracks. But you have tenure at Queens College[38] and have had it since 1983.

Gerassi: Right. I'm tenured so I can get away with saying all sorts of things. For example, next semester, I'm doing a seminar titled *The Collapse of American Democracy*, in which I'm using very "straight" books, books published by Pantheon and Common Courage and Seven Stories Press. I was a little bit leery when I suggested it as a subject for a course because I didn't think I could get away with it. But, since I get the students—which means I get the budget because in public universities, budgets are determined by the number of people who sign up for a course – since I fill seats I can get away with it. But it's also because I have tenure.

Monchinski: Did your political activism ever get in the way of your appointment at a university?

Gerassi: I was teaching journalism at NYU when Bertrand Russell[39] invited me to go to North Vietnam as part of the first investigating commission for the International War Crimes Tribunal. I had been head of the Bertrand Russell Peace Foundation here in New York.

I said yes and got someone with a PhD—the guy I made arrangements with was a full professor; I was only an associate professor—to cover my classes at NYU. Nevertheless, stories started circulating that I would be fired for violating the law, the law being you couldn't travel to North Vietnam. Turned out to be wrong. What you *couldn't* do was use an American passport to travel to North Vietnam. The Attorney General took away my passport when I returned from North Vietnam, but the Supreme Court ordered it returned.

I accepted a job at San Francisco State teaching international relations when I returned because I thought I'd be losing my job at NYU. It turned out all that information about being fired was wrong, that NYU wanted to keep me. But to tell you the truth the idea of teaching international relations appealed to me more than the idea of continuing to teach journalism. I accepted and went to San Francisco State.

At San Francisco State I was accused of leading the students in demonstration against the war in Vietnam, fired and blacklisted. It took eight years for the teachers' union lawyers to win that case.

Monchinski: What exactly did they charge you with?

Gerassi: [laughs] They initially charged me with inciting civil insurrection!

Monchinski: What did they say you were doing, attending rallies with students?

Gerassi: The students took over the university completely, and I was *with* the students. There's no question I was with them; I participated alongside them. But I wasn't their leader and I was accused of being their leader.

Columbia gets the credit but San Francisco State was the first university seized by students – December 6, 1966. There were various issues and the students were absolutely right. For example, San Francisco State allowed the military to do training for ROTC[40] and if you signed up you got half a credit for that. I suggested that myself and Don Duncan be allowed to teach a course about revolutionary training and that students get half a credit for that. I was legitimate because I had been in the 77th Special Forces during Korea so I could teach it. Duncan was military editor at Ramparts[41] and had fought in Vietnam, quitting when his three years were up. He was Special Forces too. The university administration wouldn't allow us to do it.

Another issue that contributed to this was a local San Francisco newspaper. It was basically racist. One day the black student union went in there and destroyed the place. At about the same time, the Open *Process*, an independent newspaper run by the students, ran a poem by a white man named Shapiro in which he used scatological terms to describe the racists. He was reprimanded and told he'd have a hearing; the blacks were suspended outright. So this inequality was another point.

On December 6, 1966, students from all around the Bay Area came to hear us plan for a weeklong demonstration being called Stop the Draft Week. We were going to go to Oakland to stop the recruiting of troops for Vietnam. We did that by the way and the cops were so violent they beat up everyone including the press which means we got good press because newsmen don't like to get beat up! [chuckles]

We seized San Francisco State, which wouldn't concede any of our points and condemned our participation in Stop the Draft Week. I say *we* because I was part of the students. We seized San Francisco State and declared it the first free territory in the United States.

Monchinski: So what was going on? Were you still teaching classes?

Gerassi: Yes, classes continued. What happened was it was perceived that if a teacher is part of a movement he must be the leader and I was accused of being the leader. In no way was I a leader. I was a fairly good speaker and I did speak at the open mic but so did a lot of students.

I confronted John Summerskill, the rector of the university. He made an impassioned speech about how we should keep our demonstrations off the university grounds. I grabbed the mic at that point, at the request of the students, and basically I said, "Look, it's not fair, you're allowing all sorts of research in the science and engineering departments for the army but you're not allowing for the other side. You're calling it an open university, but it's only open for the government." I also added that the vast majority of the students and faculty were against the war in Vietnam. I remember the ending very well, "I'm sorry Dr. Summerskill, but as long as you remain on the side of the murderers, we're going to have to protest."

Monchinski: What happened next?

Gerassi: It lead to the students literally taking over the administration building. And that was, in part, a mistake by my lawyer. Because things were getting so heated I had asked a lawyer friend to accompany me. Beverly Axelrod[42] was one of the greatest women I have ever known. I first met her at "Summer 2" in 1962, when we all went down south to register blacks to vote.

I got arrested and put in a cell next to Floyd McKissik, who was head of CORE, the Congress for Racial Equality We were talking and all when I saw this unbelievably beautiful woman come in and go up to McKissik. She said "I've been sent by NAACP to bail you out." So I yelled, "Hey, wait a minute, lady! I'm in here for exactly the same reason, why don't you bail me out?" McKissik turned to Beverly and said, "He's right. We got arrested at the same time." So Beverly bailed me out as well. We became great friends.

Monchinski: Beverly advised you during the student takeover of San Francisco State?

Gerassi: Yes. At one point when the students charged and seized the administration building I said "I should go. I'm with them," and I asked Beverly, "Will I get arrested for this?" Beverly's great advice was, "No, the administration has locked the doors. It's like a factory lock-out. You, as an employee of the university, have the right to be inside."

So I'm the one who broke the window and went in, which is why I was accused of being the leader. But I did that because I thought if a student did it, it would create trouble for those students, whereas—as Beverly had said—I had a *right* to do it. She couldn't handle my case so she passed me over to the greatest lawyer who ever fought for the Movement, Charley Garry[43]. He remained my lawyer all the way through all the other fusses and stuff I got into because I got arrested over and over again and he'd always get me out.

Monchinski: You knew Beverly when she was involved with Eldrige Cleaver?

Gerassi: When I first went to San Francisco State I stayed with her at her place in Haight-Ashbury[44]. She was my best friend at that time, no question about it.

Years later when she felt totally defeated in San Francisco she decided to move to New Mexico to work with the Alianza de los Pueblos Libres, an independent political party in the '68 election. Rejes Tijerina was running for president with Eldridge Cleaver[45] as his vice president on an independent party ticket in 1968.

Beverly had been very active as a lawyer in the Bay area and was crushed by what happened with Eldridge Cleaver. She had been his lawyer and fell in love with him, visiting him in his cell at San Quentin. Eventually, she managed to get people like my friend, Norman Mailer[46], to write that Cleaver had written such a fabulous book that he should be released from prison if he could get a job.

I was then on the board of *Ramparts* and we pressured *Ramparts* to put Cleaver on staff as our crime editor. He got released and was also living in Beverly's house. They were living as lovers. She's the one who really wrote *Soul on Ice*. He got the credit for it but she wrote it. In fact, there is a contract she'd signed with Eldridge that she'd get one fourth of the royalties. The publisher honored that contract and she lived off that for a long time because the book was an incredible best seller.

Let me make this clear: she didn't technically write *Soul on Ice*. Eldridge would send her these fantastic letters from jail and she'd put them together, move them around such that they made a wonderful story.

Monchinski: When you went to get jobs at universities later on, did your arrest record hurt you?

Gerassi: At Sacramento State it did. The chancellor of the university system issued decree 500 which said that anyone who had ever been fired for cause—and I had been fired for cause at that point—can never be rehired in any other educational system in California. And every other state honored that so I couldn't get a job. So I went and taught American Civilization at the University of Paris for a few years. I gave the lectures in English but we spoke French for the conversations and debates. I speak French as fluently as I speak English.

Eventually in '74, the AAUP lawyers won, but since I had been teaching all along and paid fairly well as an adjunct full professor I told the union to keep the money. The union had won my salary retroactively from San Francisco State but they hadn't charged to represent me, so I thought it was right that they keep the money. I wanted to come back to America and the very first job I was offered was to teach comparative culture at the University of California at Irvine and I accepted.

But during all of '67 and '68, before I went to France, I went around the United States speaking and I would participate in demonstrations and I'd keep getting arrested. Before being able to start the whole academic year at Irvine I was offered a job at Sacramento State and I had to fill out a form. By then Charley Garry had gotten me off all the felony charges so all I had on my record were misdemeanors like disturbing the peace.

I had to fill out a form that asked "Have you ever been arrested for a felony?" and I checked "no," but the following question was, "Have you ever been restricted or prohibited from appearing on a university campus?" and there I had to check "yes". Because after I was fired in '66 I continued to teach even though I was blacklisted.

Monchinski: How did you do that?

Gerassi: All the faculty members in my department at San Francisco State after my firing said, "We will give whatever grade you give to your students in one of our courses. Just have them register for our courses but they'll take your course."

Marcuse[47] and I had an exchange. He was teaching philosophy at San Diego. I would go down there every other week and he'd come up to San Francisco State every other week and we'd have debates in front of our students. I wanted to continue that. The chaplain of the university was a great guy and was on our side. I was forbidden to appear on land owned by San Francisco State, but the chapel did not belong to the University. So Marcuse would come and join me at the chapel. He was being careful—I don't think he was a citizen—so he asked the chaplain to give him a note saying he [the chaplain] had invited him there and not just me.

Marcuse believed that the university was a sanctuary and that we shouldn't confront the establishment at the university and on its grounds. He was opposed to what I had done and what the students had done. So I told the students to prepare well and read all his books, because we were going to have a great debate.

He came and talked for fifteen minutes and then my best students really went after him. The more heated and intense the debate became the more he would rub his hands in delight but he was losing and I couldn't understand why he was so obviously delighted. At the end he said, "You've just proved my point. How can you give up a forum like this by stupidly charging the administration building which did nothing?"

I started teaching at Sacramento State when suddenly a couple of university marshals showed up and said, "Out! You can't teach here." At Sacramento there was a private dormitory. The manager was interested in Sartre and I was teaching a course on the political philosophy of Sartre. So he said, "Ladies and gentlemen, kindly walk across the street, there is a private dormitory there where we can have class."

And what happened at Sacramento State was the same thing that happened at San Francisco State: my colleagues in the Political Science department at Sacramento said my students could register with them, they would give credit, and I could continue teaching. It was great! But even better, because I wasn't getting paid, the teachers at Sacramento chipped in and donated money for me to live on. I lived in the dorm so I asked for very little money.

At the end of that year I spoke everywhere imaginable. I got to know America as I traveled and spoke and stayed in collectives. Thinking back, the years of the movement were the best years of my life.

Monchinski: Did you ever really feel in danger during your time in the Movement?

Gerassi: I'll never forget one particular lecture. It was at Loyola University in New Orleans. I was invited to speak and the place was packed and I started talking.

All of a sudden four enormous brutes walked in. These guys were eight feet tall and six feet wide! They started heading very slowly towards the podium. It was clear they came in to beat me up. It turned out they were Cuban exiles. They approached the podium and were very menacing, dragging chains they were carrying along the floor.

Everybody was nervous. I was nervous. All of a sudden, from behind the stage, four nuns in nun garb appeared and stood in front of the podium with their arms crossed. I'll never forget it, I could have kissed those nuns if it was ethical! They were my bodyguards.

Monchinski: Blacklisted in America, when and why did you head to Europe?

Gerassi: Ralph Milliband[48] said, "Look, one of the things you don't have is a PhD. You can't do anything—you're burned—you can't teach, you can't work in journalism. Why don't you come over to England as a student at the London School of Economics." He said he'd get all the course work waived as I'd had three books published by that point. All I'd have to do was a dissertation.

This is 1969, I'm 37 years old. I go over to England and register as a student but feared I'm going to starve to death because I had no money. But in England every time you speak on television you get paid. There were a whole bunch of people who immediately organized to "feed Gerassi." I became an expert on aspirin, I was on the aspirin show; I became an expert on the Special Forces though that wasn't so strange because I had been in the Special Forces; I didn't know so much about English popular music and they wanted me to be an expert on the Rolling Stones so Granada television hired me to do the security for the first Rolling Stones in the park concert.

I went and hired the Hell's Angels[49]. Now, the Hell's Angels in England are nice. They look like brutes and they walk around with cue-sticks and no one messes with them, but they don't hurt a fly. I hired them to do the security and it went very nicely and I got to like the Stones. Certainly Jagger, he's a great guy. But to tell you the truth he was then with a Venezuelan woman and I liked her more.

I managed to survive and the following year Conor Cruise O'Brien asked me to take over for him when he completed that academic year at Vincennes and I did. I wound up teaching four years at Vincennes. I was hired as an adjunct full professor and I was paid very well. Conor Cruise O'Brien had been UN representative in the Congo and had written a great play in which he said point blank that it was the CIA that killed Lumumba—he turned out to be right, it was the CIA and Belgian secret service—but for that play the Americans put up such pressure that the UN had to fire him. Vincennes, the University of Paris, was a great experimental university. All the people who were oddballs were teaching there—Deleuze, Guatari[50], Foucault, you name them, and I loved teaching there.

Monchinski: What was Foucault like as a person?

Gerassi: I first met Foucault[51] when Sartre and Claude Mauriac decided to help the left wingers occupy empty building that the homeless were squatting in. Sartre and Mauriac hoped that their presence would keep the police from charging in and clearing everyone out by bashing heads. I was there with them. This had happened at various times before with traditional leftists in France, Gauchists, and after the photo op they all went home and the cops would come in and beat up everybody.

Sartre, Foucault, and Mauriac decided to stay and they did and during the night I struck up a conversation with Foucault and we hit it off. He started to invite me to various shindigs at his apartment where I met his lover. I was under tremendous pressure from various people who knew I was a journalist to write about Foucault's relationship but I never did.

I must also say I liked Claude Mauriac. He had all the faults of a moralist, which is to say, dogmatism. For the moralist everything is by principle instead of by circumstance. But he was a genuinely honest moralist and I liked him.

I was at Foucault's for the famous session organized by Simone de Beauvoir where Edward Siad[52] wrote an article saying how bored he was and how terrible it was. Foucault was never boring, *never*. He was always able to make the kinds of points and arguments that were much more sophisticated than his admirers'.

Monchinski: Why is Foucault's prose so difficult for many people to understand?

Gerassi: There was a quirk about Foucault when he wrote, with the sociologist-philosopher dominating in his writing. But all these guys were complicated. Just try and read Sartre's *The Critique of Dialectical Reason* once and think because you read it through once you've got it! No, you have to go over it and over it and discuss it and mull it over. The ideas that they were trying to express are very complicated ideas on the one hand, and on the other their way of presenting these ideas is dialectical. That means they present conflicting bits of thought or evidence which makes it very hard to follow. When you look at Sartre's autobiography, *Words*, it is so incredibly simple, so easy to read, but he's not expressing any profound ideas, he's just relating his life. Same with Foucault, but unlike Sartre he didn't write plays.

It was during this time that I started working with Foucault and then Sartre and Beauvoir. At the time I was working on *The Revolutionary Priest*, a book about Camilo Torres, an oligarch's son and a priest who joined the Colombian guerillas and died in his very first battle. I had met him while I was a correspondent in Latin America and had a tremendous admiration for him.

The book came out in England first and my editor there at Jonathan Cape said, "You know, it's a great book but you're not going to make any money from it. Why don't you write a book that makes money for a change? How about Fanon?" Fanon[53] was very *in* in those days. I declined and said, "Maybe I can do Sartre" and he said, "No you can't." I asked him why not and he said Sartre had turned down everybody, he doesn't want an biography.

Well, the next time I had lunch with Sartre I said, "By the way, Sartre, don't you have any vanity?" And he said, "Of course, like anybody else. Why?" And I said, "Well, apparently you don't want anybody to do your biography." And he laughed and said, "Des petits con, those little jerks from Paris Review, I would never let them do it. What about you, why don't you do it?"

I tried to decline but he continued, "No, tell me, how would you do it if you decided to do it?" I said, "Well, I guess what I would do is try to explain why it took you forty-five years to reach a position that took us five." And he said, "Yeah, not bad."

He obviously expected something else so I added, "Also I guess I would try to explain how a petty bourgeois—because that's what you are, you're a petty bourgeois through and through, look at the way you're eating", he was eating a choucroute garnie, a gory meal with pork and beans and God knows what and drinking wine. This was his lunch, okay?

I continued, "How can a petty bourgeois like you became a revolutionary?" He almost jumped out of his seat and said, "D'accord! I agree! Write it!" I said, "Wait" but he said, "No, no waiting, do a contract right now." So he called the waiter and asked the waiter to bring over a piece of paper and on that paper he wrote out a contract giving me absolute exclusivity to his documents and interviews. I, in turn, granted permission to other authors and writers because I didn't think it was fair that I alone had this access.

Monchinski: What position did it take Sartre 45 years to reach what everyone else had realized it in five?

Gerassi: That we *need* a revolution; that we could never change the system through ballots. It took Sartre so many years to realize this because he had never been in jail, he had never been beaten up. There was no way Abbie Hoffman or Jerry Rubin could levitate the Pentagon, no matter how hard they tried. The Hippie Sixties proved to me that you cannot proceed in that way. I understood a lot about how the system works that Sartre could never understand until he chose to live with the proletarian left, which included his friend Pierre Goldman. Goldman wrote the book *Growing up Jewish in Poland* and was assassinated by Zionist fanatics.

Monchinski: You were politically involved in France at this time?

Gerassi: I joined the Movement in France which was more left than that in America. The French left defined itself as "moralistic Maoists." Sartre was part of that, a speaker for them.

Monchinski: When did you take your PhD?

Gerassi: When I returned to the United States to teach at Irvine I got a letter from LSE saying they had a limit of seven years for PhD candidates, warning me I had to finish up my dissertation. I sat down and in three weeks wrote a book called *A Revolutionary Theory* as pertaining specifically to Latin America, submitted it to my advisor, Ralph Milliband who sent it back to me and said it was too *well* written, that I needed longer sentences and longer paragraphs, that I needed more "which's" and "wherefore's." So I rewrote it and sent it to him and he accepted it.

Now here's a nice little detail about British academia. Milliband told me I had to come for the defense, and I had to rush. I got Irvine to give me a week off and I hopped on a plane for England. I walked into this room for my dissertation defense. Who else was in that room? I'm sitting next to Ralph Milliband, he's my advisor and supposed to come to my defense. There are three people facing me. One of them is Hobsbawm[54], the great Hobsbawm. Another was the great Marxist historian Christopher Hill[55]. I said to myself, "Holy smokes!"

Monchinski: Did you choose your committee?

Gerassi: No! Milliband chose them. I was terrified.

Monchinski: (laughs).

Gerassi: Now Hill was an incredible historian who was still a member of the Communist Party and I had criticized the Communist Party so I thought, "Oh boy, am I in trouble!" I don't remember the third guys' name but he was head of Latin American studies at Edinborough.

The first question was from Hobsbawm and I'll never forget it. He began by saying [Gerassi mimics Hobsbawm's voice and mannerisms], "*Weeelll*, John, I was very shocked to read on page four ... " and I said to myself, "My god. He starts with page four. He's going to read all the way through like that? They're going to demand major revisions and I don't have time. I've got three weeks until my seven years are up." And then more, more questions like that.

I kept trying to catch Milliband's eye because he was supposed to come to my defense but he avoided my glances. And this went on for four hours—actually three hours and twenty minutes! I couldn't smoke; in those days I was still a smoker. They were drinking coffee. It turned out to be "red coffee" as we called it then; in other words, wine.

At the end of the whole thing Milliband said, "Well, John, as you noticed, I didn't come to your defense. The reason is we got together beforehand and decided to accept your dissertation with no revisions, the highest honors, congratulations Doctor!" Instead of jumping up and down I yelled at them, "You fucking sadists!" Fortunately they laughed and invited me to go have a drink with them.

When I got on the double decker bus that day to head back to where I was staying I was upstairs smoking cigarette after cigarette and I started to look over my dissertation, which, by the way, has to be printed beforehand in England. By pure fluke I look down in a chapter on Brazil to the footnotes and I saw "Che Guevara." I jumped, "What the ... ? Che Guevara in Brazil?"

I start looking through all of the footnotes: all were wrong! The secretary must have skipped a page in the beginning of the first chapter so all the notes were off. And these four great thinkers, some of the biggest names in academia, hadn't bothered to check!

Anyway, I got my PhD. As a result of that Irvine could put in a request for me to get tenure and I accepted, as did Stanley Aronowitz[56] who was also there. We went out to celebrate and then California passed Proposition 13 which said from now on no more money can be raised from private property to pay teachers. They put a freeze on new hiring. Both Stanley Aronowitz and I were fired in effect.

I had just gotten a Guggenheim[57] so I went to France to continue my book on Sartre; Stanley went to work with the labor unions for awhile and then we both got hired in the CUNY system where we both still are today.

Monchinski: Where were you educated, your early years of school?

Gerassi: My parents moved to Paris when I was two and I eventually went to Lycee Montaigne where I did kindergarten through third grade. All I remember about that was that at lunchtime we got wine as young as we were! It was about two centimeters in a glass, the rest was filled with water, but we got wine [laughs].

Monchinski: Was this a public school?

Gerassi: Yeah, it was a public school. Anyway, I came to the United States in 1940. My parents didn't want to come to America, my father wanted to fight in the French underground. The Francoist assassins tried to machine gun him at one point in Portugal when he went to talk to British intelligence. My uncle was working for British intelligence, set up this enormous network and got the Victoria Cross[58] from the Queen herself.

After the machine gunning my father was frightened for me and took the family to the United States. During the war he was submarined back into Spain and so I never saw him during the war. My mother put me into a private school, the Rumsey Hall School in Connecticut, with my tuition and boarding paid for by the Quakers[59].

When my father returned from the war he was shocked that I had forgotten my French so he pulled me out and said I should go to the French Lycee. But that was a very expensive school in uptown New York so he sent my mother to flirt with the owner to get me in! She did—she got me a full scholarship!

Monchinski: Were you a good student at that age?

Gerassi: I was the absolute *worst* student at Rumsey Hall my first year. The administrators said they would kick me out except the Quakers intervened and begged the administration to give me another year, saying I was all shaken up by the war.

Monchinski: What do you mean you were a bad student? Were you acting out behavior-wise?

Gerassi: Yeah.

Monchinski: Bad grades?

Gerassi: Yeah. I was a pest, a thief, a wise guy. I never did the homework. On May Day[60] I would not sit down, I stood at attention all day. I kept getting demerits and letters home to my mother. I managed to survive that first year thanks to the Quakers.

The second year I got the first prize in Improvement in Scholarship. I got a letter[61] in both baseball and football. I was still a thief in many ways. One of the things about Rumsey Hall is that you *have* to belong to a religion. I decided to be a Congregationist, which was the Church right next door to my dorm. I signed up to be the guy who passes the collection plate around during chapel services. People used to put cash in there and I would pocket some of the cash.

Everybody else got allowances from home. My mother couldn't afford that. She wasn't allowed to get a green card so she made what money she could doing facial massages for friends and things like that. I did even better in my third year so that helped me get a full scholarship to the French school.

Monchinski: To what do you attribute your turnaround?

Gerassi: I think one of the reasons I did very well in school is because of my political consciousness that I inherited from my parents. I wanted to work for people and the French school had a priest, <u>Pere</u> Farine, and his name in French means "the dough". I went to him one day and said I wanted to become a Catholic. He asked why and I said, "Well, you tell stories of what this woman is doing and what that man is doing and I want to work with them." The woman he had referred to was Dorothy Day[62] of Catholic Worker.

He said, "Well, tell me first what you believe in." So I told him. I spoke for about an hour. I told him what I believed and I never mentioned God, never mentioned Jesus, didn't mention I was half Jewish, nothing like that. All I talked about was the social work he had us do and often spoke of. When I finished he said, "Look, you're a better Catholic than any Catholic that comes to my church.

Stay an atheist if that's what you are. I'll give you a little note and you go introduce yourself to Dorothy Day."

I went and visited her and when she found out I spoke Spanish she was delighted and sent me to Harlem to work at a Friendship House[63]. That's where I befriended Thomas Merton, probably the most important Catholic philosopher. I wound up visiting him in a Trappist monastery in Kentucky later on. He died in India when a fan fell into the bathtub he was in and electrocuted him.

I met another guy there and we got along well and years later ran into each other again. When I arrived at Queens College they took me to my office and introduced me to the professor I'd be sharing office space with. They introduced us and his name didn't mean anything to me at first. I looked at him and he looked at me and I said, "We know each other, don't we?" and he said, "I think we do!" "Well, let's try to figure out when." It was Michael Harrington[64] and I had met him years before at Friendship House.

Monchinski: How do you account for your admiration of religious people like Pere Farine, Dorothy Day, and Camilo Torres when you yourself are not religious?

Gerassi: Like the genuine revolutionaries in the time of Jesus who were battling Rome, these people are fighting. By putting it into a context of something bigger than themselves, which in their case is a god, they are able to appeal to the general public. It appeals to the public before the public is educated enough to realize that actually the thing bigger than yourself is humanity. One of the greatest revolutionary writings was by Pope John the 23rd, the *Encyclical Pacem in Terres*, which says in effect, that any man who sleeps in a bed of gold when there is still a single human being who sleeps in a bed of mud is a sinner against God. Well, he's not a sinner against God, but his is a betrayal of the human trust, and I think that is why there are so many religious people in history who have fought for their fellow human beings.

Monchinski: Were you "political" from an early age?

Gerassi: The French lycee was the turning point where I became politically active. I left home because I couldn't stand my father. He was a politically marvelous man but personally was a tyrant and at that age I didn't get along with him at all.

One week before my sixteenth birthday I left home and moved into a rooming house on the West Side. I could touch all four walls from the bed. I put a board over the sink and that was my desk.

The year before I had taken the French baccalaureate[65] and passed with *bien*, which is good. There is a "very good," *tres bien*, but I didn't get "very good." I remember that because I hadn't seen my parents in about a year. They kept track of me through my best friend's parents who relayed stories about me. So they knew that I had passed with *bien*. My father knew I had passed with *bien* but I didn't know that *he* knew.

I called him after I got the results and asked if there was any mail for me and he said, "Yeah, why don't you come by at dinner and pick it up?" I'm there at dinner and I'm waiting for my father or mother to ask me how I had done and they never asked me. Finally I couldn't take it anymore so I said, "Oh, by the way, I passed my baccalaureate with *bien*" and my father says, "Oh, why not *tres bien*?"

Monchinski: Was he serious or was he busting your chops?

Gerassi: He was just busting my chops but at the time I was just floored!

Monchinski: You did your undergrad at Columbia University.

Gerassi: At the insistence of my French teachers I had applied to Columbia. I was living in a rooming house with no money, getting by through gambling, through buying and selling old cars.

One day I'm sitting on the stoop of the rooming house with a couple of buddies when a guy with a tie and a tweed jacket—he couldn't have been more of a cliché—walks up and says, "You kids know a guy by the name of John Gerassi?" I piped up, "Who wants to know?" and he figured immediately it was me.

He introduced himself as an English professor at Columbia and mentioned that I had applied to attend Columbia. All my buddies disappeared at this point. He said, "you applied pending your baccalaureate exam and I know you passed your baccalaureate exam but then you never followed up. What happened?" I told him I couldn't afford it.

"Can I ask you a couple of questions about your initial application?" he asked so I told him "Sure, if you want to." "Well, there's a space here for you to put in all the books you've read in the past year. You filled that whole space up and put 'etc.'"

I said, "Well, yeah, it's a short space." He looked at me and asked, "Did you read all these books?" I told him I read a book every week and asked him, "Doesn't everybody at school?" He laughed and said, "You mind if I ask you some questions about these books?" I told him to go ahead.

He asked me four questions which I will never forget. One was about *The Possessed*, Dostoyevsky's discussion between Kirilov and Shatov; one was about Andrei in *War and Peace*; another was about Dos Pasos' *Manhattan Transfer*; and the final question was about Faulkner's *Absalom, Absalom!*.

After I answered those four he said, "Why don't you come to Columbia?" I reminded him I couldn't afford it. He said, "Do you think you could maintain a B-minus average?" I said that a B-minus would be easy. He said, "Well, so long as you maintain a B-minus average you've got a full scholarship. Congratulations, you've just been admitted" and he extended his hand.

I couldn't believe it! Imagine how kids today have to do it with all those forms, applications and exams.

Monchinski: What kind of student were you at Columbia?

Gerassi: I did well but I wasn't a good student. I didn't work very hard except for a couple of classes. I took one class with Mathewson called *Tolstoy and Dostoyevsky*. He handed out the syllabus the first day of class and we had to read *all* the major works of Tolstoy and Dostoyevsky and write three papers! Keep in mind this was only a two credit general studies course. That first day there were thirty of us, the next session there were only seven of us. Everyone else dropped. But, among those seven, were guys that have recurred through my life ever after. They included Yvan Gold, the novelist; John Portugal the poet; Scotty Reston, who became managing editor of *The New York Times*; Arthur Gregor, another poet.

It was an incredible course and I read everything that was on that syllabus. I'd read it in the bathroom, I'd read it at night. I just went crazy but I read it all and got an A+. I still have the papers I wrote. One was about Prince Andrei as an existential hero, I remember that. Another was about the discussion between Kirilov and Shatov in *The Possessed*—for some reason in America its called *The Devils* but it should be called *The Possessed*—their discussion about the coming of the man-god.

At Columbia you had to do an apprenticeship and in Political Science I asked to do an apprenticeship with Vito Marcantonio[66]. The administration tried to stop me and I raised an incredible stink at Columbia. I went to see Vito Marcantonio and ended up working for him for his 1950 campaign.

Monchinski: Why didn't they want you to work for him?

Gerassi: Because he was a communist! Officially he was an *American Labor Party*[67] representative, and was not openly a member of the communist party. Vito was the only representative who voted *no* to the war in Korea. He was a great man, an absolutely great man.

My parents had gone to the Putney School[68] to teach in '49. They were in trouble because my father admitted he lied, that he had not been a real diplomat when they came to this country. It had been their only way for us to escape from Portugal, to lie and use the diplomatic passports Rubirosa had given them. I was separated from my parents' case. The government didn't want to deport my parents because my father had worked for OSS but I was a different story and got deportation procedures.

I went to Vito in 1952 with this deportation letter and he asked me where I lived. I was living under the elevated line[69] on 59th Street. Believe it or not the east side was incredibly poor in those days. I thought I had a very nice apartment at that time. There was a Chinese restaurant downstairs that charged *fifty-nine cents* for a three course dinner!

Anyway, Vito said, "That's Coudert's district, isn't it?" Coudert was the congressman from the Silk Stocking District. The whole area where I lived, except for my own little hole there under the El, was very rich! Coudert was one of two—the Rapp-Coudert Committee[70]—behind the blacklisting in New York.

Vito called his secretary and said, "Get me Coudert." Vito picked up the phone: "Hello? Hi. This is Vito. I want you to do me a favor. I'm going to send you over a guy who is being deported. I want you to put in a private bill for him. Yeah. Okay. Monday, first thing." He hung up. I couldn't believe it: Coudert is an arch-reactionary and Vito is a commie.

"You go there at 9:30," Vito told me, "And you sit there until he lets you in. You don't go to the bathroom, you don't go to lunch, you just sit there until he calls for you."

I went and he called me in at 10 AM. I didn't get a chance to sit down. I walked into Coudert's enormous office and he said, "I'm going to ask you two questions and I want an honest answer to both. One, are you a communist or fellow traveler[71] and don't ask me to define it?" I hesitated and said, "No, sir."

"Alright, question number two: if I put in a private bill for you are you going to vote for me?" I hesitated and I hesitated and finally I said, "No, sir."

"All right,' he said, "I believe your first answer and I'll put that bill in." And he did. But he told me as I walked out, "I'm not going to act on this bill, it's going to die at the end of the session so you better do something before the end of the Congressional session."

I went to see Vito and I told him the story and he roared with laughter and said, "You know what he meant right? He couldn't tell you because that wouldn't sound right from an arch-Republican, but he was telling you to marry an American quick!" So I did and then I got drafted.

Monchinski: After teaching at Irvine, where did you go?

Gerassi: I gave a series of lectures on the east coast. At the time I was fed up with the west coast and felt the students were all water-logged with their minds on surfing. I lectured at Bard, Hostos, Maryland, Brown and Queens.

I told the secretary when I left if I get any offers for jobs accept them all. She said, "Accept them all?" I told her yes, I'd worry about it later. As I was crossing America my secretary accepted job offers for me at Bard and at Queens College. I went to see Botstein[72] at Bard and I said, "I've accepted Queens but I'd also like to accept Bard. I'm not allowed to work at two places. How about putting me on an honorarium basis?"

He looked at me and said, "You don't get benefits on an honorarium basis." I said that was fine, that'd I'd be getting the benefits from Queens. He liked that and said okay.

I was at both colleges for two years. I worked my butt off. I liked Bard. The students read everything I assigned them and worked hard. They were all flaming lefties that were going to bring Marxism to America. At Queens the students never read, they all worked. 70% of my students at Queens College worked full time and the remainder worked part time. And they were all reactionary, all they wanted was to get their degree to get a better job.

After two years I couldn't keep it up between the two schools and I said to myself, "You know what? I know where I have to go." I told Botstein I was sorry, but I'd be resigning. I told him that my real work had to be at Queens, where,

I think, I've done a fantastic job and I love it. I keep running into students who tell me I've changed their lives and that humbles me.

You see that coffee machine there [gestures to his kitchen counter]? That cost four hundred bucks. Twenty of my students chipped in when they found out I was an espresso freak and bought me that. I'm going to Italy this summer; the guys who arranged for me to give lectures in Italy were former students.

Monchinski: Queens College has a lot of Jewish students and you're an advocate of Palestinian rights. Does that lead to problems?

Gerassi: Sure it does. About ten years ago I was picketed by people who gave out fliers denouncing me as an anti-Semitic Italian. In order to make me Italian, because I'm Sephardic, right?, they had to misspell my name and they spelled it G-E-R-R-A-S-I, which is Italian. But my name is G-E-R-A-S-S-I, which in ancient Hebrew means "from Jerez," which, incidentally, is where the liquor is made[73]. They picketed my class and handed out pamphlets signed F.O.S.

Monchinski: F.O.S.?

Gerassi: It took me a whole year before I found out that F.O.S. stood for Friends of Sharon[74]. Three years ago I was denounced as a professor of hate in a front page attack on me. In class I had said there is no solution to the situation in Palestine/ Israel except if the Israelis pull back to the pre-67 border. I said they needed to create one state in which everyone is equal. Two states[75] would never work. And that the Israelis would need to give back the land they stole in 1948[76].

Monchinski: How does this play out in the classroom?

Gerassi: Usually the students stick it out. They stick around to see if they can debate me. Last semester I gave two books as required reading. One was the Israeli lobby book[77], a big fat book, and they read it. The other was a better book actually, called *Overcoming Zionism*, by Joel Kovel.

I knew Kovel at Bard. He's a psychologist and I never knew he was interested in this topic. But Kovel is Jewish and he read and educated himself and argues that Zionism is a reactionary movement that has nothing to do with the real Jewish tradition.

I went over the syllabus on the first day, the books and films I was going to show. I do it the first day and I explain to my students that they still have time to leave the class and sign up for another one if they feel they need to. This past summer session, I had only one student walk out.

Monchinski: You were one of the first professors I had in college. Most of your fellow PhDs were coming into class in sports jackets and ties. You walked into class in jeans and a plaid shirt. Is there a reason you dress like that and has it ever been a problem for you?

Gerassi: No, I've always dressed in jeans wherever I've taught.

Monchinski: Is that a political thing?

Gerassi: No, I just never owned a suit when I was teaching. I guess it was a reaction to my journalism career. Ten years of wearing a suit and a tie at *Newsweek*, the *Times*, *Time*. I hated it. The tie always made me feel like I was choking. After I left *Newsweek* I started dressing the way I felt comfortable.

Monchinski: When I was a student in your class you didn't assign any papers but relied on an end of course "objective test" final. What does an "objective test" mean to you?

Gerassi: Theoretically, teachers are supposed to be "objective," right? Objective means *what*? You say, "On the one hand this, on the other hand that." That's supposed to be what objective means.

As far as I'm concerned, the other hand—on television, in *The New York Times*—is *never* my hand, unless the students start reading *The Nation* or *The Progressive* or something like that. But they don't read those kinds of things.

Every course I start the same way. I introduce my point of view reiterating my Henry Luce story about objectivity being neither feasible nor desirable. That was one of the only truths I heard voiced during the whole four years I was at *Time*.

Objectivity is not feasible. How are you going to be objective? On the one hand; but on the other hand; then there's this view; and let's not forget about—You're going to bore the students to death. And objectivity isn't desirable either. I always introduce Descartes and his notion of *tabula rasa*[78] and I Think Therefore I Am. That's baloney! In order to say "I think therefore I am" you have to have an incredible amount of education already.

Therefore is a connecting word and to understand its meaning think of how much education you have to have; a child doesn't comprehend *therefore*. In general you bring to the table six trunks and twenty eight suitcases if you're black, if you're poor, if you're a woman. You never make the same judgments as if you're white and rich. But if you watch television it's always the rich white man who is telling you what to say and think.

Same with *The New York Times*. Here's an example, when Clinton ran for re-election, every station, every newspaper accused him of raising the income tax higher than anyone had ever done. And indeed, he had raised the income tax on people who's income was over $200,000, so it was true. But nobody ever mentioned that he also lowered the taxes more than anyone else had ever done before for people who earned less than $32,000.

Why didn't they? Even Jennings[79] didn't; somebody in class said "Jennings." "Do you think Jennings is liberal?" I asked them. Did you ever hear Jennings say Clinton lowered the taxes on the poor? No, because he [Jennings] earns more than $200,000, and he's furious. I tell my students, "Okay, in this class, you're going to get the *other* point of view. You want to know the other side? Go watch television and read *The New York Times*." I tell them, "I'm going to give you a point of view you never hear."

I don't expect them to believe me and tell them as much. I tell them they can say I'm full of baloney and not believe a word of it, but on the exams I am going to ask them questions on what I say or on what the books I ask them to read or the documentaries we watch show. It's "objective" in the sense that no other answer is possible.

For example, if I ask them "Who started the Cold War?", their instincts would be "Russia of course!" Well, that's not true. The United States started the Cold War. It didn't like four men in a jeep in Berlin[80] and ruling together and said, "No, we don't want a mark backed by the ruble, the franc, the pound and the dollar. We're going to issue a mark backed only by the dollar." So England said, "Okay, we'll do one by the pound" and Russia said "We'll do one by the ruble." *That* started the Cold War. They had to put a division: here they use only the ruble, there they use only the pound.

Now, my students don't have to believe me, and they don't even have to look it up—though I encourage them to—but on the exam when I ask them who started the Cold War and they say, "Russia," that's wrong. *That's* what an objective test is. The reason I do this is to plant my question in the back of the students' head so when they come up with another accepted truth they think, "Ah, I've heard that before," all in an attempt to make a dent against the propaganda students are exposed to by the mass media.

I always stress that ours is not a free press. Ours is a *free enterprise* press, and that makes a tremendous difference. Have you ever read in any newspaper that the way to punish Exxon for its Valdez accident[81] was to nationalize Exxon and have the state take it over completely? No, of course not. Does the major media come down in favor of single-payer universal health insurance[82], what western Europe has? No, of course not, because capitalism is the only way.

Monchinski: What about the right that says the mainstream media *is* the left wing and guys like you are way out in left field and universities should be neutral but are bastions of left wing doctrine?

Gerassi: In the first place, the media is not liberal. It's on the right. Let's define what we mean. The right is pro-capitalist. It supports the system. You can nit pick but you do not challenge the system. *Sixty Minutes* nit picks but it isn't radical, it isn't looking to overturn capitalism, *Sixty Minutes* doesn't want to have a free education or nationalize medicine.

The minute you get to the point that public education is threatened by budget cuts, this is the right wing winning. In France, education is paid for. The only thing students pay for is the $65 registration fee so you can get your card which you can use to get half price on transportation and going to movies and the like. And that's up from $25 when I taught in France! That's the only thing French students pay—they don't pay for books. And that's true for all public education all over the west except in the United States.

Here we depend on budgets and budgets are based on property. In Scarsdale, New York, in Westchester County, they spend over $18,000 per student and nearly 100% of students go on to a four-year university. Compare that to Bayou, Mississippi, where they spend 60 dollars per student and only 12% of graduating high school seniors go on to four year colleges.

In France, Spain, Italy, Switzerland, all students get exactly the same amount. So a student in southern Italy in Calabria is getting the same amount as a student in Rome, which means they are more likely to have the same chances in life. We do not have an objective educational system. My job is to point this out, to fight the right-wing in academia.

I believe that all education should be free, and the basis for paying for that is a gradated tax system: the more you make the more you should pay. In America students have "life, liberty and the pursuit of happiness" drummed into their heads, but what do these mean? Life means being able to live. That means free medical care, equal for everybody. Liberty means freedom to choose, but what kind of choices are you going to make if you get a lousy education compared to someone who got an excellent education? That's not an equal capacity to choose. Do you think the people in Bayou, Mississippi are prepared to make good choices? We talk a lot about democracy in the United States but we don't have life and we don't have liberty, so how can we have the pursuit of happiness?

Monchinski: I remember one day in class you made a comment about cops being fascists and a student who's father and boyfriend were cops said, "My father and boyfriend aren't fascists!" You're very popular on campus even though your style can sometimes come across as confrontational. Why do you think this is?

Gerassi: Because I challenge the students to think for themselves. And I always clarify what I mean. For example, in a situation like the one you mention I tell the following story. During the Movement days my daughter was five years old and we were in the park. She was playing and a cop came up to her and was talking to her and throwing her the ball. Apparently what happened is my daughter had said, "Oh, you're a policeman. I don't talk to you," and started to walk away. So the cop asked her, "Why?" She said, "My father tells me that all policemen are pigs." This was a time in the Movement when we called all cops *pigs*.

He came up to me and he said, "Your daughter says all policemen are pigs. Is that what you told her?" And I said, "No, I told her that all *racist* policemen are pigs." He turned to her and said, "Ah, see you have to remember that. Your father is right. *Racist* policemen are pigs. I'm not racist. I'm not a pig."

Monchinski: Critical pedagogy offers that every classroom is a political arena and having sat in your classroom several times as an undergrad I know this to be true of your classes. But I would ask you what is the relationship between the politics of your pedagogy and your moral vision?

Gerassi: I have never made a distinction. To me what is political is also moral. But to me morality is to try and make life for human beings as fruitful as one can imagine. That means that any abuse of individuals – because they're poor, because they're female or black or incapacitated – that abuse is immoral. It also happens to be a political necessity to fight it, so you cannot separate the two.

THE IDEAL SYLLABUS

The Ideal Two Semester Political Science 104 ("International Relations") by Prof. Tito Gerassi: (Office hours T & Th 2–3 & T 6–6:30, room R200)

General introduction: Two great books: The first one, by a Nobel prize winner, tells us better than any where we are; the other tells us where we're going, a great book deliberately ignored by the mainstream media, which, owned by six multinational corporations, is responsible for the disaster ahead:

READ: Amartya Sen: *Identity and Violence: the Illusion of Destiny.* Verso 2007 $15.95 (Amazon $7.92) ISBN 13-978-0-32029-2

READ: Mike Davis: *Planet of Slums.* Verso $15.95 (Amazon: $9.99) ISBN 13-978-1-844676-022-2

Two historical documentaries on imperialism, which explain the division of the world in the 20th century, as seen through two great fictional films: Burn; Reds

READ: Antony Beevor: *The Battle for Spain* Penguin Books 2001. $17 ISBN 0-14-303765-x pages 1–87 (I will try to Xerox and distribute the key pages of this acclaimed very pro-English history, whitewashing US and British support of Franco & Nazis)

READ: Richard Bermack: *The Frontlines of Social Change.* Berkeley Heyday 2005 $19.95 ISBN 1-59714-000-7

Documentary on the Spanish Civil War of 1936–39 (The Good Cause)

READ: Frantz Fanon: *The Wretched of the Earth.* 1963 *(There are many editions; get the cheapest. Amazon lists it at $3.95 but will add more than that to ship it)* Read: The preface by Jean-Paul Sartre and the sections called Concerning Violence and On National Culture

Documentary: The Battle of Algiers

READ: David Halberstam: *The Coldest Winter: America and the Korean War.* Hyperion 2007 ISBN 978-1-4013-0052-4, read pages 1–250.*(It's a big fat book*

costing $35. If you can afford it, it will serve well on your bookshelf and you can *read chapters whenever there's nothing good on TV. Amazon has it for $16.86 plus postage. But why not go to a Barnes & Noble or Borders coffee shop, get a double espresso and read the first 250 pages there. The rest of the book, worth reading by skipping the endless battle scenes gives you a good idea of the war at home and in Korea, and why we lost that war too)*

Documentary: The Long March; Tankman

READ: Bruce Cumings, Ervand Abrahamian & Moshe Ma'oz: *Inventing the Axis of Evil: The Truth about North Korea, Iran, and Syria.* The New Press 2004 $14.95 ISBN 13-978-159558-038-2 (Skip North Korea, as it seems the US is not going to bomb or invade it, as of now anyway)

READ: William Blum: *Rogue State.* Common Courage Press, 2000 $16.95 (plenty of used one here) Read the introduction and sections 1–10 plus 17 & 23, which is mostly Vietnam

Documentaries: The Sixties; 2 Days October 1967; My Lai; Cover-Up: the Iran/ Contra scandals; Blowback & updates; Guns, Drugs & the CIA, Plus SOA: School of Assassins (oops, School of Americas); Panama Deception; When Mountains Tremble

READ: Isaac Saney: *Cuba: A Revolution in Motion* Zed 2004 (price blotted out in my edition, but plenty of used copies at the bookstore) ISBN1-55266-114-8 Read pages 1–90, 151–175

Documentaries: Cuba: The Accidental Revolution; 638 Ways To Kill Castro

READ: Michael Parenti: *To Kill a Nation: The Attack on Yugoslavia.* Verso 2000 $22 (Amazon $9.08) ISBN 1-85984-776-5 pages 1–36, 58–164. (If you can afford it buy it from the bookstore so Verso gets the 60%. Verso is a good publishing outfit struggling to print books refused by the mainstream media)

Documentary: The Maltese Double Cross;

READ: Father Andrew Greeley: *A Stupid, Unjust and Criminal War: Iraq 2001-2007* Orisbooks $19 ISBN 978-1-57075-732-7 pages: 1–4, 7–9, 11–13, 15–16, 24–27, 29–30, 38–40, 50–55, 66–67, 79–82, 94–95, 113–114, 125–130, 150–152, 168–173, 178–180, 197–202 (begin at the black mark and stop at the black mark on the page listed)

READ: Dahr Jamail: *Beyond the Green Zone: Dispatches from an Unembedded Journalist in Occupied Iraq* Haymarket Books 2007 ISBN-10: 1931859477

READ: Michael Ratner & Ellen Ray: *Guantanamo.* Chelsea Green Publishing 2004 $15 ISBN 1931498-64-4 Read: Intro by Anthony Lewis, chapters 1–93

Documentaries: The Torture Question; Moyers' Journal: Iraq & the Media; Yes Sir, No Sir; The Arming of Saudi Arabia

READ: Stephen M. Walt: *Taming American Power*. Norton.2005 $27.95 ISBN 0-393-05203-6 (Amazon's price: $6.48) read pages 13–108

Documentary: The War on Democracy; Endless War; Why We Fight; Chile: The Other 9/11; To Steal a Nation

READ: Noam Chomsky: *Pirates and Emperors Old and New*. South End Press 2002, ISBN 0-89608-6855-2, $18 but lots of used at the bookstore. Read the preface, pages I–80, 144–180

READ: John J. Mearheimer & Stephen M. Walt: *The Israel Lobby*. Farrar, Straus, Giroux, 2007 ISBN 13-978-0-374-17772-2. $26. A big book; read it at Barnes & Noble sipping a cappuccino, pages 24–48, 111–132, 152–167, 200–208, 233–326

READ: Joel Kovel: *Overcoming Zionism: Creating a Single Democratic State in Israel/Palestine* Pluto Press: $26.95 (Amazon $16.54) ISBN-10: 0745325696 (A key work which will set the tone and ideology of the anti-Zionist forces)

Documentaries: Robert Fisk: Beirut to Bosnia; Palestine is Still the Issue; Paradise Now; Inside Hamas; Peace, Propaganda & the Promised Land
Check Point; GITMO: The New Rules of War

READ: Understanding the Venezuelan Revolution. Hugo Chavez Talks to Marta Harnecker. Monthly Review Press 2005 $15.95. Read pages 1–103

Documentary: The Revolution Will Not Be Televised

READ: David C. Korten: *When Corporations Rule the World*. Kumerian Press 2001. Lots of Used copies. Read Foreword by Danny Glover, Chapters II–IV

READ: Naomi Klein: *Shock Doctrine: The Rise of Disaster Capitalism*. Metropolitan Books 2007, ISBN-13: 978-0805079838, $28 (Amazon $16.80) pages to be assigned.

Documentaries: WMD: Weapons of Mass Deception; Moyers' Journal: Iraq & the Media; Corporations Control the Media; The Price of Profits; Trading Democracy; Orwell Rolls in his Grave

READ: James K. Galbraith: *The Predator State: How Conservatives Abandoned the Free Market and Why Liberals Should Too*. Free Press: 978-1416566830

READ: Yasmina Kadra: *Sirens of Bagdad*. Doubleday 2007 (ask Random House) 978-030738-6168

READ: Steven T. Wax: *Kafka Comes to America*. The Other Press 978-1-590521-295-1

READ: Jane Mayer: *The Dark Side: The Inside Story of How the War on Terror Turned Into a War on American Ideals* Doubleday (Random House) 978-0-385-52639-5

THE POLITICS OF PLAYING POKER WITH JAMES JONES IN PARIS

When asked if there is a contradiction with having friends who are your ideological opposite, Gerassi replies, "There is no such thing as objectivity. A black man doesn't make the same judgment in the same way as a white man does, just as no woman can make a judgment in the same way as a man. When I come to a judgment I come with my experiences, my parent's experiences, my race, my gender, all this informs my decision. Yet I don't think there's a contradiction in having friends who harbor viewpoints different, even radically different, than your own. What it does imply is we have to have an awful lot of discussion between us."

THE POLITICS OF PLAYING POKER WITH JAMES JONES IN PARIS

I first met James Jones on my way to Europe in the fall of 1968. He, a successful writer, was routinely going back to Paris, his home for over a decade. I, a failed revolutionary, was leaving home, what I called Babylon, gambling that a brief exile would help me regain a faith I thought I had lost. We both hated airplanes. We both were addicts of the *S.S. France*, and as chance had it, we were both invited to a captain's "special" cocktail party. Not that we were special: I'm sure the suave-mannered officers who greeted us had never even heard of *From Here to Eternity*, and they certainly would not be impressed by my recent stint in jail. It was simply that their records showed that Jim and I, like the 40-odd other tourist passengers in the lounge that day, had crossed the Atlantic aboard their floating three-star hotel at least four times before. That made us "regulars," and for all our sophistication, so happy were we to be suspended in such luxury, that we put on tie and jacket to shake the master's hand. And neither of us even drank – he because of some mild heart attacks; I because the beatings the cops had offered me for twelve consecutive nights had wrecked the balance of my stomach.

"What's that pin?" Jones asked, as we were introduced. Both of us were sipping high-balls of straight Perrier soda water.

"It's the North Vietnamese emblem," I said, "made from the metal of a US Phantom jet shot down over Hanoi."

"How the hell do you know that?"

I paused, smiled mischievously, then replied, slowly articulating each word: "I was there. I saw the plane come down."

Jones bridled. He scratched the nostrils of his pug boxer's nose. "You a fuckin' red?" he said, hunching his shoulders and turned away.

That night, as I was flirting with a couple of coeds from Boston University on their way to a junior year abroad, I saw him again. We were sitting in the main salon waiting for the rock band to replace the waltz-and-foxtrot merchants when Jones strutted right past us without even nodding.

"Know who that is?" I asked the girls. I told them, but they shrugged and continued our conversation.

"I can't believe the Movement will stop when we pull out of Vietnam," Betty was saying. Throwing her long, straight, blond hair to one side, she smiled nervously. She had been very active in SDS for a year and now wanted to be reassured the struggle would still be there when she returned.

I tried my best to allay her guilt, but my thoughts were elsewhere. Why did I envy Jones, I wondered. Here I was with two beautiful, young women who admired and respected me, who had read my articles and had heard me speak when their student body had invited me as part of the visiting scholars' program. Betty had even read one of my books. And they couldn't care less about Jones. Yet he was a winner, I thought, while I ...

"Are you planning to stay in Europe long?" Carole asked me. She, too, had been active in SDS. Less pretty than Betty, she seemed more mature, and her smile more enticing. She wasn't just making conversation. She cared, and I should have been flattered.

"I dunno," I answered. Then, realizing she was expecting a full explanation, I quickly went on: "The group we had in San Francisco fell apart after we got arrested for seizing the college. Most of the students decided to join one party or another, but I couldn't. I could have continued to work for the Panthers, of course, but I felt I had to leave the Bay Area. I tried to work for the Alianza in New Mexico for a while, but, well, even though my Spanish is fluent, I wasn't Chicano. I found myself going from campus to campus, living off talks and repeating myself. Then came Chicago. A lot of people were pretty courageous there. We got arrested and beaten, and then? Nothing remained, nothing solid. All we ended up with was a sure win by Nixon in November. That's when I decided I needed to think things out, and that I needed distance to understand just where we were going. It's not like I'm going into exile – well, maybe it is – but I need ..." I paused, then added: "I just couldn't stay in Babylon."

"There's nothing wrong with that," Betty said, "Lenin spent a long time in exile too."

She was obviously trying to make me feel good. I smiled warmly and caressed her hand, and she immediately responded by squeezing mine. At that point I should have asked her to dance. But I was thinking: "For Jones, Paris isn't exile. He knows what he wants, and what to write. It may be lousy, but his life is purposeful. He's not going away from someplace, he's going to someplace. That's why he's a winner. Me, I lived by my ideals, I sacrificed a good job and a pleasant standard of living. I'm pure. But I'm leaving, not going. That's a loser."

I got off in England, Jones in France, and we forgot all about each other. While he wrote a terrible novel about the nearly-successful May '68 French New Left revolution, I floundered about London Soho espresso joints. My own royalties barely kept me in paperclips, but I managed to eat well by accompanying TV producer-friends on their expense-account Italian lunches (usually as their "assistant," sometimes, as when they worked on crime or drug documentaries, as their "body-guard.") My friends also got me on paying interview shows. I talked about my friendship with Che Guevara, my trip to Hanoi, my experiences in the Movement. I even once took on three British parliament deputies and four German-accented cosmopolitan scientists as a "socio-political moon expert" on Manchester television during the first moon walk.

None of this hurt my image, but gambling certainly did. For, after being given a free membership by some junior French diplomat who had wanted a drink one night after the 11:30 closing of London pubs, I had begun to frequent the Playboy Club. "How can a revolutionary like you justify going to that bastion of sexism?" Richard Neville once asked me. Richard was then running England's only four-colored underground magazine, Oz. I answered by taking him with me and he immediately got carried away at the dice table losing all of the magazine's stamp money he happened to be carrying around with him. But the Australian-born London equivalent of Jerry Rubin got even: he leaked the story of "a famed U.S. revolutionary last seen at the Playboy casino ..." to *Private Eye*, a top-notch politico-satirical dirt-chomping weekly. By the time the story spread the $35 I had actually lost became $5000 in the U.S. and a fantastic $25,000 win in France (which must surely be the only capitalist country where revolutionaries consider each other winners.)

Perhaps because of that, or else because I was sensitive enough to know I couldn't live off my past too much longer, I decided to leave again. I thought I was trying to get back to Babylon, but I ended up café-hopping along Paris' Left Bank.

One day, as I was having lunch with Jean-Paul Sartre and Simone de Beauvoir in a well-protected corner of Montparnasse's mammoth restaurant, La Coupole, I decided to test a rumor I had heard. "Don't you have any vanity?" I asked Sartre.

"Of course, why?" he replied, his good eye looking up from his *choucroute garnie* with twinkling expectation. Unquestionably the sharpest mind of our times, Sartre had already figured out my game, and he likes games.

"Then why have you turned down so many writers who want to do your bio-graphy?" I asked.

"Des petits cons from Paris Review? ... Now if someone like ... what about it? How would you handle my biography?" he fired back. Both of us knew the outcome. I was already thinking of all the work I was getting into.

"Well," I thought out loud, "I guess I would try to explain two things: First, why it has taken you 45 years to reach a political position we reached in five, and second, how come you became a revolutionary when you never rebelled against your own bourgeois background."

Simone and Sartre exploded with laughter. Then, focusing his good eye intensely on the hair which grows on my nose, Sartre brought down the verdict: "D'accord! When do we start?"

"Give me an exclusive statement and I'll sign it.

"Give me a piece of paper."

I handed Sartre the back of the Coupole menu and dictated the statement I would need to get a publisher's contract. When Sartre finished, he smiled almost childishly and quipped: "Thank god, I never did want to write the follow-up of The Words."

But I wasn't really sure I wanted to do it. I still thought of myself as a political activist. So, in the fall of 1971, I went back to the US to see if I could find once again a place for myself in the Movement. But the Movement, the name given to that vague entity which supposedly grouped all anti-war activists, draft dodgers and New Left militants in the Sixties, existed no longer, each sect having gone its own way. I tried to talk it over with every chum I could find. Most of my closest comrades were in jail. George Jackson was dead. Angela was becoming a folk heroine. And Jerry Rubin was already eating organic carrots. So I asked Huey: "What is to be done?" Newton's reply: "Go to Paris. Show the world why the greatest intellectual of our era had become a Maoist."

I returned to Paris, got a tiny windowless two room pad around the corner from the Coupole, built myself a king-size desk filling one of the rooms, paid a $1000 bribe to get a phone (for which I'm still waiting), and set up shop as Sartre's official biographer.

But Paris is more expensive than New York. And when you don't have a phone, you have to establish a semi-official residence at a cafe. Mine was the Select, across Montparnasse from the Coupole. It became my office from 10 p.m. to 2 a.m. every night. It had certain advantages. The waiters were nice; so nice in fact that when I ran out of advances, they often loaned me the money.

Montparnasse, as French intellectuals like to boast, is the center of the world, and true enough I rarely sat alone at the Select. Most of the time, my companions were there to look and criticize, and while they talked about dedicating their life to "helping the working class," they sipped demis and scrutinized the appearances of passers-by. If I, in turn, joked about the hefty stipend they still received from their parents at the age of 25 or 30 and wondered out loud how this furthered their dedication, my companions inevitably remembered other appointments and left. For, if sense of humor is to be defined as the ability to laugh at oneself, the French have none.

Still, there were always enough people to make me feel in the thick of it. It was at the Select, for example, that I renewed my friendship with James Baldwin when he shot through Paris on his way to Vance in the South; there that I convinced a Gallimard editor to translate and publish the books of Huey, Jackson and Bobby Seale; there that I got a two hour non-screaming primal from Arthur Janov; there that Glauber Rocha, the great but mad Brazilian movie director, agreed to direct a film script I had written about Camilo Torres, a Colombian priest who became a Fidelista guerrilla. (Rocha blew it when he tried to raise money for it from the Vatican.) And it was there that I got my phone calls, including from John Thorne, Jackson's lawyer, who used to dial collect from California every time he heard I had had a hit at a casino.

But I was not hitting. In fact, my finances were disastrous, and when the Select espresso went up from 25¢ to 75¢, my flights to the Playboy Club had to be drastically curtailed. Then one night at the Select, I ran into Bernie Frizzell. He was an old friend from the days both of us wrote Art at Time magazine, and later, when I came back from Hanoi in 1967 and he was NBC's man in Paris, he tried very hard to let me make my spiel on the network despite the fact that we remained on opposite sides of the typewriter ribbon. Bernie was now a successful novelist with lots of French monopoly money, and he told me that he regularly dropped quite a bit of it at a weekly poker game. Would I care to join? Immediately, I saw my chance to better my standard of living. All it took was $100 to sit down, he said, and besides, it was a friendly game, meaning checks were acceptable. So I went.

The game was held every Sunday at the Paris home of, yes, James Jones. A corner duplex with wings overlooking the Seine on the Left Bank of the understated but never out-classed Ile St. Louis, Jones' pad was Sutton Place nouveau riche. The master bedroom, with, naturally, the round bed, was all rug and fur. A guest toilet was so flowered I could swear perfume was exuding from the seat cover. Every available foot of wall space, along the stairs, in the living and dining rooms upstairs, was plastered with paintings, mostly gifts from Paris' almost-in American exile artists who obviously viewed the endlessly-entertaining Jones' as PR pay-offs. The round bar and dining table were made of solid wood, and the butler and maid were tempered in solid finish.

And yet, within minutes, for all the apparent ostentatiousness, I felt quite at home. I took an immediate and powerful liking to Gloria Jones, a formidable Sicilian mafia-moll who ruled over her literate society salon with ease and grace. Clearly the wittiest, most sarcastic, and often most foulmouthed woman I'd ever met, her great poise and beauty always kept her at the center of the gatherings, no matter how large. She was perfectly capable of being sentimental, motherly and devilishly teasing simultaneously. One sweltering day, for example, when I had moved into a temporary studio she had found for me, not far from her house, she came over to clean it up, took off her blouse, and scrubbed the place with such dignity that my lust for her magnificent breasts concealed only by a well-cut red bra was kept in check by a sudden gush of filial admiration.

"Have you met our bomber," she introduced me on that first day, "and he's also an excellent writer." Not only was she instantaneously injecting two subjects of conversation by such an introduction, she was also making sure, by saying "and" rather than "but," that I was being accepted on either of my two supposed talents. The former, of course, was an outrageous exaggeration. Though I had belonged at one point to a collective which, like the Weathermen group, had advocated selective sabotage, I never even held a bomb in my lily-white intellectual hands. But Gloria loved romanticizing her guests on the theory it made them more interesting and their idiosyncrasies more acceptable. And accepted I was, despite my scruffy appearance, my often vitriolic put-downs of their official friends, and my rarely hidden scorn for their literary idols. Of course, I had one asset their guests respected: money to lose.

Or so they thought. Fact is, I had barely 20 francs in my pocket. But I knew I was going to win. As I sat down at the fading green-felt poker table, I saw few dangers among my opponents. For one thing, they all drank too much. For another, they played like they talked, and the talk gave them away. James Jones, for example, issued proclamations as if he were the king. He could not let himself be exposed; hence at the table, he was tight, stiff, and always putting down his wife's extravagances. To bluff him would be easy. Irwin Shaw, Jim's most famous rival present, was too successful to be impressionable; he went into almost every pot, showed his booboos, and laughed off his losses. Sidney Chaplin knew his limitations; he would never match his father. But he rollicked in second place, and loved the game. That would make him a big winner or a big loser. Annie Farge, the ex-actress who brought musical comedies to France and produced or co-produced Hair, O Calcutta and Godspell, was too ambitious to be concerned with anything but the big hit: she would be vulnerable in hi-lo games. Harry Mayen, a successful German producer/director, was introduced to me only as the husband of Romy Schneider; shy and slow, his lack of self-confidence made him the natural fish. Greek financier Tassos Fondaras, who had married New York Timesman Tom Wicker's ex-wife, was too rich to care. If he had the cards he'd win; if not, he'd feed us all. Rafael Hakim, who with his four brothers, had been dubbed "five of the ten plagues of Egypt," was a lovable scoundrel, horse-owner, movie producer and professional gambler; that meant he expected to win. So, I told myself, hit him hard when he's griping. And then there was Gloria. Instinctive but shrewd, I figured she had the daring to wipe us all out, so I decided to avoid major confrontations with her.

As the game proceeded, my preliminary judgments were confirmed. Jim hated Gloria every time she took chances, and Gloria took many of them. For a while she lost, and Jim both gloated and bled at the sight of the disappearing chips, which, of course, he would have to cover. He himself was winning and thus was getting more and more pontifical, puffing on a Havana given him and cursing. Gloria began to pick on him, questioning his manhood when she wanted him to chase her, pitying him when she wanted him to fold. Irwin was losing and drinking, but enjoying it. And me, well, I had it all down pat, so nothing could go wrong.

When the game was over at 4 a.m., Gloria was the big winner, Chaplin second, Bernie third, and everyone else a loser. I issued a check for $300 on my French account.

Next morning I covered the deficit by getting my French bank to buy a check from a US account. I then sent my US bank an English check. I calculated I could continue the round-robin until the next Sunday, when I would win it all back. But I lost again, this time $200. By the third week, when I lost $100, I must have had a dozen checks flying the Atlantic.

But I won Gloria's sympathy. She began to invite me to their pre-poker spaghetti dinners, which, I thought at the time, must have cost Jones all of one ante, and sometimes to their equally unvaried non-poker meals as well. Inevitably still introduced as "our bomber," my presence was never really much of a success. For one thing I kept visibly cringing every time Gloria tinkled the little bell to call the butler, and Jim was never pleased when I went off into long-winded conversations with the help, especially since, after some 15 years in Paris, Jim's French was fluent only when he wanted to know if such-and-such a critic was important or if such-and-such a producer had backing. But Gloria liked me just the same. She even invited me, on condition I forsook my usual jeans, to accompany her to Longchamps, where her nearly-infallible instinct made her a steady winner. As for me, I always read the poop sheets meticulously, expertly handicapped every horse, and lost.

So my finances kept getting worse. For game No.4, I borrowed 2000 francs from Sartre and purposely left my checkbook behind. I now knew every mannerism of each player and was determined to make a comeback. But as soon as I got there I found the odds were again against me. Neither Shaw nor Tassos showed up, and Chaplin was off filming a French soft-core. In his place was an old regular just back from the States, Jack Egle, who ran the Paris bureau of some students-abroad outfit. A happy-go-lucky Frenchified Midwesterner, he too lived on Ile St. Louis, but in a one-room studio. He played the horses from his office, worked the craps table in England, and always managed to stay in a good mood. The other new face belonged to Tony Azzi, a Cuban-Lebanese nightclub operator who managed well by putting on transvestite shows in Paris and nude reviews in Las Vegas.

On the very first hand, with Jack Egle, Tony Azzi, Jim Jones going for low, Rafael Hakim, Harry Mayen and I for high, I discovered the game would be expensive, as Jack raised on every card. Jim and I split the pot, and our share was almost 2000 francs each ($400). On the next hand, five card stud, I raised Rafael's king with a six, announcing I had a pair of them. He assumed I was lying and was only hiding an ace. We fought it out till the fifth card, when my two (I did have the sixes) pairs defeated his pair of kings. He was furious, and from then on dropped ashes from his cigarette on his immaculate blue suit. A few hands later I bluffed Jim out of a big one, and on the next one, split a huge pot with Jack. By the end of the first hour, I was up almost $1000 in chips.

But then Bernie Frizzell arrived and we made room for an eighth player. Gloria's luck changed, and she started coming into every pot. Jim became angry. "What are you doing?" he snapped each time she lost a chase. Rafael, now losing the most, kept trying to shut everybody up. "Let's play," he kept insisting. Ever-smiling Tony refused to stop telling nightclub stories which Gloria and Bernie loved. Harry Mayen started taking more and more time to make up his mind on almost each card, irritating Jim who wanted everyone to move fast though he himself often brooded before making a decision.

Once, in a heavy pot between Harry and Gloria in which she wanted him to come in, she stared at him with Pigalle eyes, slipped her hand under the deep cleavage of her fiery red dress, and while massaging a breast, voluptuously whispered to him, "Come on Harry, it's just you and me." Harry saw and Gloria won.

At another point, it was Tony's turn to hesitate against Gloria. While thinking, he had automatically dropped a hand to scratch his crotch. She threw him a languishing smile and purred: "You can do that after you lose your pants to me, Tony ..." Tony paid and lost. Everyone except Jim laughed, Tony most of all.

The game ended early, at 2 a.m. Rafael, a heavy loser, insisted we play another round. Most of the rest of us had enjoyed the game too much to want to quit, whether we were up or down. But both Jim and Gloria had won so Jim brought down the ax: "No, I have to work at 8 tomorrow." And that became a pattern. If the Jones' were ahead, no reprieve. If the Jones' were behind, the game was always extended, one, two hours. But I was the big winner. I went home almost as pleased as the first time I had hit a cop.

"Don't you feel dirty just being in that house," a Trotskyite friend of mine asked me the next day as I paid for his steak-au-poivre at the Coupole. "Look," I answered, "it's an easy way to make a living." But I was lying: it wasn't the money. I had enjoyed myself, even on my previous three losses. What's more, I was beginning to like everyone there, even Jim with his morose self-torture. He could be generous with his time and helpful with his contacts. And for all his pose, his insecurity was based on his conscious self-doubts; he knew he wasn't what he wanted to be, and he had the guts to admit it, not to others, to himself. When he read the review in Time which began "Everybody knows James Jones can't write …", he bled, like anyone would, but then shut himself up in his office and wrote six hours straight. Away from the poker table and alone with a peer, he was neither dogmatic nor regal.

"But they're all a bunch of fascists," exclaimed a Maoist friend of mine, as he let me pay for his mixed-grill at the Module the next day. "Sure," I replied, "and they know that someday, when the barricades go up, I might be shooting at them. But meantime they're pretty funny." What I didn't add was that they were also pretty nice. Not only Gloria, who was as generous with Jim's money as he was tight, but also Jack, who turned out to be a very good poker player; Tony, who never let his losses interfere with his boyish charm; and Bernie, sensitive, warm, and open. Jack became one of my closest chums.

"You're switching sides," an Anarchist friend of mine accused me one day, as he ordered another round of drinks on me at the Select. "Bull shit," I shot back, "but while we are sitting around in cafes waiting for the revolution, all we can talk about is why so-and-so is a fink, a discussion we call political. They, would you believe it, also talk about novels, movies and sex." He ordered *another* drink.

I won the next four times. I squared my accounts, paid off my debts, put aside a bundle for the Playboy Club and went off to London. The craps table was jammed when I got to the third floor casino, but as soon as the pit boss saw me he diplomatically made room not only for me but for my girlfriend and an American couple I had invited for dinner as well. When I got the dice, I laid my bundle on three-way, eleven and the win line, and rolled snake eyes. Paid 33-to-1. I now doubled the stakes. Eleven. This was it: I was going to win everything I had ever lost in 20 minutes. I pressed, rolled, Seven. Pressed again. Seven. Once more. Nine. I covered the numbers and started shooting them: six hard, four, five, five again, ten, ten hard. Each time I pressed. I now had close to two hundred pounds backed-up on each number. "There's a year salary riding there," I heard my friend whisper to his wife. Didn't I know it. As I shook the dice, I told myself: "Now the nine and I'll take it all off." I fired. Seven.

"He was good while he lasted," the croupier bellowed as he scraped in the chips. Off we went to the VIP Room. After tipping the waiters with the remaining chips – the meal was on the house, of course – we staggered out – and bumped into Jack Egle and his girl. "I figured I'd catch you here," he beamed.

"You're too late," I answered. "I'm clean."

"Then how come you look so happy?" he asked.

"Don't you know about him yet?" my friend replied. "He doesn't play to win. He likes to lose. So he's happy."

"That's because you were playing with your own money," Jack said. "Come on, let's go back. I'll stake you and we'll split your winnings. With my money, you'll win."

We did, and I did. I won it all back plus some, in three short minutes at the craps table. "Well done," the pit boss patted me on the back as I cashed in. The dealers too were smiling. "Don't stop at a table on the way out, Mr. G.," the floor manager laughed.

Back in Paris, an exiled ex-Weatherman asked me: "How does it feel to be a winner?" He was the first leftist friend of mine who wasn't putting me down.

I thought about his question. I hadn't written a word in three years. I had screwed up my sex life. I hadn't even gotten a telephone. Like any Parisian, I had become a food fetishist. Having finished interviewing Sartre, I was even beginning to think I should first write a novel, a best-seller like Jones or Shaw, and so what if my friends thought it was junk. Then what would happen? Would I buy a castle on the Rhine, hire a staff I couldn't communicate with, offer spaghetti to my guests, suffer every time my wife or girlfriend lost at the races, and waste precious time buttering up to the local critics?

"You know." I answered my comrade, "the truth is, winning this way is really losing. It's time I went back to Babylon."

– Written at the Seleet Cafe, Montpamesse, Paris, in May 1974

CHAPTER ELEVEN

THE SECOND DEATH OF JEAN-PAUL SARTRE

No intellectual, no writer, no man is more hated by academics and newsfolk, by eggheads and politicians on both side of the Atlantic than Jean-Paul Sartre. Nor is this new: Sartre has been hated by them for half a century. But as long as he was alive, his pen easily deflected their pricks. In France, where he could take to the podium or even to the streets if they tried to stifle his counterattacks, the media had no choice but to report his retorts. In England and in the US however, Sartre was dependent on the fair play of his critics. He got none. They smeared him, distorted him, ridiculed him. When all else failed, they tried to silence him altogether – by ignoring him in the US, by murdering him in France.

At first, after the war, Sartre was turned into a "national asset;" in *What is Literature?*, he even complained that "it is not pleasant to be treated as a public monument while still alive." But he was soon damned by left and right. In 1946, Britain's censor banned his play *No Exit*. In 1947, Pierre Brisson, editor of the rightwing Paris daily Le Figaro, expressed delight that "the cohorts of Maurice Thorez (longtime head of the French Communist Party) insult him and proclaim him to be the writer of the failures, while the warring faction of the rightwing talks of exorcizing him, of covering him with sulphur and setting him on fire on the parvis of Notre-Dame, which would be the most charitable way of saving his soul." In 1948, Pope Pious XII put all of Sartre's works on the index – meaning that any Catholic reading any part of them is automatically ex-communicated. That year too, the Soviet Government officially objected to a production of his play *Dirty Hands* in Helsinki on the grounds that it was "hostile propaganda against the USSR." The play remained forbidden throughout the Eastern bloc for decades, and when it opened in France, it elicited this judgment from the Communist daily *L'Humanite*: "Hermetical philosopher, nauseated writer, sensationalist dramatist, demagogue of the third force [earlier that year, Sartre had helped launch and was principle spokesperson for the R.D.R., the Revolutionary Democratic Assembly, which hoped to keep France divorced from the aggressive policies of both Russia and America.], such are the stages of Mr. Sartre's career." Added that year George Lukacs, the highly touted Hungarian Marxist philosopher: "Existentialism reflects, on the level of ideology, the spiritual and moral chaos of the current bourgeois intelligence." Summarized Fadeev, head of the Russian Federation of Writers, at the 1948 Wroclaw Peace Conference: Sartre is "a hyena armed with a fountain pen."

But in France by then, the communists had already condemned him. The most "learned attack" came from Henri Lefebvre, that professional party hatchetman who had smeared his closest friend, the novelist-journalist Paul Nizan, as a police informer because Nizan had refused to soften his anti-Nazi stance when Stalin signed the Russo-German pact. Now, in 1945, Lefebvre went after Sartre, defining him as "the manufacturer of the war machine against Marxism." (No longer a communist by the Sixties, Lefebvre never apologized to Nizan or Sartre, yet is still respected as a great intellectual in France – perhaps precisely because of that.)

In 1945 meanwhile, the French Government had thought enough of Sartre's wartime resistance activity to offer him the Legion of Honor; Sartre had refused. Four years later, André Malraux, onetime communist sympathizer turned Gaullist mouthpiece, denounced Sartre as a collaborator even though he, of all people, knew better. (Sartre had tried to entice Malraux into joining his resistance group in 1941 when Malraux was then still enjoying the good life on the French Riviera.). In April 1949, Catholic writer François Mauriac intimated in print that Sartre was a foreign agent. The very next month, he offered Sartre a seat for "immortals" by having him elected to the most elite 40-member Académie française; Sartre scoffed at such a chance to "learn equality" among those who spend their waning years bragging about their "superiority." He also turned down an offer to join that other prestigious bastion of French culture, the College de France.

But the worst insults from fellow French intellectuals while Sartre was alive were provoked by his rejection of the Nobel Prize for Literature in 1964. In private correspondence to the Nobel Committee, Sartre had said that he would turn down, with equal intransigence, the Lenin Prize, were it ever offered to him, and on the same public grounds, that the Lenin and Nobel are equally politically motivated. When the Nobel Committee ignored Sartre's warning and awarded him the prize anyway, and Sartre published the correspondence, ex-communist surrealist Andre Breton nevertheless denounced Sartre for being part of "a propaganda operation in favor of the Eastern bloc." But that sally was nothing compared to the onslaught unleashed by the usually mild-mannered Christian philosopher Gabriel Marcel. Said he, presumably with Christian charity: Sartre was an "inveterate denigrator," a "systematic blasphemist" with "pernicious and poisonous" views, a "patented corruptor of youth," the "grave-digger of the West."

By then, Sartre was used to much more formidable attacks. After *Paris-Match* had run an editorial entitled "Sartre: A Civil War Machine," hundreds of war veterans marched down the Champs Elysees chanting *fusiller Sartre! Fusiller Sartre!* ("Shoot Sartre!"). On July 19 of the next year, a bomb went off in his apartment at 42 rue Bonaparte (but did little damage). Six months later, on January 7, 1962, a more powerful bomb, detonated on the wrong floor, destroyed much of the apartment and either obliterated various unpublished manuscripts or gave the in-rushing firemen the opportunity to pilfer them.

None of these attacks stopped French students from reading Sartre. And as they did, his reputation and influence grew. In the Anglo-Saxon world however, they had their effect. His plays were rarely performed, his novels badly read, his philosophy almost totally ignored. Dominated by logical positivists and empiricists, Anglo-Saxon university philosophy departments have long been reluctant to take seriously any epistemology or ontology, much less Sartre's, which is based on phenomenological descriptions of reality. A.J. Ayer, for example, dismissed all of existentialism as "an exercise in the art of misusing the verb 'to be.'" But then

Ayer, like his analytical colleagues, limited the task of philosophy to analyzing the language of propositions and "must be content to record the facts of scientific procedure." In a Columbia University philosophy class taught by the eminent Ernest Nagel, I remember spending hours on deciding whether Bertrand Russell's sentence "Is the present king of France bald" was a meaningful question (whether the verb "to be" predicated existence). Similarly, both Iris Murdoch and Mary Warnock put Sartre down for not playing the game the way they do, that is, by using logic as a philosophical method rather than description. Warnock, who dismissed Sartre as "not original thinker," objected to what was a proof for Sartre, namely "a description so clear and vivid that, when I think of this description and fit it into my own case, I cannot fail to see its application."

What bothered Ayer, Nagel, Russell, Murdoch, Warnock, et. al., about Sartre's approach, indeed any approach which began with the "I" situated *in* the world, is that it risked defining truth according to its human relevance, which is precisely how Sartre defined it. In other words, the approach transformed the so-called dichotomy between object and subject into a dialectic in which each had its own being yet were inseparable—exactly what Sartre hoped to show (not prove) through his phenomenological description. For Anglo-Saxons who want to uphold the purity of "objectivity," this method is very dangerous because it may lead to interpreting speeches, events, indeed all of history, according to class interest. The conclusion may well be—and Sartre emphatically thought so—that for all their liberal, even perhaps socialist pronouncements, such intellectuals as Ayers, Warnock, et. al., were part and parcel of the bourgeois state and that their work ultimately defended that state.

But these philosophers were at least respectful. They sometimes even disagreed with each other. Thus while Ms. Warnock claimed that philosophy "has perhaps always been something of a sideline for Sartre himself," Denis O'Brien, an expert on Hegel and president of Bucknell University, insisted that, on the contrary, "Sartre was fundamentally, uncompromisingly, and incessantly a philosopher." But then, analytic philosophers never did like Hegel very much; during my ten year under- and graduate stint at Columbia, he never once earned the right to his own course. Still, better rejection at Columbia than praise at Berkeley, where Denis Hollier had this to say about Sartre's trilogy: "The war puts an end to the clinical narratology of the hypnagogic story." (That phrase may have put Professor Hollier's students to sleep but it sent Professor Alexander Leupin, another high-minded critic this time down at Louisiana State University, into orgasmic ecstasy—and Yale to print it).

In the US, Sartre's most efficient assassin was Germaine Bree, an expert on the contemporary literary scene in France. Infatuated with Albert Camus, Bree felt that she therefore had to demolish his main critic, Sartre. So, in a popular text, *Sartre & Camus*, which gained immense influence in academia, she condemned Sartre for dealing with authority "callously," "pompously," "typically." At least Camus, she wrote, never was guilty of making a judgment on the basis "of class." On the other hand, "Sartre's hatred of bourgeois life," she went on, "reveals the streak of irrationality that underlies many of his judgments." (Bree also had to attack Simone de Beauvoir because she had written in *Force of Circumstance*: "Camus became a more and more resolute champion of bourgeois values.")

Bree ridiculed Sartre for his supposed fear of psychoanalysis (page 33) but then scoffed at his supposed neuroses when she learned that, on the contrary, Sartre quite welcomed the idea of analysis (page 114). She passed off his opposition to General Ridgeway as head of SHAPE as "trite" because in her views no one could seriously have objected to the general's war-making in Korea, then tried her best to discredit Conor Cruise O'Brien for correctly calling Camus a "colonialist under the skin." Finally, she damned Sartre because he "never to my knowledge supported any political candidate who had the slightest chance of winning nor has he ever supported any action taken by the French government" – thus naively handing Sartre the best compliment he ever received.

The effect of Germaine Bree was somewhat offset, it is true, by such erudite critics as George Steiner in England, Arthur Danto and Robert Denoon Cumming in America. Cumming, for example, tried to explain why Americans, who want to turn everything, including poverty and exploitation, into a personal, individual problem, are disturbed by Sartre for whom "nothing is sacred ... not even the Freudian theory of the superego."

But such counterattacks could never dislodge Camus from the pinnacle of the literary hierarchy in England or America. There he is admired mostly because he focused on individual despair and individual hope, never on class conflicts. He disturbed no conscience. On the contrary, he soothed the self-involved and the self-indulgent by generalizing individual problems (whereas Sartre concretized the universal problems, forcing each of us to be responsible for all). No wonder, then, that someone like Bobby Kennedy discovered Camus "in the months of solitude and grief after his brother's death," reported Jack Newfield. "By 1968, he had read, and reread, all of Camus' essays, dreams and novels ... He memorized him, meditated about him, quoted him, and was changed by him." Bobby Kennedy's favorite passage from Camus' *Notebooks* (which he underlined): "Living with one's passions amounts to living with one's sufferings...When a man has learned— and not on paper—how to remain alone with his suffering, how to overcome his longing to flee, then he has little less to learn." The passage eloquently reveals Camus as an Algerian *pied-noir* (French colonial descendent), as a metaphysical sufferer who never understood the human causes of pain—which is why he never supported the Algerian people's struggle for independence.

It got worse after Sartre died. One British "expert," David Caute, cast off Sartre as an incestor *manque*. (Too bad Sartre didn't have a sister, he wrote). Then he added that the only reason Sartre chose to write about Flaubert was because the latter "had left behind 13 volumes of correspondence."

Concealing the fact that Sartre carefully avoided her because, he said, she was "an arrogant imperialist witch," Mary McCarthy told the *New York Times* that Sartre "didn't care for people." Which elicited this brilliant non sequitur from the "New Philosopher" Marcel Gauchet: "we want the Christian West to be on top." After which, most French reactionary critics felt free to let loose. The best, perhaps, was issued by the writer Olivier Rolin, who decided that "Sartre lacked courage" because he always maintained the unpopular viewpoint, and by Clement

Rosset who bewailed the fact that he could never find in Sartre's work "a solid philosophical or clear political position."

Even the editors of *Liberation*, the Parisian daily Sartre had kept alive for years with his own money and scores of exclusive interviews and articles, now turned against him. Re-interpreting his end-of-life musings, they decided that Sartre had abandoned the poor and the powerless, the rebel and the revolutionary to support the French reactionary Left, which he had always despised. Or was it that the *Libe* editor now wanted to court the powerful and established in order to be more "relevant"?

And wasn't that similar to the contortions performed by *The New York Review of Books* writers? Do they really think that "Sartre was entirely wrong" in his feud with Camus, as one of them affirmed, or do they simply like the fact that Camus never dirtied his hands (by avoiding commitment), thus giving the *Review* its "moral" justification to do likewise? Is it true that "Sartre has not been forgiven for the retrospective embarrassment caused the leftists intelligentsia for his visceral hatred of 'bourgeois' society, an attitude that now seems corrosive of democratic values," as one *New York Times* critic concluded? Or is it that today's "leftist intelligentsia," who inject morality into yuppie avarice, are lusting for bourgeois respectability—and bourgeois honors?

Sartre did hate bourgeois society and did reject its honors—from the Legion to the Nobel (which compelled *Time* magazine to snort stupidly: "reverse snobbery"). To his death he insisted that the job—and the excuse—of the intellectual was to criticize the powerful and defend the voiceless. Few famous and no rich ever agreed, then or now. But today, they are not afraid to praise their perks. Thus, in France and in the US, the new "intellectuals," those servicefolk of the established media, must show that "the ideology" of commitment of their immediate forebears, as the *Times* put it, "is indeed dead and that for them, private life is worthy of literary celebration."

That celebration of private life, decided David Leitch with acute plebian depth in the *London Sunday Times*, is why Sartre had lost touch with the young. He so wrote on the very day that 50,000 of those young gathered spontaneously to pay their respect the day of his burial. As they marched across Paris, they attracted another 50,000 more middle-aged mourners—the greatest testimony to the relevance of an intellectual the world has ever seen.

So, why their hatred—and our love? "How is it possible," asked Istvan Meszaros, "for a solitary individual, whose pen is his only weapon, to be as effective as Sartre is—and he is uniquely so – in an age which tends to render the individual completely powerless?" The answer: his "passionate commitment to the concerns of the given world." With Sartre, there were no escapes, no ivory towers, no retreat into false "objectivity." Those of us who had no power knew he fought for us and with us. Those who hid knew they could never say "I can't help it." The job of the intellectual, Sartre said over and over, is to criticize, to oppose, to denounce. And he cheerfully accepted his resulting solitary fate, just as Andre Chamsom had moaned during the Spanish Civil War that "the duty of the writer is to be tormented." For Sartre, as Hazel Barnes said, "literature is a means; at its best it is a form of praxis."

Sartre offered the intellectual no peace, no self-satisfaction, no contentment, nothing but hard work—and not even the hope of victory. In *The Words* he wrote: "For a long time I took my pen for a sword; I now know we're powerless. No matter. I write and will keep writing."

But he was wrong. He had a lot of power. The proof? All those who hate him. All those who followed him to the cemetery of Montparnasse. All those who love him. Like Francoise Sagan. Listen to her "Love Letter to Jean-Paul Sartre":

> ... You've written the most intelligent and honest books of your generation, you even wrote the most talented book in French literature—*The Words*. At the same time, you've always thrown yourself doggedly into the struggle to help the weak and the humiliated; you believed in people, in causes, in universals; you made mistakes at times, like everybody else, but (unlike everybody else) you acknowledged them every time ... In short, you have loved, written, shared, given all you had to give which was important, while refusing what was offered to you which was of import. You were a man as well as a writer, you never pretended that the talent of the latter justified the weakness of the former ...
>
> You have been the only man of justice, of honor and of generosity of our epoch.

CHAPTER TWELVE

THE US EMPIRE AND THE DEATH OF DEMOCRACY

Throughout history, no empire has survived if it tolerated dissent. It was just as true in Ancient Rome as it is in Modern America. From the day that US policy makers, representing big business and finance capital, decided to control world trade, that is, to become the empire of the world, it has had to eliminate dissent, and therefore genuine democracy. But it did so slowly, within its potential, and always when the pliant media was willing to tout its lies as facts.

Thus in 1825, when President James Monroe proclaimed his famous doctrine of freedom for the Americas, by which he meant, and every Latin American well understood, that the Americas would hereafter be colonies of the US, the media hailed the declaration as a stoic anti-imperialist doctrine. But then there never was an established free press in America; it was always a free-enterprise press, owned mostly by the same business and finance capitalists who controlled the government. Which explains why every newspaper and journal of the times heralded "Manifest Destiny" by which god himself had proclaimed that the Caribbean must become "an American lake."

And so it almost unanimously applauded when the US went to war against Spain to "help" the Cuban revolutionaries when they had already defeated Spain. Nor did the establishment object when the US imposed on Cuba total tutelage through the Platt Amendment, took over the Virgin Islands, Puerto Rico, the Philippines and various other Spanish colonies which lusted for independence. When it came to Europe, it had to act more slowly, less belligerently, always within its strength and potential. During World War I for example it had to be certain that the European powers were too exhausted to object, and hence waited until 1917 to enter the war. And when it did, it claimed to side with the democracies, forcing the press to mimic its pronouncements that England and France were the good guys and Germany the bully, when in fact it was the allies who started the war to stop Germany's rapidly expanding industrialization. Nor did our media tell Americans that there was much more democracy in Germany than in the so-called allies. In fact Germany then, with its legal Socialist parties, its massive union movement and its workingmen's bill of rights (including three weeks paid yearly holidays), was much freer in 1914 than England is today.

After the war, the US ruling class frightened dissenters by launching nation-wide witch-hunts, first against anarchists by tossing their leader Salcedo out the window of police headquarters, then framing two rank-and-filers, Sacco and Vanzetti, to their death. It jailed Socialists and framed the Wobblies, executing some of its leaders, for opposing entry into World War I. To make sure Americans did not realize the truth, the US elites next went after public universities, the only bastion of academic freedom. One of the worst such witch-hunts was in New York, the Coudert-Rapp Committee, which "investigated" public schools and universities for "subversive" teachers, and arranged to have them drummed out of their schools. For all the talk about democracy, it was little by little disappearing.

The US constitution correctly defines the fundamental prerequisite for democracy: life, liberty and the pursuit of happiness. But no country can be democratic if all of its people do not have access to life, that is health. Nor can a country be free if its citizens do not have easy access to choices, the result of free, equal education. And no people can pursue happiness, unless they are healthy and educated.

But the US, while proclaiming itself the bastion of freedom, quickly made sure that the poor, the worker, the sharecropper, the non-white, the immigrant would not have access to either prerequisite; it made health private and expensive and education financed by local taxes. The result of course was that the rich went to the good schools, the poor to the mediocre ones. Today in Westchester County, where the rich pay the local taxes, every student is allotted a yearly $17,520; in Bayou, Mississippi, where folks are so poor they own nothing and survive by catching cat-fish, as the CBS "Sixty Minutes" program documented, each student must do with $60, a State subsidy at that. The last science book purchased by the high school's library is dated 1961.

Though many of the idiotic Republicans never understood that Franklin Roosevelt was saving their capitalism for them, it was he who decided to make the US a two-ocean power, by turning Japan into an enemy to stop its industrialization. FDR imposed boycotts on Japan of steel, manganese, oil, bauxite, thus forcing the mineral-void island to invade other countries for its needed minerals. And it was FDR who set up the machinery of state to crush serious dissent in America, which his heirs employed to the fullest. The arbitrary arrest and incarceration of Japanese Americans, even if they were born in the US, would later give impetus to Colonel North and his NSA henchmen to set up concentration camps all over the West, and frighten the Latino population into submissiveness when his boss, President Reagan, and the fascist team working for him (Poindexter, McFarland, Weinburger, Perle, Abrams, *et al*) decided to crush a legally and very fairly elected Nicaraguan government, calling it Marxist-Leninists, because it had the gall to institute the first minimum wage law of Central America ($1.27). The OSS (Office of Strategic Services) which FDR allowed to operate all over the world without oversight, stimulated President Truman to enact the National Security Act 1968 (that's just a number, the date was 1946), creating the CIA and the various loyalty boards under which 1.2 million people lost their jobs without being able to confront their accusers.

Senator Joseph McCarthy's "anti-Communist" crusades did the US ruling class a disservice for a while by overdoing it, causing some newsmen (Edward R. Murrow) and academics (Harvard President Pusey) to fight back, especially after two more rank-and-filer dissidents, in this case the Communists Rosenbergs, were executed. But the US ruling class never lost track of its main goal: pervert, intimidate, or force all other countries to accept the US 's criteria for world trade.

Bush II's infamous "if you're not with us you're against us" is not new to US policy. Nor was it new with President Eisenhower's Secretary of State John Forster Dulles, who was the first to affirm categorically that the US had a right to demolish any country opposed to "our new order". No, even before him, that great statesman whom every liberal adores, General George Marshall, made it quite clear in testifying before the House Foreign Relations Committee that his objective (known since as "The Marshall Plan") was to rekindle Europe as a market for US goods, and any neutralist opposed to it was "as dangerous as any communist."

No poor country can develop its infrastructure, build low-cost housing, hospitals, universities, self-defense forces without capital accumulation. No poor country can achieve such accumulation by allowing foreign companies to run its utilities, its banks, its mines. Latin America has 75% of the goodies the US needs to maintain its industrial might, under its ground. The US does not have enough iron (steel), cobalt, bauxite (aluminum), manganese, diamonds (industrial), to keep its imperial machinery running. Hence it wants what Latin America has. To get it, it supports every dictator it can bribe, and it opposes every independent government which dares to try to develop its own country's economy. So the US plotted against Argentina's Peron (a "Nazi" it said), Frondizi (a "Communist)", Brazil's Vargas (another Nazi), Quadros (too conservative to be a red so a "nut"), Goulart (another communist), etc., and of course Allende, and supported all the petty dictators in Central America and the Caribbean, from Somoza to Trujillo.

To succeed, the US had to create death squads, organize Operation Condor assassination teams, plan dirty wars, foster vicious military coups and, as NYTimesman Langguth so eloquently described in his book, teach all the two-bit gangsters corralled into the local police force, how to torture. Always to support US corporations exploiting Latin lands. With what results? Every year, 5 million kids under the age of 14 die in Latin America alone from lack of potable water where that water is used and polluted by American mining (especially nitrate) corporations. Hitler may have killed over 50 million people with his drive to create a thousand-year Reich, Stalin 20 or 30 million to cater to his paranoia, but the US has murdered more than 100 million people in the last century alone just to satisfy the greed of its corporate executives. It can do all that because it is not a democracy, its elected officials are whores, embedded to whatever corporations give them the biggest re-election booty.

Does the average American know any of this? Does the mainstream media report any of these facts? No wonder then that when a Latino rebels or an Arab blows himself up with a few US soldiers, the average American thinks the Latino is an ingrate, the Moslem a fanatic. What paper tells him that only 14 percent of suicide bombers are religious? What TV anchorman tells him that the CIA murdered every decent leader the Third World ever had, incorruptible leaders who wanted to better the lot of their people? Egypt's Nasser (heart attack by poison), Iraq's Kassem (shot by CIA employee Saddam Hussein), Algeria's Frantz Fanon (leukemia by poison in a US hospital), Guyana's Cheddi Jagan (heart attack by poison), Congo's Lumumba (by CIA and Belgian local gunmen), Che Guevara (by Cuban CIA employees), Indonesia's Sukarno (by Japanese World War II collaborator Gen. Suharto under CIA orders), the Cameroon's Felix Moumie, Um

Nyobe and Osende Afana (by French CIA thugs), Guinea's Amilcar Cabral (shot in the back by a local CIA operative), *ad infinitum.*

Most of the people of the world (not in the US) know that it was the US which started the Cold War in 1946, by violating the Berlin treaty whereby each of the victorious powers would rule the city together, backed by a currency defended by the four. But the US decided to issue a mark backed by the dollar. So the English did the same, and so too the French. When the Russians decided to follow suit, the West cried foul. Why did the US want the war? Because it could then launch an arms race and have its citizens pay for it, by frightening them with the coming nuclear war. Those of you old enough will remember all those alarms and tests, where we had to scamper under the nearest table to "protect" ourselves against the A-bomb dropping on our heads. Fear! That was the object, and it made the industrial-military complex rich. Nothing better than weapons: once one is built it is obsolete, so let's build another. And another. And another. Who is going to object to paying taxes for our defense? Building hospitals is profitable to the builder, but it can't be rebuilt every year. But weapon systems can, and do. And just to make sure we stayed in fear, the CIA lied to us; for 20 years, it claimed that Russia was way ahead of the US in arms build-up. For 20 years it lied, so the complex could keep making money – on average-Joe's taxes.

To get the American public to buy US intervention in the Middle East, the Russians gave us Afghanistan. The co-called Communist regime which came to power during Breshnev's reign was quite good, better than Afghanistan ever had. It built schools, hospitals, roads. It allowed women to work, to walk the streets without shadors or burkas if they wanted, to demand that their husbands have only one wife. The fanatic tribesmen were outraged and launched a counter war against Kabul. Their operations were on the border with Soviet Russia, which was worried that fundamentalist Moslems would sweep into Russia as well. So Moscow intervened, and our ruling class warmongers immediately called the Kabul regime "Marxist-Leninist." The only Marx its leaders had ever heard of was probably Groucho. President Carter surely knew that, since all he did was condemn the Soviet intervention by boycotting the Olympics scheduled for Moscow that year. But Reagan and his cohorts jubilantly saw their chance to start dominating the whole area. The CIA poured weapons and money ($44 million to what was to be Taliban) to the worst fanatics in the whole Middle East. And the Pentagon set up the most advanced base it could build in Saudi Arabia.

How would Americans react if, on the guise of helping the US stop Cuban exile terrorism, Fidel built a huge modern military base in North Carolina? As President de Gaulle told a worried British Prime Minister Macmillan on his way to meet JFK and hoping to resist US domination: "Too late. England is now nothing more than an aircraft carrier for US goods and policies. No country can be free if it has a foreign base on its territory." The effect of the US base in Saudi Arabia was immediate. Every Moslem whose creed opposes foreigners stationed on their land and every Saudi who hopes one day to be genuinely independent rallied to those who denounced it. But don't castigate the Reagan administration for that. On the contrary, that's what the US ruling class wanted: a "war of religion". If only the Moslems got really angry, maybe they might resort to a bit of terrorism. And then the politics of fear would continue. Instead of a Cold War, the US would now fight the War on Terror. And once again, taxes would go for weapons, military bases, cops, agents, torturers, assassins, with no money left for hospitals, schools, entitlements, invalid children, AIDS, for anything human. Thanks to "Terror", taxes would continue to go for death. Because death makes more money for the rich. And to "defend ourselves," the ruling class could tighten its repression.

Anyone who looks Moslem could now be jailed. And any foreigner the US didn't like could become an "enemy combatant." The US could now torture anyone it wanted to at home or, if some lawyers objected, send them to Egypt, Pakistan, Uzbekistan or some other dictatorship-run friend of the US, where they might be tortured without interference, secretly. It is called "rendition". How many of the 1500 American Moslems whom the ACLU has identified as "disappeared" are being rendered abroad? Every day we learn of a new case. The Canadian citizen taken off a plane at JFK airport, sent to his native Syria, tortured there for three years. The German Moslem, "not tortured only severely beaten" for nine months and held long enough to force his family back to Lebanon. The American Lebanese picked up in the street by FBI goons who refused to notify his family and held him *incommunicado* for three years, compelling his wife and two kids to abandon their lives in Queens, New York. Not to mention systematic torture in Guantanamo, Abu Graib, US detention camps in Afghanistan and, we now are told, in US prisons as well. Amnesty International defines the US camp at Guantanamo as a "Gulag." Logic and careful analysis of the facts tell us that the US runs Gulags wherever it dominates a country.

Some of that information is now known to the average American. But not all. Not enough, thanks to a pliable media, for average-Joe to understand that the FBI, CIA, DIA, NSA, and most local US police corps are today no better than the Gestapo or the KGB goons. And to make sure that average Joe does not get to know the extent of US atrocities, the government is now trying to silence even defense lawyers.

So for you and me, who don't look Moslem or Latino or Hindu or Apache, beware: one wrong word and, under the US Patriot ACT, we will face the charge of aiding and abetting the terrorists. And we will find it harder and harder to find a lawyer willing to defend us, that is if we are not simply "disappeared" to Tashkent or Ryad. Under the War on Terror, nothing can stop the empire. Years ago, the State Department hawk who invented the rational for the Cold War, the former ambassador to Moscow who invented "containment," euphemistically meant to give an acceptable term to the US policy of surrounding Soviet Russia (and making the Russians so scared of our first strike policy that the US, in effect, created and is responsible for post-war Stalin), the great statesman George Kennan said:

We have about 50 percent of the world's wealth, but only 6.3 percent of its population. In this situation we cannot fail to be the object of envy and resentment. Our real task in the coming period is to devise a pattern of relationships that will permit us to maintain this position of disparity. To do so we will have to dispense with all sentimentality and daydreaming and our attention will have to be concentrated everywhere on our immediate national objectives. We should cease the talk about vague, unreal objectives, such as human rights, raising of living standards and democratization. The day is not far off when we are going to have to deal in straight power concepts. The less we are hampered by idealistic slogans, the better.

In other words, said this great American statesman, forget democracy. We don't have it, we don't want it. And let's stop pushing it on our totalitarian friends.

ANSWER TO QUEENS COLLEGE SMEARS

When asked about the circumstances behind this piece, which ran in Queens College's student newspaper, *The Knight News*, Gerassi explains:

"Today we lionize the French resistance fighters during World War II. I announce on the first day of class that I am pro-Palestinian. I explain that I believe that Israel is an occupying-power much like Nazi Germany was an occupying power in France. The French used 'terror' in the same way as Palestinians do today. There were a lot of suicide bombers in France. In the French underground they made it a point to shoot and kill German officers even though they were told that for every German officer killed the Nazis would execute ten, then fifty, then one hundred people. The French underground had to accept the fact that they end up being murderers, but they continued to struggle, and we praise them today.

"I make the point in class on the first day that when one country occupies another, every unnatural death in the occupied country, by whatever means it is perpetrated and by whomever it is perpetrated, is the responsibility of the *occupier*. So for every suicide bomber who kills, who is responsible? Israel, not the Palestinians.

"I explain to the students that I say all this up front on the first day because if they cannot accept this kind of criticism they are free to leave the class and still have time to choose another class. Queens College's newspaper, The Knight News, ran a front page story claiming fifty students got up and left my class. Only one got up and left, and that was the guy who wrote the article. I continued to teach the course. I had Zionists in the class who argued with me but there was no problem.

"The guy who left, left right away, the first day of class, and he later wrote an article where he made up all sorts of things he claimed I said. He gave the article to a reactionary columnist at the *New York Post*. She tried to interview me but I refused to be interviewed by her. I said, 'Murdoch is the Goebbels of Bush; I don't talk to Goebbels, I don't talk to Bush, and I'm not going to talk to you working for Murdoch.' She then made things up and said she interviewed me at my 'swanky east side apartment,' but she guessed wrong; I've never lived on the east side and never would. This piece [Answer to QC Smears] was my answer, which ran in *The Knight News*, and only because the President of the University called the editor-in-chief and asked when they were going to run my piece. That seemed to have provoked *The Knight News* to run it; I don't think they were going to otherwise."

MY ANSWER TO THE SMEARS IN QUEENS COLLEGE'S ZIONIST-RUN PAPER
KNIGHT NEWS

Ever since I denounced JFK's invasion (by so-called "advisers") of Vietnam, I have been smeared by bigots, American-firsters, racists and just plain idiots who believe what they read in the mainstream media. I have never bothered to answer them on the simple grounds that such yokels never listen to anyone else's point of view. I will this time to Rubin's hysterical diatribe but only because he cites for support one of the most despicable lawyers the pro-war, pro-Israel fanatics have produced: Harvard's Alan Dershowitz, who has publicly praised the use of torture by US forces, even while Bush was trying to deny that the US did so.

I was right about Vietnam. Right again when I denounced LBJ's invasion of the Dominican Republic in 1965 to save his friend Ellsworth Bunker's Jack Frost Sugar; LBJ named the top ten "constitutionalists" as communists, but I pointed out that two were dead, four were in Paris, one was studying at Columbia, and said so, in *Newsweek* to boot. That made me "unAmerican" in the News. I was right when I denounced the US for organizing the coup that crushed Brazil's democracy in 1963 and printing that the US ambassador actually congratulated the top general by telegram the day *before* the coup; that got the New York Times mad because they loved the ambassador, liberal Lincoln Gordon. I was right when I printed evidence that the US helped the generals destroy Argentina's fledging democracy and instill, helped by the CIA, the "dirty war" which resulted in 30,000 "disappeared" and which all the media now condemns (without, of course, saying who made it possible). I was right when I called Kissinger a murderer (now so indicted in Spain) at the service of the exploiting copper companies for his fomenting the coup against Chile's democratically elected government. I was right when, as the first investigator for the International War Crimes Tribunal, I photographed and reported (in the full issue of the New Republic and in my book *North Vietnam: A Documentary*) that the US bombed dykes in North Vietnam, which the media kept denying until Walter Cronkite went there, saw it, and said so. I was right when I showed proof (the British 4-hour documentary film) that the US and its NATO allies bombed Serbia because its president, Milosevic, would not privatize its utilities, which US and European firms coveted; Milosevic was certainly guilty of crimes against humanity, but even more so were the Nazi-heirs Ustashis who run Croatia and the Bosnians, but they were perfectly willing to privatize everything and did so. (It was the Ustachis who started the ethnic cleansing, not the Serbs). And I was right to denounce the US for using anti-personnel fragmentation bombs against civilians in Vietnam as crimes against humanity (as also characterized by the UN, Amnesty International and Human Rights Watch).

I research my facts carefully. Every day I read two British papers, France's *Le Monde*, Spain's *ABC*, Argentina's *La Prensa*, even the *India Monitor*, plus seven weeklies, ten monthlies (even such esoteric revues as Switzerland's *Illustre*) and I comb the web. I receive information via email from dozens of folks all over the world, even Indonesia. Nevertheless, I tell my students that the facts they will hear in my courses are one-sided, facts never or rarely available in mainstream media. If you want that point of view, I tell them, watch TV, read *Time*. I tell my students: "You don't have to agree with me. I cannot penalize you if you do, as I give strictly objective exams." Ask any student. That's why I am a good teacher. That 55 of them walked out of my class as the Post's hysterical columnist reported is a lie. The only student who walked out had not even registered for the course.

Speaking of lies, lets deal with them. I was not interviewed by that Post columnist. I hung up on her three times, once explaining that to me Murdoch, her boss, "was Bush's Goebbels and that I do not talk to Bush, I do not talk to Goebbels and I won't talk to you working for Goebbels." Nor have I ever lived on the upper (or lower for that matter) eastside, as she reported. I certainly know better to believe in a Jewish control of the media; capitalists own the media, and when I say so I always give the examples (e.g. GE owning NBC, Viacom owning CBS, etc).

Now let's deal with Israel and what I said and say. Zionism is an imperialism. The policy of every Israeli government has always been to regain "greater Israel" (whatever that may be) and eliminate all Palestinian characteristics. On Face the Nation (CBS, June 11, 1967) Moshe Dayan (then the Israeli Defense Minister) made that quite clear: "... We can absorb them [Palestinians] but it wouldn't be the same country ... we want a Jewish state like the French want a French state." But the French state don't want a Catholic state or a Huguenot state or a Shinto state. They want a French state. Quite a difference.

From its inception, Israeli leaders have lied, taught well by their mentors, the US. They claimed and by and large still claim that the Palestinians left Israel on their own accord, when in fact they were driven out, and all the belongings they could not carry were confiscated by the "Jewish" state. They claimed and still claim that those who remained were and are given equal rights, when in fact they suffer an apartheid regime. And Israel receives more aid, more free arms and technical support from the US than any other nation in the world, proportionally and in absolute figures. Israel is an occupying power, and I stress in my class, never judge a poor people trying to win freedom by the same criteria as you judge the powerful, the dominant power. We didn't judge the Norwegian underground or the Polish ghetto insurgents or the French Maquis by the same criterion as we judged the Nazis. So don't do it now, I tell my students, either in Afghanistan (where the US helped Taliban come to power) or Iraq (where Saddam Hussein was a paid CIA agent when he was head of Iraqi intelligence) or in Palestine. And I add: "When one country occupies another, all deaths, no matter how committed or by whom, are the responsibility of the occupier." When freedom fighters have neither tanks nor planes, neither missiles nor canons, anything they can do against those who do have them and who try to subdue them into slavery is absolutely justified. Those freedom fighters who then blow themselves up to attack their dominators are not only justified, but fantastic heroes. And the deaths, those innocent children on the bus? The murderers are the occupiers.

From that to pretend I said such an inane remark that I thought Hezbollah would win in 40 years, is the epitome of stupidity. I did say and maintain that Hezbollah had the right to defend itself. I did say and maintain that Israel's cruel devastation of Lebanon has resulted in such hated of Israel among all Arabs and

Moslems that peace now is impossible, that no Moslem will ever forget it, and that perhaps in 40 years, 400 million Arabs may decide to get even by driving the Israelis to the sea. Nor will they ever forget that Israel used the same weapon, the anti-personnel cluster bombs that the US used in Vietnam. They know as we all do but never read in our mainstream media that Israel is just as guilty of crimes against humanity as was/and is the US. They know but can never read in our mainstream media that only the weak, the losers, the helpless are tried for such crimes.

CHAPTER FOURTEEN

WILL THE TEARS EVER STOP?

The day after the events of 9–11, explains Gerassi, "I wrote this and sent it to the New York Times, which refused to print it as an Op-Ed piece. A friend put it on Z Magazine's website, and it spread like wild fire. It's been translated into over fifty seven different languages. The only version that was edited was the version that appeared in *L'Humanite*, the French communist newspaper in Paris which took out all my references to Israel-Palestine because they don't want to come across as pro-Palestinian." As we went to press Gerassi was excited to report that this piece had just been translated into Urdu.

WILL THE TEARS EVER STOP?

I can't help crying. As soon as I see a person on TV telling the heart-rendering story of the tragic fate of their loved-one in the World Trade Center disaster, I can't control my tears. But then I wonder why didn't I cry when our troops wiped out some 5,000 poor people in Panama's El Chorillo neighborhood on the excuse of looking for Noriega. Our leaders knew he was hiding elsewhere but we destroyed El Chorillo because the folks living there were nationalists who wanted the U.S. out of Panama completely.

Worse still, why didn't I cry when we killed two million Vietnamese, mostly innocent peasants, in a war which its main architect, Defense Secretary Robert McNamara, knew we could not win? When I went to give blood at St. Vincent, I spotted a Cambodian doing the same, three up in the line, and that reminded me: Why didn't I cry when we helped Pol Pot butcher another million by giving him arms and money, because he was opposed to "our enemy" (who eventually stopped the killing fields)?

To stay up but not cry that evening, I decided to go to a movie. I chose Lumumba, at the Film Forum, and again I realized that I hadn't cried when our government arranged for the murder of the Congo's only decent leader, to be replaced by General Mobutu, a greedy, vicious, murdering dictator. Nor did I cry when the CIA arranged for the overthrow of Indonesia's Sukarno, who had fought the Japanese World War II invaders and established a free independent country, and then replaced him by another General, Suharto, who had collaborated with the Japanese and who proceeded to execute at least half a million "Marxists" (in a country where, if folks had ever heard of Marx, it was at best Groucho)?

I didn't go to the movies but watched TV instead and cried again at the picture of that wonderful now-missing father playing with his two-month old child. Yet when I remembered the slaughter of thousands of Salvadorans, so graphically described in the *Times* by Ray Bonner, or the rape and murder of those American nuns and lay sisters there, all perpetrated by CIA trained and paid agents, I never shed a tear. I even cried when I heard how brave had been Barbara Olson, wife of the Solicitor General, whose political views I detested. But I didn't cry when the US invaded that wondeFEDDDDDDDDEXDXXrful tiny Caribbean nation of Grenada and killed innocent citizens who hoped to get a better life by building a tourist airfield, which my government called proof of a Russian base, but then finished building once the island was secure in the US camp again.

Why didn't I cry when Ariel Sharon, today Israel's prime minister, planned, then ordered, the massacre of two thousand poor Palestinians in the refugee camps of Sabra and Shatila, the same Sharon who, with such other Irgun and Stern Gang terrorists become prime ministers as Begin and Shamir, killed the wives and children of British officers by blowing up the King David hotel where they were billeted?

I guess one only cries for one's own. But is that a reason to demand vengeance on anyone who might disagree with us? That's what Americans seem to want. Certainly our government does, and so too most of our media. Do we really believe that we have a right to exploit the poor folk of the world for our benefit, because we claim we are free and they are not?

So now we're going to go to war. We are certainly entitled to go after those who killed so many of our innocent brothers and sisters. And we'll win, of course. Against Bin Laden. Against Taliban. Against Iraq. Against whoever and whatever. In the process we'll kill a few innocent children again. Children who have no clothes for the coming winter. No houses to shelter them. And no schools to learn why they are guilty, at two or four or six years old. Maybe Evangelists Falwell and Robertson will claim their death is good because they weren't Christians, and maybe some State Department spokesperson will tell the world that they were so poor that they're now better off.

And then what? Will we now be able to run the world the way we want to? With all the new legislation establishing massive surveillance of you and me, our CEOs will certainly be pleased that the folks demonstrating against globalization will now be cowed for ever. No more riots in Seattle, Quebec or Genoa. Peace at last.

Until next time. Who will it be then? A child grown-up who survived our massacre of his innocent parents in El Chorillo? A Nicaraguan girl who learned that her doctor mother and father were murdered by a bunch of gangsters we called democratic contras who read in the CIA handbook that the best way to destroy the only government which was trying to give the country's poor a better lot was to kill its teachers, health personnel, and government farm workers? Or maybe it will be a bitter Chilean who is convinced that his whole family was wiped out on order of Nixon's Secretary of State Henry Kissinger who could never tell the difference between a communist and a democratic socialist or even a nationalist.

When will we Americans learn that as long as we keep trying to run the world for the sake of the bottom line, we will suffer someone's revenge? No war will ever stop terrorism as long as we use terror to have our way. So I stopped crying because I stopped watching TV. I went for a walk. Just four houses from mine.

There, a crowd had congregated to lay flowers and lit candles in front of our local firehouse. It was closed. It had been closed since Tuesday because the firemen, a wonderful bunch of friendly guys who always greeted neighborhood folks with smiles and good cheer, had rushed so fast to save the victims of the first tower that they perished with them when it collapsed. And I cried again.

So I said to myself when I wrote this, don't send it; some of your students, colleagues, neighbors will hate you, maybe even harm you. But then I put on the TV again, and there was Secretary of State Powell telling me that it will be okay to go to war against these children, these poor folks, these US-haters, because we are civilized and they are not. So I decided to risk it. Maybe, reading this, one more person will ask: Why are so many people in the world ready to die to give us a taste of what we give them?

CHAPTER FIFTEEN

REVOLUTION BY LIFESTYLE

So we call ourselves revolutionaries! So we want a radical transformation of society! So some of us – more than ever before in the history of the world – are so fed up with the way we're *supposed* to live, that we spend our whole waking day talking. reading, planning, plotting revolution. Yet we – at least most of us white, middle-class, educated dreamers and drop-outs – have all the basic necessities we need to live more comfortably than ever before. We have more physical freedom, to move, escape or roam about. We have more sexual freedom. We are even freer than ever to say what we feel like. At least in the developed capitalist world, which we consider the real enemy and want to destroy. So, why *do* we want a revolution? What kind? What would we do with it?

Ask these questions of any 'traditional' revolutionary, one who thinks he is a 'Marxist-Leninist', and you'll get the traditional economic-political answers: the capitalist exploits the working class by blah-blah. But we're not working class! Yes, but we're intellectuals, and the role of the intellectual revolutionary elite, conscious of the ti-da-ti-dum, is to papim papam. Why? Because that elite, realizing that it profits from the greed ... Ho hum.

I don't know about you, but that's not why I'm a revolutionary. Sure, I can make those tedious analyses. Sure, I even think such analyses have to be made, as fuel to bring about evolutionary situations. In order to thrive in my kind of society, I know I've got to convince others to view it as groovy. And in order to make them receptive to my future, I've got to make them conscious of our present. So, I guess I'll keep trying to explain why we live in a dehumanizing society, the direct and necessary consequence of capitalism, and its mode of operation, capitalist bureaucracy. But, were I a Russian, I'd try just as hard to show why its system, which the world calls 'Communism' but is really State Capitalism, is just as dehumanizing, the direct and necessary product of the managerial bureaucracy built into its elitist revolutionism. The cause is the same: material incentives.

Once one posits material achievement as the only valuable (or the most valuable) drive of man, the consequences – whatever one's ideology – are inevitable. Why should I work harder to produce a bigger and brighter and faster car? Because you pay me for it. The harder I work, the more you'll pay me. If you're going to pay me more and more, you'll have to charge more and more for the car. So you, capitalist or government, are you going to try to get rid of the other guys or govern- ments who make cars; that's so you can have a monopoly and charge what you want. Well, sometimes you'll succeed – via mergers, *coups d'etat*, invasions, boycotts, control of the money markets, exchange rates or whatnot. Sometimes, you won't. That's when you'll come to terms. 'Why don't we get together,' you'll say to the other guy, 'you can have that market, I'll have this one. And we'll get together on prices, okay?' Net result: capitalism, state or private, based on competition, ends up as competition-less monopoly. And who gets screwed? Me. I can't buy a car that's safe, that doesn't pollute my air, that doesn't break down after X number of miles. I know safe, non-polluting, indestructible cars *can* be made. But I can't get one. In America or Russia.

But then, that ain't the worst *of* it. It's not enough just to build bigger and brighter and faster cars, one has to keep selling them, too – more and more every year. So the capitalist, state or private, has to keep expanding markets, which means controlling more and more countries – the underdeveloped world. That's got to be done in a special way too: these countries have got to produce more rich people *to buy* the cars but not rich enough *to make* them. That is. the countries have to stay underdeveloped, or, more accurately, unevenly developed.

Well, you say, too bad for the people there, but that doesn't affect me. True. I don't believe in revolutionism by guilt. But there's a catch. In order to keep the underdeveloped world's economies unbalanced – money from mines, plantations, assembly plants, export-import, but not from steel mills and factories which could produce cars – the capitalist has to keep a tight control on the manner in which that world develops. When he does, some local patriot is going to say no! He'll find others and they'll fight. That's when the capitalist needs help – from you and me. We have to be his henchmen, his soldiers. We've got to go there and do his fighting – in Vietnam, the Dominican Republic, the Congo, Thailand, Laos, the Philippines, Czechoslovakia, the U.S. black ghettoes (they function the same way) And that *does* affect us: You want to die in Vietnam?

Even if our dying becomes unnecessary in the future, if the U.S. – Russian capital experts devise a way to press some button and – whammo! – those nasty rebels are zapped off the face of the earth, do you think we wouldn't be involved? Just how do you think they'll get those gadgets and experts? And who, pray tell, will rationalize their necessity? Who will explain their political value? You and me. They need us more than we need them. We are the ones who must think up these things in their labs, the ones who must explain their value in books, the ones who must show their appeal on television, the ones who must defend them in their courts. That's why we've got to go to *their* universities, join *their* factories and institutions. Otherwise? Well, just imagine, as Abbie Hoffman put it recently:

> *'What would happen if large numbers of people in the country started getting together, forming communities, bustling free fish on Fulton Street, and passing out brass washers to use in Laundromats and phones?*
>
> *What if people in slums started moving into abandoned buildings and refusing to move even to the point of defending them with guns?*
>
> *What if this movement grew and buoy salesmen sweating under the collar on a hot summer day decided to say fuck the system and headed for welfare?*
>
> *What if secretaries got tired of typing memos to the boss's girlfriend in triplicate and took to panhandling in the streets?*
>
> *What if when they called a war, no-one went? What if people who wanted to get educated just went to a college classroom and sat in without paying and without caring about a degree? Well, you know what? We'd have*

ourselves one hell of a revolution, that's what? Who would do the work?
Fuck it. There's always some schmuck like Spiro Agnew lying around. Let
him pick up garbage if he's worried about the smell. We'll build a special zoo
for people like that and every weekend we'll take the kiddies over to Queens
to watch them work'.

Obviously, if the modern world's universities came to a standstill – or if we all refused to get educated 'their' way – the whole capitalist-bureaucratic world would collapse. And it would do so faster than with guns and barricades. This is true not only because of what they teach us but why as well. In order to make us 'experts' they have to separate us, compartmentalize us. We have to be segregated, pigeon-holed, divorced from one another so totally that we cannot relate to one another (outside of our own in-group) except through *their* institutions.

The only way to make an 'expert' is to dehumanize man. How else could a sociologist deal 'objectively' with types? A political scientist predict behavior? A psychologist concoct the stimuli for desired responses? Only if a man is coerced or conditioned into living with his peer-group in his peer-place, with peer-things, on his peer-salary, influenced by peer-produced television, peer-programmes, can pollsters predict his voting pattern, can admen channel his lust, can presidents appeal to his 'patriotism' to spend 60 percent of the country's budget to defend him against non-existent enemies while increasing the profits of the industrial military complex – which, in turn, finances elections, including the President's. What would happen to our society if a worker actually like to sit and talk with intellectuals? If children were allowed to masturbate together instead of watching television? If a housewife's value system told her that the cheaper a product the better it is?

But that still isn't all. What our education system does necessarily force us to enter and propagate the vicious circle which dehumanizes us, which teaches us that material achievement are the only valuable things in life. To make us 'good' experts, we must prove our merit. How? By passing tests better than anyone else. By competing. In other words by considering our fellow-men as our personal enemies. This is true in Russia as well as in America

We've got to 'prove' ourselves – first in class, then in the army, then in the factory. Every value we have is based on individual achievement, on some rags-to-riches tale, on some poor bloke finding his god in the desert, overcoming his obstacles *alone*, struggling with *his* soul. Who wrote that book? What was the name of that painter? Was that composer influenced by that other one? Who's the leader? Where's the best car, the stand-out, the valedictorian, the Rhodes scholar?

The so-called communists are just the same. All Power to the Soviets! Yes, but later: First, let's be as good as the capitalist world. So Lenin rules. Then Stalin. Then what's-his-name. The Soviets can wait. They're made up of ordinary people, and some ordinary people are stupid and everybody knows stupid people don't count. Because they don't want to get to the moon first. And niggers don't count either because they love sex too much and are lazy. But they'll be okay when they get our values, when they understand that the meaning of Life is to get ahead. Until then society can tell them how to live – with the police. Police are the same in every country. Their job is to protect their bosses – those who have property or those who make laws, have power. Did you know that in America, 'Nearly all the violence that has occurred in mass demonstrations has resulted not from the demonstrators' conscious choice of tactics, but from the measures chosen by public authorities to disperse and punish them?' And that's no radical who said that but President Johnson's hand-picked National Commission on the Causes and Prevention of Violence.

I'll tell you why I'm a revolutionary. It's very simple: I just don't want that kind of life. I want to live in a world – where I don't have to stand while my boss or the commissar sits; where I can talk to a black man as an equal; where I don't get asphyxiated by fumes or killed by shoddy cars; where no one wants to shoot me and I don't want to shoot anyone; where I can enjoy a painting without caring about who did it, just as I don't care who made the sun-set. I want to know what my neighbor thinks about the school where we both send our kids, even though he likes music written by some guy named Beet Hoven while I groove to Jimi Hendrix. I want to be free to ask a girl to go to bed with me knowing that if she doesn't she'll feel free enough to say 'no thanks' and then we can still rap about a book we both read – and vice versa. I want to smoke pot if I like it. I don't want cops telling me where I can sit, but I do want to be able to listen to my neighbors, all kinds of people, and if they all feel that it's good for us all for me *not* to sit there I won't, and I won't feel my manhood is bitten off for going along with them. I know I can't participate in every decision, that I can't be everywhere at the same time and I don't want to – I'm lazy – so I want to be able to have some guy represent me there and another guy over yonder. But I want to be able to recall him anytime. I don't want to worry about food or clothing or a roof – I know the world is rich enough to give me all that, me and everybody else – and I'm willing to do my share of the work, but not for somebody else's profit. I don't want to accumulate property. I want free education, as I and the people I rap with think it important or pleasurable. I'm no masochist; I don't believe I have to sacrifice myself in order to have a vacation or enjoy myself. I don't believe pleasure and work are antithetic; every man ought to enjoy what he does. I want free medicine, free transportation, free rent, free leisure, free theatre, free eye-glasses, free pot. I'll work, sure, I'll do my best. I can write – sometimes. I can teach. I'll do it, with pleasure. Or, if you all think it's a waste of time, well, I can make pretty good tables and dressers, with sliding doors that really slide. Maybe I can hoe potatoes. Why not? If a bunch of us do it together, singing, laughing. Well, not every day maybe. So, we'll take Mondays. You take Tuesdays.

Most important, I guess, I want to know what you think and feel, and why. And I want you to care about me. I don't care if you have an IQ of 20 and me 120 – that's luck. You have blond hair, I got brown. That's our human condition. If you have an IQ of 20, you're just as much a man as I am, me with my potato nose and you with that straight, delicate one. Your experiences are worth mine and mine yours. Let's rap, brother. Let's see what we want from each other, what we have to do in private, what we agree on and can do together. Let's run our schools together. And our factories. And if, after a while, there's no Spiro Agnew to pick up the garbage, and we agree that we want it out of our community, maybe I'll pick it up on Tuesdays if you can do it on Wednesdays.

I know one thing already, even before you and I start rapping, and that's that neither of us wants to die in Vietnam. Or go in the army. And if we don't own that goddamn factory over there, the one that is spewing all that junk in the river and killing the fish and stopping us from enjoying a swim in it, or if we *all* own it but none of us is better off than any other for owning it, then we'll sure put an end to the pollution, even if we have to tear it down. Chances are, though, that we'll find some way to keep it going, make better cars without pollution. There's no reason technology has to be used against men. It's man-made, let's put it to the service of man.

I don't want customs, or passports, or work-permits or foreign exchange. Of course, since we'll all be equals, we won't need any of that. True, there's always that guy, the one who invents a new way to fly and won't tell us unless he gets two cars to our one. Well, the hell with him and his invention. Suppose, though, what he invents is a pill that prolongs life for fifty years. We'd all like to live until we're 130, but then, what can he do with his invention? Together, you and I, we'll have fun. We'll laugh and enjoy ourselves and we won't have any reason to distrust each other, even if you do have a prettier nose and I envy you for it, and I have a higher IQ (which you won't envy since it won't get me more things). (I might have a prettier wife though.) Still , we'll relate. He'll be an outcast. Let him live till he's 130, lonely and bitter. We'll die when we're eighty. But it was fun. That's what I want. That's what a lot of people I know want. The blacks aren't there yet; they can't think that far ahead, because the white world won't let them live with the basics. They've got to fight for those still. And the poor, too, in all those underdeveloped countries which my country rules. But me? I got taught by having it. That's right, I'm a product of capitalist society. I've had the fancy home, the maid, the car, the expense account, the titles and the Bigelows on the floor. What I didn't have was happiness. I was bossed, cajoled, coerced, manipulated, pigeon-holed. I was so frustrated I competed against my friends, my wife (ex–now), even my child. I lived by the values of this society and they taught me to drive, drive for more, rush and rush some more. I was told not to think about happiness as a feeling, only as a thing, a possession, a warm blanket like Linus always has.

I didn't work. I had to have pills and more pills, yet I still wanted to be happy. And all those possessions, those paintings and rugs and French-imported wines, just weren't it. The last stage of capitalism is when they can't buy off anybody any more. We're getting there. I didn't have the memories to keep me quiet. I hadn't suffered from the Depression or World War 2. I just couldn't be fooled any more. And there are thousands, perhaps millions of kids today who won't be fooled either. Brought up under the material incentives of capitalism, we are the product of capitalism's greatest contradiction – that it simply doesn't satisfy. And so we can no longer be manipulated by capitalism, at least not for very long.

But we can be repressed by it. That's why we need a revolution. We *are* being repressed by it, by its police, its universities, its television, its 'democracy', its parliamentism, its secret services, its apologists and especially by its myths, most importantly the myth that change must be peaceful and that only we revolutionaries are violent. (Even the National Commission on the Causes and Preven-tion of Violence can't stomach that myth. It says: 'Like most ideologies, the myth of peaceful progress is intended at bottom to legitimize existing political arrange-ments and to authorize the suppression of protest. It also serves to conceal the role of official violence in the maintenance of these arrangements.'

Let's settle a few things first. Sure, we're violent. We want to throw out those in power to establish a new society. Now if you think that elections can change anything, you just aren't with it. Those who have power are not those who are elected but those who set up elections. Max Weber once said that "one can define the modern state sociologically only in terms of the specific *means* peculiar to it, as to every political grouping, namely, the use of physical force. 'Every State is founded on force' said Trotsky at Brest Litovsk. That is indeed right." That is, what we must overthrow is capitalist (state or private) parliamentism, not the Democratic or Republican, Labour or Conservative parties. We have as much right to do so as the Americans who overthrew the English, the French bourgeoisie who overthrew their aristocrats. As Abe Lincoln put it: "This country with its constitution belongs to us who live in it. Whenever they shall grow weary of the existing government they shall exercise their constitutional rights of amending it or their revolutionary right to dismember or overthrow it."

But then, influenced by a lifetime of debates between 'majority' and 'minority', you might say that we're the minority, and that there are a lot of innocent bystanders, too. For one thing, every revolution, the English and American included, was started by a minority, a tiny one at that. It became a majority only as it proved it meant what it said. For another, we're the young. Among the young, we're probably the majority. In any case, the argument of numbers is irrelevant. If you feel strongly about saving your capitalist regime, defend it. You will, anyway, just as Spiro Agnew will. If not; then you don't care that much one way or another. Or you're just waiting to see how we'll do. But don't call yourself an innocent bystander. There is no such thing. An innocent bystander in the American Revolution? To Hitler's occupations? Or, as Abbie Hoffman puts it: 'If you are a bystander, you are not innocent.'

So we agree, it's a fight to the finish. Well then, why doesn't the Establishment hound us, arrest us, kill us? Because that is not what modern capitalism is all about.

It is not George Wallace, the KKK and Minutemen, the four colonels of the green beret calypso. No.

The Establishment is IBM, Xerox, the Kennedys, the *New York Times*, Harvard University, the courts – the liberal corporatists who, *to survive*, must maintain the semblance of fair play and reform-mindedness. It is no accident that no modern, developed capitalist state has ever resorted to dictatorship, not even in times of trouble. For as long as the libero-corporatists can maintain such a semblance, protesters tend to remain isolated and unpolarized. Destroy the verbal meaning of corporate liberalism – silence the *New York Times*, arrest the Eugene McCarthys – and the whole structure becomes threatened overnight. It can then he maintained only by an armed phalanx who are just as apt to bump off the Kennedys and the chairman of Xerox, IBM, and the universities (who are often the' same) as they are to cut my head off. In fact, more apt to do so; for the colonels (or police chiefs, as would be more likely in America) have more to gain from liquidating the former, the loot. Thus, it is no accident that in the French revolution of May-June, 1968, the power elite did not bring in the troops to open fire on students and workers, even on May 29 when it could fear total collapse of the corporative state apparatus.

The enemy is not going to kill us all. Some, here and there, by assassination, but not all, and not systematically. It will repress us (and is doing it) by massive individual arrests, tying us here and our resources up in their courts, while simultaneously trying to buy off some of us here and there by paper reforms, changes in degree but not in kind. (For, suppose that they did let us run our universities, what would happen to their counter-insurgency, biochemical and ghetto-control research? What would happen to their moon-projects, their executive training and recruiting operations, their future civil servants, media-men, computer experts?)

But let's not kid ourselves their form of repression is the most efficient yet devised. It is far better than guns or clubs. Useless car-safety legislation or an amendment to lower the voting age to eighteen is far, far wiser than HUAC intimidations. Indeed, the best-thing that happened for the Second American Revolution is Mayor Daley.

Well then, what can we do against this monolithic liberal corporativism which bathes itself from head to toe in a pluralistic myth? Lenin once gave this answer: 'Give us an organization revolutionaries, and we will overturn Russia!' And he did. But with what results? Never mind what he said, what did he *do?* He got his organization – the revolutionary party and with it the elite corps that went on to rule Russia, creating Stalinism, Czechoslovakia and the trials of Daniel and Siniavsky. History has judged Lenin right. His methods were the only ones capable of overturning the Czarist State. And ever· since, like scholastics mimicking St Thomas, 'Marxist-Leninists' have insisted that every revolution must be carried out in the same way. Yet Lenin wouldn't agree. He would say, as he did, that conditions determine tactics and that tactics are subservient to the reasons for the revolution. His reasons were land bread, freedom. His revolution never got the third, but two out of three is a pretty good batting average in any league.

Almost. Not in ours. We're more ambitious, We want a perfect score – or else forget it. But don't, because we'll get it.

There are certain laws about revolutions. Not many, but a few. One is that a revolution is made by people, i.e. a movement . The other is that it must (and does) function within two awareness's: (1) the nature of the adversary; (2) the kind of structure, at least in general, which the movement wants to set up. The first is easy: liberal corporativism, which we all know or should. The second is harder. I've described my structure above. Other revolutionaries have other descriptions. But we'll agree on one basic characteristic: that it be a humanizing society. That means that Lenin's elitist organization is out. Also, then, is his 'party' as defined by modern-day "Marxist-Leninists", I put that in quotes because Marx never talked about a ruling party hierarchy such as Lenin put into motion. Marx, for example, spoke of' the party arising spontaneously from the soil of modern society'. And

Engels, in his best work, *Anti-Diihring*, said that the role of a revolutionary party is to destroy the state; not only the old state but all further states. After seizing power he wrote: 'State interference in social relations becomes, in one domain after another, superfluous, and then, withers away of itself; the government of persons is replaced by the administration of things. The state is not "abolished". It withers away.'

Even Lenin insisted that once the revolution is victorious 'a "special force" for suppression is *longer necessary*. In this sense the state begins to wither away.'[10]

Where Lenin went wrong was to believe in short cuts. There are none, neither to justice nor truth. Just as a revolution from above is bound to fail (since they do not participate in it, the masses do not consider it theirs and will not work for its post-victory success), so is the one that forgets its principles in order to strengthen itself (once the value of man is 5, relegated to second place it stays there). No matter how 'good' and just a cop's intentions may be, no matter how much he believes in the rationalization that he is being efficient in order to become chief whence he can have the power to humanize the whole force, by the time he *is* the chief he will have institutionalized his actions: every cop on the force will act as if man is an object, to be treated as such. Once manipulation is a way of life, human lives become manipulatable. The Russia of today is not the fault of a Stalin gone mad; it is the necessary consequence of a revolution that did not trust people for whom it fought. Because it was under attack from both a reactionary within and a capitalist without, it may have had no other historical choice. But that does not change the fact that today Daniel and Siniavsky are in jail because Lenin believed in discipline and that Russians are stratified and compartmentalized because Lenin reintroduced material incentives with his 'temporary' New Economic Policy.

Our revolution, then, must not cherish the principle of efficiency. It must not build leaders who build followers. It must not sacrifice participation for effect-tiveness. It must not judge what is relevant according to doctrine. Nothing that is relevant to you or me can be considered irrelevant by the revolution. The only way we will ever see a New Man is by valuing all men. Men not theories. Men not programmes. Is this heresy, as the Marxist-Leninists' yell? To their scholarly dogmatism, perhaps. Marx himself, however, was no dogmatist. 'Every step of real movement,' he wrote, 'is more important than a dozen programmes.' By real movement, of course, he meant *people.*

No party? No ideology? No programme? How in hell, then, do we make this 'humanizing' revolution?

By living it. By fighting for what's relevant to you, not to some theorist. You want to turn on, turn on. You want to drop out, drop out. Groove to the MC5 singing John Lee Hooker's *Motor City Is Burning* ("All the cities will burn. ... You are the people who will build up the ashes") or the *Lovin' Spoonful's Revelation: Revolution '69* (I'm afraid to die but I'm a man inside and I need the revolution'). Live in a commune. Be faithful to *your* values, not your parents'. (Remembered Bob Dylan's) *The Times, They are A-Changin':* 'Your sons and your daughters are beyond your command; Your old road is rapidly aging.') Don't be afraid to he happy. As Abbie Hoffman wrote: "Look, you want an outlet for your creativity, then get out of school, quit your job. Come on out and help build and defend the society you want. Stop trying to organize everybody but yourself. Begin to live your vision."

Sure, there will be hard times. Sure, you may have to go to jail. Sure, some of us may even die. But are we alive when we proclaim one set of values and live according to another, which we despise? The little bit you live the revolution by being the revolution, you thrive. Yeah, man, it's exciting. Let the 'Marxist-Leninists' laugh at you. All they can do is argue among themselves, anyway. And when they're very strong, like the CP in France, all they can do is play the established parliamentary game, campaigning on a platform of 'We are the party of Order' and help crush the revolution. (But wait: it'll succeed yet, despite the CP). The combat is the only effective activity,' said Clausewitz, 'even when the combat does not actually take place.' The May 1968 French revolutionary students put it another way. On the walls of the Sorbonne and Censier, they painted: 'Don't buy your happiness, steal it.' Or one might say: Make the Revolution by living it. If we do, there's a great pay-off: once we win we won't have to worry about somebody having perverted the Revolution. Because the Revolution will be us.

PART III: THE POLITICS OF THE WORD AND THE WORLD

THE POLITICS OF THE WORD AND THE WORLD

INTERVIEW

Monchinski: Were you a writer as a kid?

Gerassi: No. I started writing in Columbia for the Columbia Spectator[83].

Monchinski: What made you want to write at that point in your life?

Gerassi: The maintenance men went on strike. Columbia University then ordered all its fellowship students to take over. For example, engineering students had to run the boiler. Stuff like that.

Monchinski: They were forcing you to be scabs[84].

Gerassi: Right! I was on a full scholarship but I refused to work while the maintenance staff were on the picket line. The editor-in-chief of the Spectator was Max Frankel[85], who went on to become editor-in-chief of *The New York Times*. He was a stringer[86] for the Times even back then. He ran an editorial in the Spectator condemning the University's policy and calling on all students on fellowship to refuse to work.

I did likewise in an article reporting what had happened. I wrote everyday during the strike, which if I remember correctly lasted a couple of weeks until Columbia gave in. But not before Max Frankel and I were suspended for the duration of the strike. After that I started writing little pieces about Columbia and I'd send them to Liberation Magazine[87]. The reason I chose Liberation was because the war resistance people were all affiliated with it. One man I greatly admired was A.J. Muste[88]. But I didn't write anything I'd consider "serious" until I got drafted.

Monchinski: Drafted to serve in Korea?

Gerassi: Yes. My family came to America with forged diplomatic papers; we came here illegally. Because my father was immediately asked to join OSS he told the truth that we were really political refugees.

My father was very active in OSS, first as a spy in Argentina finding out which way Argentine businessmen would go if the United States entered the war because of Argentine's ties to Franco who was pro-Hitler. After the United States entered the war my father was sent to Spain to set up an underground to blow up bridges and so on in the event that Franco allowed Hitler to cross through Spain to attack the Allies in the event of an African landing. General Bull Donovan and my father's immediate boss Arthur Goldberg said, "Oh don't worry, OSS is part of the US Army, you have the rank of colonel, so you'll be a citizen automatically." But when the war ended, not only did my father *not* become a citizen, deportation proceedings started against him. Years later we found out he was being black-mailed to work for the CIA, which he always refused to do. When I became 21 in 1952 they separated my case from my parents' and proceedings started against me—they weren't trying to blackmail me, they were going to ship me right out! So I married a friend, a fellow student. The marriage was never physical. It kept me in the country, but as soon as I let the draft board know I got married I got drafted!

Monchinski: What did your parents think of that?

Gerassi: Well, I wasn't living at home and I didn't say anything until I was actually in the military. I called up and told my mother—my father and I were not talking at that point—I told her, "By the way mother, I've been drafted." I had put off calling because I kept having my call-up deferred until I finished my Masters Degree in Philosophy. I didn't actually enter the military until the end of '54, beginning of '55, and by then there was a truce in Korea. Then, at Fort Bragg who do I run into? Max Frankel! He hated Fort Bragg and he hated the 101st Airborne. He didn't want to wear the green beret[89]. We both had been drafted into psychological warfare which was part of the 77 Special Forces and we had to wear green berets. A green beret meant you were a volunteer and you were a parachutist. He pulled strings—I guess *The New York Times*—and got out but I had no strings to pull.

I did my three jumps and won my wings. But what I hated was having to wear the green beret. Eventually I organized in a sense the first successful strike in the Army—it wasn't really a strike. I just got everybody that was drafted into psychological warfare to sign a petition objecting to having to wear green berets on the grounds that they don't deserve them because they had not volunteered and are not doing any more than the three required jumps. The officer in charge, Colonel Rapp, approved our motion.

I lied about my journalism experience, which, aside from the Spectator I didn't really have, and convinced Colonel Rapp to send me on temporary duty to the *Fayetteville Observer*, and that's where I learned the trade. The technical trade, like how to be able to read upside down, because with the old cold press system you had to set it yourself.

Monchinski: Were your colleagues at the Observer in a situation similar to you or were they regular North Carolinians?

Gerassi: I was the only one from the military. The managing editor of the *Observer* asked me not to come in uniform. I told that to Colonel Rapp and he said it was alright, go in civilian clothes. I loved it there. I started dating the boss' daughter. I learned the trade and I learned to write under deadline and fast. During my second week Colonel Rapp saw an article with my name attached to it and said, "Hey, listen, try to cover Army baseball games. We have a lot of games. Don't just submit it to the Observer, try submitting them to the Army Times[90] and let's see if we can get them in."

I started applying myself and suddenly realized that it isn't that hard to write as long as you remember certain rules. The rules have changed but back then they were to write in the first paragraph who, what, when, where, and why. Second paragraph, same thing, but you elaborate, and so on. By doing this you have gravity feet. What that means is if a 140-line article is ordered trimmed you cut from the bottom and therefore aren't taking out anything important.

Somebody complimented me on my vocabulary and I remember the managing editor saying, "God, you sure know a lot of words. You never repeat yourself and know all these synonyms. How did you ever learn so many words?" I thought about it and the answer was very simple. I'll say this to anyone who wants to be a journalist: read! I was an avid reader since I was a kid. That's where I got my vocabulary, I just read a lot. I loved the Russians, Dos Pasos, Steinbeck.

Monchinski: What were your politics in those days?

Gerassi: None. I mean, I had some, but I just didn't know it. You don't read *Black Boy*[91], you don't read Dos Pasos or Hemingway and not have politics. All of these novelists were on the left at the time.

I got the politics little by little at Columbia. During the strike with long discussions on the picket line. And a professor who was teaching Anthropology 101/102, Donald Freed. He was a great anthropologist. He had survived the red baiting that McCarthy started at Columbia before he took it to Harvard.

The difference between the president of Columbia, Courdier, who'd replaced Eisenhower, versus the president of Harvard, Pusey[92], was that Courdier said anyone who doesn't answer the questions and invokes the Fifth Amendment obviously doesn't believe in academic freedom. Whereas Pusey said anybody who *does* answer the questions doesn't believe in academic freedom and doesn't belong at Harvard. Everybody gives credit to Edward R. Murrow[93] for the breaking of McCarthy, but it was really Pusey. He was the first one to really fight the blacklisting and all that. Academia should be proud of the fact that it was academia that broke those red-baiters.

Anyway, Anthropology 101/102 was a massive course with three hundred students in the auditorium. Freed's assistants would take the attendance record by noting which seats were empty. The seats were numbered so if somebody was sitting in seat forty-two the student registered in that seat was there. I say forty-two because that was my seat, and I paid somebody a dollar to sit in it for me and I never went to class.

Fortunately I did go one day, a great day which made me fall in love with Freed and which began my political education. We were all sitting down and Freed walks in. He goes up to the podium and tells his teaching assistants, "All right, go ahead and collect the papers." We all started looking at one another. Papers? What papers? He hadn't assigned any papers. He sees there's a general consternation in the audience and he says, "What's the matter? Didn't you remember to do the paper?" Somebody said, "You didn't assign a paper."

Freed said, "Oh my god, I gotta treat you like children? Alright, get up and line up in twos on the side." We all obeyed and he said, "Okay, now follow me," and he lead us out onto the picket line. Of course everybody laughed and a few who were politically conscious on the right walked away. But most of us stuck around and picketed with the Columbia maintenance people and those who had turned out in response to Max's editorial. So that, my internship with Vito, Pere Farine's example, all these helped politicize me.

Monchinski: Did you do a lot of writing in the military?

Gerassi: While I was in the Army I really tried to polish up my writing. I thought if I could become a reporter for Army Times they'd never send me overseas. That was the idea at least, though it backfired, but at least it backfired in my favor. About halfway through my stint in Fort Bragg my whole unit was sent down to big maneuvers at Sage Brush in Louisiana, including me. I had to say goodbye to my girlfriend and the owner of the *Fayetteville Observer*. In Sage Brush, thanks to Colonel Rapp, I immediately managed to get a job reporting on maneuvers for the *Army Times*.

The idea of camping out in the woods in Louisiana where there were snakes and god-knows-what didn't appeal to me at all. We were warned about little black snakes that were absolutely deadly that liked to climb into warm places like your sleeping bag! So I got myself a "green" card; the Sage Brush maneuvers were between two teams, the reds and the blues, and green was neutral so with a green card I could visit and write on both sides.

I had a jeep and a driver and we could run around reporting on the maneuvers which were supposed to last two weeks. I remember on the very first day I said to my driver, "You want to go around like this from one side to the other? We're always going to have to sleep in fields in our sleeping bags." He said, "Hell no. Why? You got a better idea?" I said, "Yeah, I got a better idea. Why don't we drive to New Orleans, find a garage where we can hide the jeep, get some civilian clothes, and spend our time in New Orleans?" He agreed of course and we got to New Orleans and found a garage. I remember it cost ten dollars a day and we gladly paid it. It was a garage that closed so no one could see what was parked inside.

Monchinski: And how would you write the stories?

Gerassi: For ten days I was royally drunk, and so was my driver. But drunk or not drunk I wrote my stories. I made them up. It was incredible. I wrote eight stories in that two week period, four of which got on the front page of *Army Times* because they were so fascinating.

These included one I think really happened but couldn't have happened. I described it so well that it entered my head as a reality when in fact it was a complete fabrication. The story of Private Jack Richardson of the 82nd Airborne who woke up one morning with something warm on his chest. I describe all this and I describe his fear and his commanding officer coming and saying "Don't move" and they very slowly unzipped his sleeping bag back and, sure enough, curled up on his chest is this black snake.

The lieutenant assesses the situation very gravely and pulls on gloves—I gave this fictional lieutenant a name and Army Times ran a little aside, a "hat" as they call it in the trade, thanking him for his valiance. "On the count of three," the lieutenant tells his men, and on three he scoops up the snake and throws it aside. Richardson rolls away and two other G.I.s trample the evil snake and save the day. That story made the front page and no one checked, no one verified, no one said let's go find this Private Richardson or the lieutenant. All those stories were made up!

When we got back to Fort Bragg I knew I was in trouble. Everyone of my buddies was furious that I had spent a two-week drunk in New Orleans while they really were sleeping with snakes in the fields. I knew somebody was going to rat on me.

On the day we arrived I asked to see Colonel Rapp. His adjutant said, "Look, he just got back from Sage Brush. Can't you let him rest and come back later?" but I said it was very, very important. I heard him talking to the Colonel and the Colonel saying, "Ah, tell him to fuck off, I can't be bothered—what name did you say?" "Private Gerassi, sir." "Oh, yeah, he's that guy who wrote all those front page stories. Send him in."

I was ushered inside and saluted him and told him that I learned something from the Sage Brush maneuvers. I told him I knew that I was a good reporter, I knew that he was pleased with how I was doing with Army Times. But, I told him, I'd like to go to officer training class and make a career of the Army. He said, "Sure, just fill out the application and I'll sign it." I said, "Just a minute sir. The trouble is I don't know if I'm a coward or not. Could you send me to Korea?"

He stood up and saluted me and said, "Boy, if all my soldiers were like that!" I knew they were already talking peace in Korea, and I also knew he'd sign the orders and that they'd send me through Japan to get to Korea. I figured the officer in placement headquarters in Japan would look at my M.O.T. which describes what I do and he'd send me to psychological warfare right there in Japan, and that's what happened.

In psychological warfare my job was to write propaganda. We had a radio channel and were expected to turn out enough stuff for eight hours in Korean, eight hours in Mandarin and eight in Cantonese. There were four writers, and each of us had to write two hours worth every day, then the translators would do their job. That's not easy to do; it's very hard.

During a furlough my father and I had started talking again so I sent him a packet of propaganda scripts I had written. He stacked them on the night table of the guest room. In 1956, I'm still in Tokyo writing propaganda, and my father had a big art show at the Panoras Gallery[94]. The main Time Magazine art critic, Alexander Eliot[95], did a story on my father. He'd traveled to Vermont to interview him at the school where he was teaching but it was late. My father said, "Look, it's very late. We have a guest room at the house. Why don't you spend the night?"

Apparently before he went to sleep, Eliot happened to see the stack of pieces I'd written so he started reading them. Underneath the propaganda scripts was a one-act play I'd written. While in Tokyo I'd directed Sartre's *No Exit*. I directed it at a very fast pace and it didn't make a whole evening of theatre. So I decided to write a curtain raiser. I thought to myself, "*No Exit* is about responsibility; I should write something about how you get there."

I wrote a one-act play called *The Choice* about three sons of a family who's village is occupied by an enemy force of some sort. The leader of the enemy comes to the father of the family and says, "If resistance doesn't stop by tomorrow night I will shoot one of your sons, and you pick him. If you don't choose one, I'll shoot all three." The point of my play was not to choose is a choice.

Monchinski: How'd it go over?

Gerassi: We only had one performance because the Army put it off limits to any Army personnel and all my actors were military personnel. They didn't like my play or Sartre's. Only that one night, but it got great reviews! Alex Eliot reads *The Choice*. The next morning he comes down and at breakfast tells my father, "This Tito Gerassi, is he your son? If he can write such crap like the propaganda scripts so well, and then a play like this, he's obviously perfect for *Time Magazine*. Tell him when he gets out of the Army if he wants a job I'll get him a job." That's how I got my job with *Time Magazine*.

I started out with a three week try-out writing sections like *People*, *Milestone*, that kind of stuff. When I was successful at that I was hired permanently. At that time Alex Eliot took off a year to write *Three Hundred Years of American Art* and I was taken on as the third art critic.

In those days *Time Magazine* was absolutely incredible! I mean, I requested a trip through Latin America on the grounds that I didn't know Latin American art and they wanted me to talk about it. *Time* said "Sure, go ahead." For two months I'm galavanting throughout Latin America on the expense account. Every art book I own I bought on that expense account.

Monchinski: Had you had any training as an art critic at this point?

Gerassi: None.

Monchinski: How did you pull it off?

Gerassi: While I was doing my training, Alex Eliot warned me that he might be taking off. He said, "You know what I'd suggest you do? Do some art stories that I'm not going to do. I'll give them to the senior editor." I sat down and read every major story Eliot and others had written and educated myself. I also realized how *Time*-style was. *Time*-style isn't really that hard. It has to be punchy, it has to have a kick at the end. The ideal punch line comes after a dash. "And so he ran," dash, "until he died!"

At *Time* back then permanent came after a year. And after a year I got a huge raise. I was invited to have dinner with the owner, Henry Luce. I got the invitation two weeks in advance and was told I'd be picked up by a limousine on such and such a time that day. There was the managing editor, the head of foreign correspondents, all their wives. Our wives were not invited. During dinner art came up only once when Henry Luce turned to me and said, "What do you think of Andrew Wyeth[96]?" I said, "Ehhhh, slick and sentimental." Then, during coffee and cigars—Cuban cigars—and cognac—Remy Martin – that I remember these details, it's incredible—in the lounge, no women, Luce asks me what I thought of Jackson Pollack. I replied, "America's first great classic painter." And he said, "Oh that's very interesting."

When I showed up for work, somebody is sitting there. I said, "Who the hell are you?" He said, "Oh, you must be Gerassi. You're in Latin America now." I barged into the senior editor's office and before I could open my mouth he said, "Why didn't you tell me Luce invited you?" I told him I thought I was being discreet.

"You stupid jerk," he continued, "I would have told you he's going to ask you only two questions, what do you think of Andrew Wyeth and what do you think of Jackson Pollock? If you'd answered correctly you'd have been an art critic for the rest of your life!" And it was a great two day job—you visit a gallery one day and write it up the next.

When Luce called the managing editor and said "Get him out of art" the managing editor called the administrative head and asked for my file. He found out I spoke Spanish so I ended up in Latin America but I didn't know the difference between Uruguay and Paraguay.

At first I was furious, but it was the best thing that could have happened, because suddenly I became political. You can't learn about Latin America without becoming political. By political I mean there's these terrible things that American corporations and multinational firms do to the people of the region and that's why they rebel. The minute I started traveling around Latin America and taking notes I knew I would write a book. I didn't write that book for four years until I left *Time Magazine*.

Monchinski: The book would be *The Great Fear in Latin America*?

Gerassi: Yes, but I didn't do it at *Time*. I worked there and became very pro-Castro, because Castro to me represented the revolutionary spirit of the whole of Latin America against the exploitation that was taking place. I did a cover story which is Castro superimposed on Leone. Leone was president of Venezuela and pro-America. The question was *Whither Latin America*? Basically I said as long as we get more Leones there will be more Castros.

My end at *Time Magazine* came this way. The senior editor got this file—we called it a file, the reports from the correspondents. The correspondents would send in twenty pages and the editor would rewrite it into one column to which he would add his own research and what his own researcher would add.

There was this twenty page report from this correspondent in Cuba who turned out to be a CIA agent. He sent a twenty page file back on the executions Castro was carrying out[97]. We knew this correspondent was reactionary as hell and we knew he was anti-Castro, but he wrote "In this case I have to say that Castro is doing the right thing." Because at these open trials everybody could talk and testify for and against these Batista cops; it was an incredibly cathartic experience for all the people who had suffered under the Batista dictatorship. 360 people were executed; they were the Batista torturers.

During these trials it was proven as a matter of fact that they were guilty and even our correspondent was in favor of the trials. But the senior editor called me in and said, "Look, the editorial board got together and we've decided to go after Castro, call him a dirty commie." I said, "Why? Even our own correspondent is in favor." He said, "Yes, but Castro is *executing* them. That means he's *serious*. And if he's serious"—I'll never forget this, it's the way he put it, the senior editor's name was Bill Forbis, "—and if he's serious, he's going to find out that American companies like United Fruit were behind Batista and then he'll denounce us and we'll call him a dirty communist and he'll ask for Russian aide. So let's call him a dirty communist before he does that."

I said I wouldn't do it. He said "Well think of it, go to your office." Then they left me alone for three weeks. Each day Bill Forbis would call me up and say, "You feel like writing today?" and I'd say, "No, I feel like I am going to have a stomachache." Finally I saw on the story list a piece *Time* was going to do about communism in Uruguay. Now I had married a Uruguayan woman, and I knew there was no communism in Uruguay. There was a lot of socialism but no communism.

I called up Bill Forbis and told him I was familiar with the Uruguyan story and I'd write it. "Oh great," he said, "welcome back!" I wrote the story that "there is no communist problem" in Uruguay, that this was the imagination of such people as the missionaries and I mentioned various missionaries by name. One of them was Henry Luce's brother[98]. Henry Luce himself was the son of missionaries in China. I knew that and I did it on purpose and it worked, because I wanted to get fired. The reason I wanted to get fired was because *Time* in those days gave a whole year's salary as severance pay.

I wrote the story, the story passed through the copy desk and every top editor got a copy, so everybody knew. All of a sudden I got a call from the administrative manager who said, "Tito, you finally did it! You got your severance pay. Congratulations!" And he added, "By the way we're giving you a party next Tuesday."

They gave me a really nice party and a suitcase, a nice gift. I took the administrative manager on the side and asked why they hadn't given me severance pay right away. He said, "The Union is asking severance pay for anybody who leaves voluntarily. If we had given it to you the union would have used that as an example. So we waited until we had proof that you were legitimately fired—that article on Uruguay makes us legit!"

I went to see Herbert Matthews[99] at the *Times*, and got a job. I got sent to Uruguay with my wife who wanted to do her dissertation on Uruguay and did.

I went and covered the Alliance for Progress conference where Kennedy's secretary of the treasury, Dillon, presented Kennedy's idea about thirty billion dollars to feed all of Latin America.

Cuba's representative was Che Guevara. The *Time's* correspondents were Tad Szulc from the Washington desk who came down especially for that and Juan de Onis, who was the chief Latin American correspondent and my immediate boss. I knew Juan and I knew Tad quite well and I thought we had the same basic politics. But at the conference to get rid of me, because he knew that Che would never talk to the American press, Juan told me to cover him [Che]. But Che was late, so Juan and Tad traveled ahead to Punta del Este and I'm stuck at Montevideo airport waiting. Che arrived and there are a thousand students there screaming their heads off and demanding that Che go to the university and make a speech. I'm the only correspondent, they had all gone on to Punta del Este—AP, UP, API, they were all gone.

I went with the students to the university. Che made this fantastic speech. There were so many people they put loudspeakers in the esplanade because so many couldn't fit in the auditorium. Then we drove up to the conference.

At one point I went up to Che and tried to interview him and he said point blank, "I don't talk to the imperialist press." He's sitting there with about twenty people at his round table laughing and talking and I'm at my table eating my dinner alone, straining to pick up their conversation. They're talking about their individual countries and I don't know what they're talking about. They're talking about people with funny names like Allende, Corbalan[100], names that don't quite ring a bell yet.

All of a sudden Garcia Lupo arrived. He was a correspondent for La Prensa, which is to the right of Attila the Hun, but he was a good friend of mine. He and Che were very good friends. They'd been in Tacuara together, a student organization that was anti-imperialist. The United States considered it right wing because it was anti-British, but the imperialists in Latin America were the British, not the Germans.

Anyway they hug each other and go to sit down and as Pajarito—Garcia Lupo was called *El Pajarito*, "the little bird"—sat down he saw me and called out, "*Che vos*, what are you doing all alone over there?" By the way, "*che*" means *hey*, "*vos*" is *you*. Every Argentine says "*che vos*" all the time; that's how Che got called *Che*, he'd say "che vos" to everybody.

Che said, "You know him?" Pajarito says, "Yes, we're very good friends." Che goes, "He works with the imperialist press." Pajarito says, "I work for *La Prensa*, it's much worse! He's a good guy." Che waved me over and I spent the rest of the conference, six more days, at their table.

Now, at that table was every left wing correspondent of Latin America. There was *Punto Final*, the greatest magazine Chile ever had until Pinochet got rid of it. There was the guy who died with Allende, his press attaché Ojeda. We called him El Negro because he was so white. There was the head of Allende's ministry of information, Olivares; we called him El Perro, the dog. Rodolfo Walsh, who disappeared. He wrote a fantastic book about America's planning and plotting the counter-revolution in Argentina. Representing Colombia was some guy I'd never heard of named Garcia Marquez. Representing Mexico for the Monthly Review was a guy called Carlos Fuentes. The cream of the crop[101] was all there and I became friends with all of them.

The day before the conference ended we were all eating lunch together. Che asked me what my plans were and I said I'd gotten word that I was no longer with *The New York Times*. He asked me what I was going to do. I told him I knew that might happen so I had signed up to do a series that would cover me financially for the *Baltimore Sun*. It was going to be a no-edit series and I could arrange that because when I signed the contract nobody knew I was going to be fired from *The New York Times*.

Che turns to the twenty people there and said, "I want you all to give me your word of honor ... now when Tito comes to your country, you show him what the gringos never see." That's what made *The Great Fear in Latin America* so powerful.

Monchinski: How was *The Great Fear* received in America and world-wide?

Gerassi: After the Punta del Este conference, two friends of mine had left *Time Magazine*. They were right wingers but they were honest. They started a magazine called *USA One*. They asked me if I would write an article on the conference. I did. It was a thirty page article called *Alliance for Regress*. They were impressed with the article and sent me a wire saying, "We're going to run the article, but we're sure you understand and won't mind if we run a little hat on it saying this is your opinion and not necessarily the opinion of our editors"—which I agreed with of course.

The magazine folded before the article could come out. But one of the two guys decided the article shouldn't be wasted so he passed it along to *Vintage*. Morris Philipson, the head of *Vintage*, went to see Bennett Serf, who ran *Knopf*. Serf told him "Ah come on, Latin America doesn't sell" so Philipson sent the article to Peter Ritner, who was head of *DoubleDay*.

Ritner was a right wing libertarian, and when *DoubleDay* tried to say Latin America doesn't sell, he said, "You're not turning down a book on Latin America. You're turning down my judgment." So *DoubleDay* agrees to publish it.

I don't know any of it. I'm in Uruguay, minding my own business, preparing my first article on Argentina for the *Baltimore Sun*. I get a telegram. It says, "Have read your *Alliance for Regress* story. Please answer following questions by prepaid cable. One, can you write 85,000 words or more on it? Two, how much money do you need to go to each country to lend it an *I-was-there* feel? Three, who the hell are you?" [laughs].

I very modestly said three thousand dollars, which was a lot of money then, but I didn't think of asking for ten thousand. I got it by return mail, by wire, and so I went to every country in Latin America. Each of those people who had been at that round table met me at the airport -- and introduced me to Allende; introduced me to the head of the Colombian revolutionaries, Fabio

Vasquez; with "Tiro Fijo" Marulanda, head of the FARC. These Latin America journalists[102] opened the door to everything.

Monchinski: How long were you in Latin America doing this?

Gerassi: Once I got the money I did the tour in seven months. When I got back to the States I went to Vermont and rented a little place where my wife could teach Spanish at the Putney School and I started writing *The Great Fear*. When I'd finished I handed it to Peter Ritner and two days later Ritner calls me up in Vermont and says, "We're going to need you for publicity, because we just sent your manuscript—unedited except for typos—to the editor."

Ritner was told a few weeks later by *DoubleDay's* legal team that the book was going to cost them a fortune.

Monchinski: Why?

Gerassi: Three people had gotten advanced copies of the manuscript and were suing DoubleDay. The first was Andrew Heiskell, head of *Time Life* and *Freedom of the Press Committee*. He sued because I said at one point when I was talking about Brazil that the Freedom Committee always white-washed censorship by the right and yelled bloody murder when it was by the left.

Macmillan's lawyer went to court and asked the judge "How many cases do we have to prove to get this thrown out?" and the judge said "if you can prove one then there's no maliciousness and they cannot prove libel." I had the documentation on Andrew Heiskell that shamed everybody and the judge looked at it and threw the case out.

The second lawsuit was from Cero De Pasco, a Guggenheim monopoly on nitrates in Peru, which claimed that they only made 18% remitted income while I said that they made 3,000%. Our lawyer said "We have a document here that is on official stationary of the Peruvian Ministry of Hydrocarbons." The prosecutor said, "Yeah, but it's not signed." Macmillan's lawyer retorts, "Yes, but notice it bears the official stamp."

The judge tells Guggenheim that now it behooves *them* to prove that the official stamp is a forgery, otherwise the case is dismissed. And so we won that.

The third lawsuit came about because I had said that Jules Dubois, the chief Latin American correspondent for the *Chicago Tribune*, an arch-reactionary, had sent a telegram to his newspaper suggesting that something not be mentioned at the Punta del Este conference because it put the US in a bad light. Dubois denied ever sending the telegram.

But the clerk at Press Wireless was lefty and he had handed me a copy of his dispatch. So I'm sitting in court with the copy trying to contain my smile while Jules Dubois makes this long speech about how he'd never do such a thing. The judge turns to our side and asks Macmillan's lawyer if he wants to cross-examine. The lawyer says, "No your honor, we just want to present this one page document to the court."

Jules Dubois's signature was on the bottom of the Press Wireless cable. The judge read it, showed it to Dubois, asked him if wanted to contest the signature. Dubois sat down at his table, mumbled something to the *Chicago Tribune* lawyer, and the *Chicago Tribune* lawyer said, "We withdraw." None of these legal proceedings, by the way, cost me a penny.

The book was published and it died. Nobody reviewed it except the *Columbia Spectator*. A few other reviews here and there dismissed it as "terrible" and "way out in left field." The phrase "way out in left field" was actually used by a friend of mine, Tad Szulc. He was convinced that if he could review the book and say something that the *New York Times* would accept, with a review of Lincoln Gordon's book[103], that he could get it in the *Times* book review. He reviewed Gordon's book very favorably. He reviewed my book very factually. But at the beginning of the article he put it down this way, "*The Great Fear* has absolutely no interest to American readers unless they want to know what Latin Americans think about the United States."

Tad told me later "I thought that would do it" but it didn't. It helped kill the book. I was furious at Tad and everybody.

Next thing I know I get a phone call from Peter Ritner saying, "You know, we've remaindered the hardcover edition of the book a little too soon. There seems to be a little bit of demand for the book on campuses. So maybe we should come out with a paperback edition. But since demand is so small we have to make a new deal. Theoretically now you get 7½ % per book; if we make a deal where you accept half of that, 3 ¾ % we'll publish a paper edition."

What I didn't know was that student newspapers all over America were saying read this book. Also a former student of mine was now editor-in-chief at the *Columbia Spectator* and he ran a review of *The Great Fear* in which the last line was "The Robert Alexanders are dead; the Gerassis are taking over." Robert Alexander was a famous historian at Columbia and was still teaching at Columbia when that ran in the *Spectator*. *The Great Fear in Latin America* became the biggest selling book on Latin America ever and is still to this day. It sold 198,000 copies.

Monchinski: Wow. How much of that did you see?

Gerassi: 3 3/4 % of $1.50, what it cost at the time. So 5 cents a book! [laughs] I barely made ten thousand dollars on the deal!

Monchinski: What came next

Gerassi: Pete Ritner gave me *The Boys of Boise* to write thinking it would make us some money, but it didn't make as much as he thought it would. It went over well with academics and was re-published in 2001[104]. *Latin American Radicalism* sold fairly well. *The Great Fear in Latin America* was selling and being reissued in Mexico, Argentina, Brazil, elsewhere, but I never got a penny from those editions. The editor-in-chief of the company that published it in Brazil went to jail for it when the military arrested him. Then there was the Camilo Torres book. It didn't make me any money but the movie script that I wrote of it, *The Revolutionary Priest*, optioned[105] eight times for five hundred dollars each time. It was never made into a film. I did a biography of Che that was published by *DoubleDay*. It was meant to be a children's biography of Che but *DoubleDay* said it was so well written they would issue it as regular book and of course it never sold. I was one of the people chosen by Bertrand Russell to travel to North Vietnam to investigate war crimes. I did *North Vietnam: A Documentary*, which has been translated into many editions. But you don't get money from their sales, you get an advance, like the Scandanavians will send you a few thousand dollars. But you never get an accounting of how that edition sold. It's even less so in Latin America. You don't even get an advance there, you get a contract promising an advance but you don't see the advance.

Monchinski: How did *The American Way of Crime* come about?

Gerassi: *New York Times Books* came to me and asked me to do a book. I suggested I do it with a reporter because I was teaching regularly and didn't have the time to do the research. Frank Browning was a guy I knew since I had been an editor at *Ramparts* and he was one of our reporters. Frank and I settled together in a house that Leonard Weinglass[106] owned in Echo Park in Los Angeles. It was a very poor Latino neighborhood.

Leonard had bought a house on top of a hill, very cheap, next to a Latino-black musician. When his neighbor was trying to sell the house the guy came to Leonard and said, "You know, the people who want to buy my house are interested in developing it and think they'll bring gentrification to Echo Park and chase all the Latinos and working class out. I think you should buy it." Lenny, an old friend of mine from the days when he was a Movement lawyer in Jersey, bought the house.

Lenny offered me the house if I could pay the mortgage, which was only six hundred a month. He didn't want to make any money off the deal. So I was contracted to write *The American Way of Crime* and I asked Frank Browning[107] if he wanted to work with me and then move in with me. We lived there and worked on the book. I commuted to Irvine to teach while Frank worked on the book.

Monchinski: What were the politics of publishing *The American Way of Crime* at home in America?

Gerassi: I thought *The American Way of Crime* would make a big splash here in America because it was contracted by *The New York Times Books* and their books were always well reviewed. But New York Times books sold out to *Putnam*. Mrs. Putnam, who ran the company, was an arch-reactionary and didn't like the book. I once got a ride with her in a taxi. I was down at Putnam's offices in New York City picking some stuff up and she was getting into a taxi, told me she was going uptown and asked if I needed a lift.

So we shared a taxi and I asked her if she knew what was going on with the book. She said, "Why yes, I know what's happening with your book. It sold out."

I asked, "The whole printing?" She said they'd only printed five thousand copies. I said, "Oh, well that's why I'm having so much trouble even getting reader's copies. Hey, wait a minute – aren't you going to reprint it?" She said *no*. I asked why not. She said she told them not to. "You did?" I asked, "Why?" "I own this company," she said, "I decide what goes." I asked her why she wasn't going to reprint it. "Because it's a commie book," she said.

However, my agent did sell it to a major French publisher, Fayard. When the French edition was going to come out I was asked to go over to France and appear on French television to help promote the book. My agent told me they weren't going to foot the bill for my going over there but he told me I'd probably more than make up for it while I was over there. So I went to France.

I was on Pivot's program, *Lire*[108], "To Read", which was at the time the most popular program on French television. It ran ninety minutes without advertisements except for the books he had picked to promote that evening. An hour and a half of talk about books.

Monchinski: During prime time?

Gerassi: During prime time! It was incredible the difference in audiences between France and America. Could you imagine an hour and a half prime time network television show here in America where books are discussed? Anyway, I found out there were going to be six American authors on that night's program. That night the managing director of Fayard takes me out to dinner, preps me on what he feels I should stress during my time on camera, and as we walk into the studio nudges me and on the side says, "You know, every minute you're on the air sells a thousand copies."

It was a rectangular table with Pivot at one end and no one across from him. Three authors on his one side, three on the other, and I'm first! When I leaned over to my right I could see the teleprompter below the table. The questions were just hints for Pivot and it was obvious he had actually read all six books. So I see the questions, right?

The show starts and he asks me my questions and I'm doing fine, I answer them and I talk and I talk. I'm still leaning that way and on the teleprompter screen I see flashing the cover of the next book by the lady sitting to my left. I realized that was it, this was my last question I was answering and my time to talk was drawing to a close. So in the process of talking I dropped something like, "Yeah, yeah that's something every American knows. I knew it when I worked for the Mafia."

Pivot was immediately like, "You what? You worked for the Mafia?" I described how I worked for the Mafia. I started telling some fantastic stories, very few of which were actually true. I did work for the Mafia in the sense that I did collect the chits for a friends' number racket for about seven months, and he did use Frank Costello's lay-off operation[109]. There was another American sitting there facing me, Bill Evans, one of two guys who wrote *The Longest Day*. At one point or another he helped me out because I said something like, "Nobody can open a store or business today without first clearing it with the Mafia." Of course Pivot immediately turned to Evans and said, "Is this true, Bill?" Evans didn't want to leave me hanging so he nodded and said, "It is certainly true in the laundry business." He didn't want to hurt me because we'd been friends since we worked together at *Newsweek*.

Pivot came back to me and I continued and held the screen for sixty-seven minutes and *Le crime a l'Americaine* sold, believe it or not, sixty-seven thousand copies. At a dollar a piece in those days Frank and I got over thirty-three thousand in royalties and lived off it a whole year.

Monchinski: So what's next? You're writing your autobiography, no?

Gerassi: Yeah, but, it's very hard...I mean, when I compare my life to my father's it doesn't add up.

Monchinski: Maybe in your eyes it doesn't.

Gerassi: Until Kent State[110] the white movement in America didn't feel it was risking its life. After Kent State, Jerry Rubin[111] quits. He told me point blank, "Now I realize they'll kill whites as well so I'm quitting. I don't want to die." I didn't quit, that's true. But I didn't really think I'd get killed. It's different.

The people who went to Spain expected to die. Sartre confronted my father and asked, "So, any chance you're going to win in Spain?" "Oh no, we've lost," my father replied. "Wait," continued Sartre, "You've said that with such assurance. You know you're going to lose?" "Of course. We know we're going to lose. Franco's going to win. It's fait acompli." And Sartre said, "But you're going back to Spain?" "Of course." "You're crazy, why go back if you know you're going to lose?" And my father answered, "You don't fight fascism because you're going to win. You fight fascism because they're fascists."

MURDER INCORPORATED

I ask Gerassi if today's Ralph Nader is a mockery of himself and what he once was, to which Tito replied, "I continue to think that his ideas are right-on; Ralph Nader continues to be in the forefront of perceptive thinkers in America. My objection is he doesn't use that perceptiveness to realize that without a very active organization you cannot change things in America. What I object to with Nader is that during the four years between elections he doesn't exclusively spend his time on preparing an organization that can win more votes."

MURDER INCORPORATED

We March on Washington for Peace in Vietnam; we picket the House Un-American Activities Committee for freedom of thought; we organize freedom rides for justice in the South; in sum, we are outraged whenever and wherever man's dignity is trampled upon, whenever his civil rights are violated, wherever his civil liberties are denied. But what do we do-we Liberals and Radicals who pride ourselves on our dedication-when we are confronted by a massive, organized, legal apparatus that kills us at the rate of forty-seven thousand persons a year? Why do we not stand up for Bodily Rights? Is there something tainted, something crass about demanding the right to live when the victims are not being killed out of discrimination or political ambition ? Should we not oppose, with equal fervor, those who kill us indiscriminately for only one reason-money?

And yet, we do not. We talk about cybernation and automation, about public works and public power, about intervention in the Dominican Republic and extermination in Vietnam, because there, the issues are clear and, yes, for us, safe. Not that some of us do not risk our lives or at least our livelihoods to fight on such issues. But in our image of ourselves, we are backed by the knowledge that our cause is right, and therefore pure.

But to take on the greatest criminal syndicate in the United States, the most powerful corporation in the world, there, we hesitate. That corporation is General Motors, and the syndicate is the automobile industry. It is directly or indirectly willfully or negligently responsible for more unnatural deaths than any other man-made or man-controlled enterprise. At the present rate, one out of every two Americans will be injured or killed in automobile accidents. In 1964, 47,700 Americans were killed in such accidents, and more than four million were injured. In accidents involving all modes of transportation (ships, trains, planes, etc.), cars account for over 92 percent of deaths, 98 percent of injuries. Automobile accidents are now the fourth leading cause of death, after heart disease, cancer and strokes.

Why then is the true Liberal reluctant to fight, to expose this Murder Inc.? Because, he says, "it is the fault of the driver." Wrong! Like Americans in general, like even the father of the little girl who casually bumped into the tail fin of a parked 1962 Cadillac and was immediately pierced through the heart, the Liberal has been brainwashed by Detroit public relations men. Accidents are perhaps unavoidable; some drunk will always crash into some innocent. But there is a great difference between collision and injury, between accident and death. And G.M., Ford and Chrysler are fully aware of it. They can make safe cars, cars that will not kill their occupants or even injure them in collisions. But they don't want to. Safety is not profitable; it has always been sacrificed for style-and planned obsolescence. Listen to G.M.'s vice president, William Mitchell: "The motor car must be exciting and create a desire and not become mere transportation, or we will have just a utility and people will spend their money for other things, such as swimming pools, boats, hi-fi sets, or European vacations." Or education, medical care, food, and housing.

The Liberal, of course, is wary of denouncing G.M. lest he sound like a Marxist. After so many years of McCarthyism, fear of using such dirty words as "economic determinism" has remained deeply rooted. It is "socialistic" to attack G.M., whose gross receipts (about $19 billion in 1965, $17 billion in 1964) are more than all of Canada ($6.5 billion), all of Japan ($12.6 billion), more even than all of West Germany ($14 billion). But the facts are absolutely clear, and provable in court. They are documented beyond question in the recent book "Unsafe at Any Speed," by Ralph Nader. Nader, who has been researching his expose since 1957, is a lawyer, a former consultant to the Department of Labor's Office of Policy Planning and Research, an adviser to the Senate subcommittee that investigated auto safety last summer, and the author of "Automobile Design Hazzards," Proofs of Facts, Volume 16, Bancroft Whitney, 1965 (San Francisco), which shows lawyers how they can sue the real criminal whenever accidents occur-the automobile maker. This technical counterpart to "Unsafe at Any Speed" is crammed with legal information and procedures and has been distributed to twenty-five thousand law firms. "We have one great advantage in this country," Nader told me recently, "the fact that lawyers can sue on contingency fees. But of course, if they lose, they get nothing. There should be an American Bodily Liberties Union to carry on these suits. What good is A.C.L.U., ultimately, if there is no A.B.L.U.? A man must first be alive in order to fight for civil liberties."

Nader's book, *Unsafe at Any Speed,* is a bombshell. Not because he documents what we Liberals have known (and ignored) for so long, namely that the automobile industry purposely builds cars that will hurt, injure and kill, but because it shows there is no check whatsoever on that industry. G.M. could make a fuel tank out of onion skin if it wanted, and no G.M. official could be held responsible. If a drug kills a patient, the drug company can be held accountable. In fact, drugs are inspected by the government; so are foods. But there is no inspection of cars outside the industry itself. The automobile industry is not exposed to statutory criminal penalties; lethal defects knowingly produced are not punishable under statutory law. The industry is an outlaw in its fundamental sense-totally outside the law.

How can the automobile industry get away with such a status? Nader has the answers. First, it is a concentrated industry, meaning that there is no true competition, that prices (which are administered according to target returns and not according to supply and demand) are set by policy, and that the product is then manufactured to conform with that policy. Second, it is a perilous industry, dependent not on utility but on style, like Dior fashions. The auto makers must convince consumers that they should go along with the fads. Just as it is possible to produce a dress that can last and look new for twenty years, so it is possible to build virtually indestructible cars and totally unwearable tires. But what would happen to the industry if consumers did not buy new cars-or new dresses-every season? That question alone frightens most economists from even suggesting government controls. And third, since one out of every five retail dollars is spent on automobile products (which makes the U.S. economy completely dependent on the automobile industry), government has been reluctant if not outright opposed to any checks or controls against the industry. John Kenneth Galbraith's famous Theory of Countervailing Power, which has been wrong in so many cases but which Liberals like to cite when they feel compelled to defend capitalism, becomes plain hogwash when it is applied to the auto industry. In fact, the government, which encourages and in part finances-the auto "establishment," as Nader calls the community of associations and organizations supposedly defending the consumers' interests, actually helps the auto industry maintain its grip on the economy, and cooperates fully with its brainwashing operation that claims that safety is a question of educating the driver.

This simply is not so. A leading crash researcher and biochemist, Dr. Carl Clark of The Martin Co., states:

> Instead of the forty-mile-per-hour barrier collision survival being a "spectacular accomplishment," it should be a routine requirement of proper car and restraint design. Indeed, without major modifications of car structure and size, by applying what we know about crash protection, a fixed barrier impact of forty-five m.p.h. should be experienced without injury, and crashes at higher speeds should be survivable.

(A forty-five m.p.h. crash into a fixed barrier, like a tree or a stone wall, generates, for example, the same force as a car striking the rear end of a stationary vehicle at more than seventy-five m.p.h.) This is especially significant when we remember that three-fourths of all injuries and deaths are caused at impact speeds under forty m.p.h.

But G.M. couldn't care less. It built a Corvair, for example, that had to go out of control at a particular degree turn or under certain conditions, whatever the speed. On May 18, 1956, almost a year before the Corvair project was launched, the former head of research and development for the Chevrolet Division, Maurice Olley, filed a patent application (issued as #2,911,052 on November 3, 1959) where he said what he thought of the Corvair-type suspension:

The ordinary swing axle, under sever lateral forces produced by cornering, tends to lift the rear-end of the vehicle so that both wheels assume severe positive camber positions to such an extent that the vehicle not only "over-steers" but actually tends to roll over. In addition, the effect is non-linear and increases suddenly in a severe turn, thus representing potentially dangerous vehicle handling characteristics.

But Olley's judgment was ignored. Reports Nader: "It took General Motors four years of the model and 1,124,076 Corrvairs before they decided to do something for all unsuspecting Corvair buyers by installing standard equipment to help control the car's handling hazards." Meanwhile, of course, hundreds of people died or were injured, and some one hundred suits against G.M. are now pending.

The same kind of willful negligence, this time on the braking system, was applied to the 1953 Buick Roadmaster, resulting in one suit where the court (Judge Thomas Murphy) asked Elmer Krause, general service manager of Buick, why "you didn't call them [Buick dealers] up and say, get all these cars in and have them repaired?" The case went to the Michigan Supreme Court where a unanimous decision insisted that "Prompt warning to him [the claimant] would in all likelihood have meant repair before any brake failure occurred. Prompt warning could easily have prevented this accident." G.M. then quickly settled out of court for $75,000. But neither in the Buick case nor in the Corvair case did G.M. pull the cars back, and Nader is currently fighting a one man battle to get various states' attorney generals to do this.

If every car owner, every police officer and every lawyer involved in accidents would learn to check the cars at the scene of the crime, and then to sue the manufacturer for causing, through built-in defects, the accident in question, many lives would be spared, because Detroit would then have no alternative but to eliminate the danger.

Pressure and publicity is a weapon, and it can be effective. Reports Nader:

In the sale of buses, buyer choice is almost synonymous with whatever General Motors chooses to offer. G.M. has over ninety percent of the bus business in the country. Since 1957, the Southern California Rapid Transit District has desperately tried to persuade G.M. to improve the braking system of its buses. It was not until 1965 with competitive bidding of a small Ohio bus manufacturer and the district's threat of public denunciation, that General Motors stated it would install better braking capabilities on new buses sold to the District.

But so far, very little exposure has taken place. Consumer Reports does an honest job of trying, but since it lives off its small number of subscribers, it cannot afford to test cars much beyond five thousand miles, and it cannot put them through collision tests. Nevertheless, it did conclude from its research that, despite the auto makers' claim that cars are safer than ever, "the condition of the 1965 cars Consumer Union has bought for test is about the worst, so far as sloppiness in production goes, in the whole ten-year stretch of deterioration that began in 1955, the first year in which U.S. new car sales first approached eight million." Road Test magazine has also spoken out occasionally, most specifically against Ford's Mustang which is simply "a hooked-up Falcon with inadequate brakes, poor handling and marvelous promotion."

One courageous Congressman who has long fought for safety, says Nader, is Alabama's Kenneth Roberts, who started introducing bills in 1956 but never got the support of the Commerce Department. Though his bills passed the House, they kept getting defeated in the Senate Committee until its chairman, Senator Smathers, stepped down in 1964. The passed bill, mild in comparison to what Roberts originally wanted, instructed the General Services Administration to set up standards for the thirty-six thousand cars, purchased by government agencies, hoping thereby that these standards would become incorporated into all cars manufactured. Naturally, this never happened.

There have been other attempts to force G.M. and its weaker cohorts to emphasize safety, including the much publicized hearings held last summer, during which Senator Robert Kennedy asked G.M. what was its net profit ($1.7 billion), how much it spent on safety research ($1 million), and then commented: "If you just gave one percent of your profits, that is $17 million." But the Senate Committee, chaired by Abraham Ribicoff, went on to urge the auto industry to place greater emphasis on safety by itself. In other words, once again, it was left up to G.M., Ford and Chrysler, killers though they are, to police themselves.

But then, this has always been the general attitude in Washington. Even the President's Committee for Traffic Safety, which has the prestige and bears the stamp of the White House is a phony. Its chief officers are paid by the President's Action Committee for Traffic Safety, which is a tax-exempt organization that gets most of its funds from the Automotive Safety Foundation and the Insurance Institute for Highway Safety, which in turn represent the interest of the auto manufacturers. "The traffic safety establishment," Nader told me, "is not a conspiracy in the old Marxist-type lingo. It is nevertheless a conspiracy in effect. No one can challenge it, and it serves the industry. Those who pay for it all are we drivers who are condemned to drive in death traps."

And it is we, the consumers, who foot the bill. Writes Nader:

Highway accidents were estimated to have cost this country in 1964, $8.3 billion in property damage, medical expenses, lost wages, and insurance overhead expenses. Add an equivalent sum to comprise roughly the indirect costs and the total amounts to over two percent of the gross national product. But these are not the kind of costs which fall on the builders of motor vehicles (excepting a few successful law suits for negligent construction of the vehicle) and thus do not pinch the proper foot. Instead the costs fall to users of vehicles, who are in no position to dictate safer automobile designs.

Meanwhile, the auto industry rakes in the loot. In 1964, for example, Ford had a net income, as a percentage of sales, of 5.6 percent and an 11.3 percent return on invested capital. General Motors, with more than 50 percent of the market, made

10.2 percent and 20.4 percent respectively. "It is this success," says Nader, "that stops the industry from changing its ways." G.M. sets the standards, and the others follow the leader-what is called by economists "protective imitation." An oligopoly, such as the car industry, does not compete. Each year, a few features in style are changed in order to make believe that the car itself is changed. But these features are only the visible ones. As Gene Bordinat, vice president and director of styling for Ford, said: "Styling serves to make the public aware that there is a new product ... If they buy the car, they don't want its best features to be concealed. They want identification where it is visible to one and all. It's the same sort of urge that causes some girls to wear tight sweaters."

And so, year after year, new sweaters are designed-with new and bigger falsies. But the oligopoly remains the same, never offering a radical departure from its normal line. Success breeds standardization. Unsafe dash boards continue to kill about eight thousand people a year. The wrong kind of seat belts (the industry opposed any kind for ten years) continue to fail to prevent heads from smashing through windshields at speeds as low as 12 m.p.h. Protruding nobs continue to blind, maim and kill pedestrians and drivers in "freak" accidents such as the one in which the Cadillac fin killed the little girl. Individual complaints continue to be ignored, as when Howard Gandelot, G.M.'s chief engineer, reacted to the Cadillac complaint by saying there "always is a likelihood of the few unusual types of accidents." And the public at large continues to believe him and all the other auto engineers who are guilty of what can only be described as "petit Eichmanisms" since they know better.

What is terrifying in all this is that we, the so-called Liberals who willingly fight for civil rights, accept G.M.'s violation of our bodily rights. We are either afraid to challenge G.M., or we simply do not care. Perhaps that is because we pretend to be non·materialists, or perhaps simply because, brainwashed as we are, we cannot shake off the feeling that if we really do obey traffic laws we will avoid accidents. Thus we let the world's biggest and most powerful oligopoly (one of whose former directors, John Connor, is currently Secretary of Commerce) establish a totalitarianization of a huge sector of the market. And we do not even form an A.B.L.U., an American Bodily Liberties Union, to fight it in the courts, to generate the atmosphere for a counterattack against the most vicious organized outlaw empire in the world.

CHAPTER EIGHTEEN

THE CELL
(A PLAY IN ONE ACT)

Directed by Ha'rold Herbstman and starring Jaimie Sanchez as the Cop, Raul Davila as the Professor and Allen Garfield as the Guard, "The Cell" was given eight weekend performances at the Off Center Theater, at 152 West 66th street, New York City, from March 31, 1967, to April 16, 1967. The play will reopen on June 1st for six performances (June 1, 2, 3, 8, 9, 10) at St. Peter's Episcopalian Church at 346 West 20th street in New York. Dil'ected by Harold Herbstman, it will star David Milton as the Cop, Raul Davila as the Professor and Jerold Brody as the Guard.

TIME: The present

SETTING: A cell in Havana's "La Cabana" prison. One small barred window high on left wall. A heavy iron door center, with a foot-long, half-foot high slit at eye level; the slit is usually closed by a wooden shutter on the other side of the door. Inside the cell: two stools, one on the right and one on the left, and a toilet, on right, which is just a bowl and has no flush. There is no light. A weak glow shines through the window-just enough to illuminate the cell while making it clear it is night. The glow must increase steadily during the play so that at the end the cell is well lit indicating the dawn. Whenever the slit or the cell door are opened, a dull yellowish light shines into the cell.

CHARACTERS: Guard
                      Cop
                      Professor

AT RISE: A fat, dark-skinned, unkempt middle-aged man sits, his back to the audience, on the stool at left. He is dressed in an army uniform stripped bare of all insignias and decorations. The uniform is dirty and slightly torn, indicating past struggles of some kind. Only his boots, knee-high and in good shape, testify to the fact that he is-or was-a fairly high ranking army or police officer. He sits face in hands, elbows resting on his knees.

After a few seconds of total silence, noise is heard off-stage center, gradually increasing until the slit is opened and a pair of eyes peer into the cell. There is a rattling of keys, the cell door is unlatched and is thrown open. A tall, lanky man in

145

his mid-thirties is pushed inside. Slightly balding, immaculately dressed and wearing thick-rimmed glasses, he stands proudly but not contemptuously. In his jacket pocket, a three-pointed handkerchief is clearly visible. A bearded khaki-uniformed Fidelista guard, holster on his hip, crowds the doorway. He stares at the man on the stool (who has not moved), then at the other who remains standing at the center of the stage.

Guard: (HALF SNEERING, HALF LAUGHING) I hope you'll be comfortable-for the next few hours ... Just keep an eye on that window: when you see light, make your prayers! (HE TURNS TO LEAVE, THEN STOPS AND NODS TOWARD THE NEW PRISONER) Heh, Professor, you want a priest? (PAUSE) Don't be ashamed-the best of them breakdown ... How about it?

Prof: (CALMLY BUT COURTEOUSLY) No thank you.

Guard: Okay, okay-but as it gets lighter ... Well, if you change your mind ... don't be afraid to call ... that's what we're here for. Besides, there is a priest on duty all the time-and, after all, he's got to work for his living ... So just call, you hear?

Prof: (A BIT TOO POLITE) Yes, thank you, I hear.

Guard: (TURNING TO MAN ON LEFT) Heh butcher! That goes for you too! (SILENCE. BOTH GUARD AND PROF LOOK AT THE THIRD MAN WHO DOESN'T MOVE. GUARD TAKES A STRIDE TOWARD HIM, HESITATES THEN STOPS, SHOUTING) Butcher? Child-killer! I'm talking to you! (PAUSE, THEN GUARD STEPS BACK, TURNS TO PROF) Well, if he wakes up, tell him he can have a priest if he wants one (A SECOND THOUGHT) Of course, I'm sure he knows the gates of heaven are closed to him-too many of his victims are there! You know how many people he killed? Guess! (PROF SHRUGS HIS SHOULDERS) Eleven! Yeh, that's what they say, but I'll bet it was a hundred-and-eleven – He was the cruelest cop in Oriente. Tortured children too! (HE GETS EXCITED, TIGHTENS HIS FISTS) One old woman at his trial said she saw him do it. Saw him take a six-year-old girl and push his cigarette into her breasts and her belly button and even into her hole! And you know what else, he (POINTS TO THE COP) ordered his men to hold the girl's mother, forced her to watch. And butcher there kept at it until the little girl died. For two hours she cried. The whole damn village heard her-and her mother had to see it all. And then he killed the mother. Just like that! Ran her through with his knife (MAKING THE GESTURE) But you'll get it now, alright, Butcher.

Cop: (JUMPS TO HIS FEET, SHOUTS) It's a lie, a lie! I followed orders! I followed orders! (HE STOPS SUDDENLY, AWKWARDLY FROZEN, HIS BACK STILL TO THE AUDIENCE, THEN SLOWLY SINKS BACK ONTO

HIS STOOL. HIS VOICE IS NOW WEAK AND LAMENTING) I ... followed ... orders.

Guard: Like hell! You gave them! Child torturer! That's what you are. The old woman saw it. She was hiding in the sugar field. She saw you! (HE STARES AT THE COP BUT THE COP HAS RETURNED TO HIS ORIGINAL POSITION. AFTER A FEW SECONDS, THE GUARD TURNS TO THE PROF AND STILL FULL OF HATE, SHOUTS) They say you're even worse! He killed children – you wanted to kill Cuba!

Prof: (SMILES AWKWARDLY, TURNS AWAY, WALKS TO THE TOILET, INVESTIGATES IT, NAIVELY) No paper?

Guard: (RELEASED FROM HIS TENSION, OVERLY AMUSED) Ha! You aristocrats are all alike. No paper! That's a good one! No paper! Use your hand-kerchief! In a few hours (HE POINTS TO THE WINDOW) it'll all be the same, heh? (LAUGHING) No paper! (HE EXITS LAUGHING, SHUTS THE CELL DOOR BUT CAN BE HEARD REPEATING) No paper! No paper! (THE LAUGHING DIES OUT, SILENCE)

Prof: (STARES AT THE DOOR, SMILES AGAIN, BEGINS TO WALK AROUND THE CELL LIKE A DOG SNIFFING A NEW HOME. HE STOPS IN FRONT OF THE IMAGINARY WALL FACING THE AUDIENCE, DECIPHERS AN IMAGINARY BIT OF SCRIBBLING, CHUCKLES THEN POINTING AT IT, TURNS TO THE COP) You know what someone wrote on this wall? He said ... (SEEING THE COP CROUCHED IN HIS SAME OLD POSITION, HE STOPS, STARTS HIS WANDERING ANEW, LOOKS AT THE WINDOW, GETS HIS STOOL AND MOVES IT NEXT TO THE LEFT WALL BETWEEN IT AND THE COP. PROF STANDS UP ON THE STOOL, LOOKS OUT THE WINDOW AND WITHOUT TURNING) Well, at least it's a clear night. (THE COP LIFTS HIS HEAD SLOWLY, LOOKS UP AT THE PROF, THEN BURIES HIS HEAD INTO HIS KNEES AND BEGINS TO SOB, SLOWLY, QUIETLY. THE PROF, HEARING HIM, LOOKS AROUND AND COMES DOWN FROM HIS STOOL. HE HESITATES, FINALLY PUTS HIS HAND ON THE COP'S SHOULDERS) Courage, my friend, courage (THE COP CONTINUES TO WEEP) ... You must try to take yourself in hand ... come, my friend, come ... We must accept our fates. It's hard, I know, it's the hardest task in our life, but we must accept it, we must pull together all our resources, all our strengths ... Come, my friend, try, force yourself...

Cop: (GRADUALLY STOPS SOBBING, STRAIGHTENS OUT AND TURNS TO FACE THE PROF-AND FOR THE FIRST TIME, THE AUDIENCE. HIS CHUBBY CHEEKS QUIVER. HIS EYES ARE RED AND SWOLLEN, TEARS HAVE CAUSED THE DYE OF HIS HAIR- LINE MOUSTACHE TO SMEAR

IDS UPPER LIP) I ... I can't help it ... It's unfair ... I was a cop ... that's all ... I took orders. Why should I die? I wasn't crooked! The others, they robbed and filled their pockets all the time. All I took was a few bribes here and there. Everybody did that! Batista expected us to do it. It was the only way to live. The others, they stole so much they could afford to bribe their way out of the country. And they did, too! They all got away. They're not going to die! They're in Miami or on the Riviera! Why should I die? Why? I didn't kill that girl! I wasn't even there! I told my men "that Gonzalez woman has seen the guerrillas. Get her and find out where they are." That's all I said, I swear it, I swear it! (SOBBING AGAIN) I don't want to die! I'm willing to work for Fidel. I'm not guilty! I don't want to die! Why should I die while the others are safe in Miami, why, why?

Prof: (COMPASSIONA TELY) I don't know, my friend, I don't know, but it won't help you to think about it. You must forget the others, you must forget the past. It's hard, but you've got to try. Everything is too late now. Right or wrong, our acts are classified, our fates are sealed. We're not even human beings anymore. We're objects, historical data. Nothing more. Our public reality is no longer in our hands.

Cop: (MISUNDERSTANDING) Public? I didn't even get a public trial. It was the army, the army ...

Pro: I didn't mean ... I mean all we can do now is try to face death bravely. It's only a gesture and rather meaningless at that, but it's all we've got left. But you'll see, my friend, if we make that our only purpose, our only essence, it will give us a sort of satisfaction. It's not much, but it's all we've got.

Cop: It's not fair, it's not fair...

Prof: I know, I know ... but death is never fair. The human condition is defined in terms of an arbitrary death-and that makes it already unfair.

Cop: Huh?

Prof: I mean that morally speaking death is never justified-no matter what the circumstances or the rationale. No one has the right to kill.

Cop: But I didn't do it, I tell you! I didn't do it!

Prof: No, no, my friend, you misunderstand me. I mean that no one has the right to judge you and send you to your death.

Cop: They're (POINTING AT THE DOOR) doing it, aren't they? Why? Why me?

Prof: (STILL TRYING TO GET ACROSS) That's exactly what I mean, that death is arbitrary, that is, that there's never a reason for it. It just happens and we must try to accept it without trying to understand why it does. Like a newborn child that dies, there's no moral reason for it, is there? And that Gonzalez woman ...

Cop: (WITH A START) She refused to talk!

Prof: I didn't mean it that way, I meant, well, no matter what she did, from a point of view of moral justice, she shouldn't have died, should she?

Cop: (VIOLENTLY) That was an accident! My men didn't mean to kill her, I swear it! They just wanted to frighten the mother, force her to talk. That's all, I swear it to God, nothing more!

Prof: I understand, I understand, but what I'm trying to explain is not that. It's about your desire to understand death, and the incident of the girl is valid ...

Cop: I don't know what the hell you're talking about! I told my men to make this woman talk and they used this girl to frighten her and then the girl died! What does that have to do with me? (POINTING TO THE DOOR AGAIN) They judged me for the wrong reasons.

Prof: Exactly. And the woman too died for the wrong reasons, didn't she?

Cop: How the hell was I supposed to know that she hadn't seen the guerrillas? My ...

Prof: (HORRIFIED) What?

Cop: (SUDDENLY AWARE OF HIS SLIP, MEEKLY) Oh, well, yes, that's right, she ... she ... Never! And they told me she had seen the rebels! They said she had even given them food! It's not my fault they made a mistake this time, is it? I acted in good faith, didn't I? It's not my fault the girl died! The men didn't mean to kill her! And then, well ... (SLOWING DOWN) well, after she did, what could they do? (RAPIDLY AGAIN) They had to kill the mother, didn't they? (PLEADING) Don't you understand, they had to! The mother saw the little girl die! They had no choice: But it was all an accident, an accident: It wasn't my fault, was it? Tell me, was it? Was it? (BREAKS DOWN, SOBS)

Prof: (MOVED, PUTTING HIS ARMS ON THE COP'S SHOULDERS). Courage, my friend, courage. Few men can bear such a cross without pain. I understand, I understand ... Come now, it's all over, try to forget the past, try. Very few men live moral lives, and no man is free from the sin of faulty judgment. If there is a

God, my friend, he will understand, and he will surely feel compassion for your suffering.

Cop: (VIOLENTLY) I don't give a damn about God: It's them (POINTING TO THE DOOR) I care about! Why should they convict me, why? Why should they want to kill me? They did the same thing to their prisoners: It's one thing to kill in battle or out of duty, it's another to judge, to sit on your ass and judge you're so goddamn better.

Prof: They are men, my friend, and men make mistakes, many mistakes. Sometimes mistakes are fatal. You've made yours, now they are making theirs. You must try not to think of reasons or causes. You must try only to be strong, to show them that you are a man. They may hate you but they will also respect you.

Cop: What the hell do I care?

Prof: It's the only thing we have left I'm afraid, our honor.

Cop: (COOLING DOWN) Honor, bah! What good is it in front of bullets! And why do you care what others think of you, anyway?

Prof: Perhaps it's because I hope to make them think about themselves, about the rightfulness of their acts, not in terms of moral justice but in terms of human relations.

Cop: Bah!

Prof: I mean it. I think my death might make them think a little. It's possible. Very little, but it's possible. Anyway it's all we've got left.

Cop: So what?

Prof: Well, I guess I'm an incurable idealist ... But down deep, don't you think man does eventually achieve the moral progress he seeks?

Cop: No! And furthermore, I don't think a man seeks anything except his own personal good life.

Prof: That's because we don't see enough evidence of progress in our lifetime. But men do seek it. So do you, I can tell by your troubled soul.

Cop: (VIOLENTLY) Shut up! Shut up! (SILENCE, THEN THE COP LOOKS UP AT THE PROF WITH CALM, ALMOST KIND EYES, WALKS UP TO HIM

AND PATS HIM ON THE BACK) I'm sorry ... It's just that I've never met a man, any man, who cared about anything but himself. Frankly, I don't think it's possible.

Prof: (PLEASED) I don't blame you for being bitter, but your only chance now is to be forgiving, really. After all, we do know that some of these rebels (POINTING) died for something they believed in besides themselves ... There is progress in the world. It's slow, incredibly slow, and it has its setbacks, but it's there. And you know how it starts? Whenever individual men stop to think about themselves.

Cop: Maybe, but not these guys (POINTING)

Prof: Oh yes, even they. That's why we've got to try to be brave. You see, to me, my death is my last lecture, and they (POINTING) are my last pupils. All men are afraid of death, and therefore all men are fascinated by death. So they will watch us very carefully. They'll hope to see us cry and tremble and beg for mercy. And if we do they'll think they were right to kill us. But if we don't they'll feel uncomfortable. No man can kill without being insecure, and now they'll feel even more insecure. And maybe they'll ask themselves Why? Maybe they'll even ask themselves why they kill. And then, who knows, maybe they'll stop killing. So you see, my last lecture may be my greatest.

Cop: Nonsense! ... Forgive me, sir, but that's ... These guys (POINTING) are butchers, just like Batista! Do you think those ex-cops living it up in Miami are going around talking to themselves asking themselves questions?

Prof: Maybe. Maybe a few of them are, or just one or two, that's enough for a start ... You are, aren't you? You couldn't kill anyone anymore, could you? Well, that's a beginning of progress – not material progress, moral progress. And in time ...

Cop: Time! Time! I don't understand you-don't you realize you're going to die in ... (HE TURNS TO THE WINDOW, IT'S A BIT LIGHTER) in ... an hour or two?

Prof: Yes, I know. But it's easier if you think it isn't in vain, don't you think so? If all men are brothers, and you know the rest of them will be better off-in some small way or other – by your death, doesn't it make your death more tolerable? Just a little?

Cop: No!

Prof: Perhaps not, but it's the only thing that can help us – now.

Cop: Dreams can't help a dying man

Prof: Some dreams can.

Cop: Then I prefer the one of a golden paradise. At least in that one I come out ahead.

Prof: That's not a dream, my friend, that's wishful thinking. I can't recognize what is not human. I can't – and I won't – think of what is not firmly planted in the human condition. A paradise on earth, yes. That is worth working for, fighting for, even dying for.

Cop: I thought you wanted to stop killing.

Prof: I do.

Cop: But you want to fight for your paradise.

Prof: Sometimes peace must be won by a sword.

Cop: That's what they (POINTING) say too.

Prof: Yes, but their sword is one of vengeance, not peace, and vengeance only leads to more vengeance.

Cop: Doesn't killing lead to more killing:?

Prof: Some kind is inevitable.

Cop: But you said death is never justified.

Prof: (SLIGHTLY NERVOUS, BEGINS TO PACE) It isn't, not on moral grounds. But there are differences in degree between killing for profit and killing for a future ideal.

Cop: Man always kills for what he wants, what's the difference what he calls it. I've learned that from experience. Haven't you? What are you here for anyway?

Prof: I plotted.

Cop: What?

Prof: I tried to arrange a coup, ah, a sort of revolution.

Cop: Because you wanted something you didn't have?

Prof: (INCREASINGLY AGITATED) Not at all. I had all I wanted personally, but to me Cuba was suffering. I wanted Cubans to have freedom, that's why I plotted against Fidel. He's not good for Cuba, he's …

Cop: That's what Fidel said about Batista.

Prof: And he was right too-about Batista. But that doesn't mean Fidel is right about Fidel!

Cop: And so you fought against them both?

Prof: That's right.

Cop: How?

Prof: Well, I'm a teacher, I taught history at Havana University, and as long as I could I told my students the truth about Batista. I tried to teach them between right and wrong. I tried to make them understand that no man should ever dominate another, that no one should …

Cop: And Batista let you get away with it?

Prof: For a while, yes. I had, ah, well, I had sort of a big name in my field. Batista warned me, and then he finally threw me in jail, but I got away to Miami and there I continued to fight him the best I could. I bought arms and ammunition and I smuggled them to Fidel in the hills.

Cop: So why are you here?

Prof: Because things changed. After Fidel won, I came back. I started teaching again, and then Fidel changed. What could I do? I had risked my life for freedom and that same freedom was being raped by someone else. I had to keep on fighting, and stay faithful to what I stood for. So I started buying arms again.

Cop: For the counter revolutionaries?

Prof: (CURTLY FOR THE FIRST TIME) Bah, that's what Fidel calls them-because they fight against him! But most of them fought with him as long as he represented freedom. We fought for Cuba, not for Fidel.

Cop: (AFTER A PAUSE, REFLECTIVELY) So that's the reason you're not afraid of death – not because of progress or lectures.

Prof: What do you mean?

Cop: Well you think justice is on your side. My father – he was an ordinary peasant but he wasn't stupid-he told me once: "Only those who are guilty are afraid of death."

Prof: That's too negative. Man has to have a justification for his life, he has to think he did something positive and worthwhile. It's not enough to say I didn't do anything bad.

Cop: I guess it's how you feel about it, I mean how you feel about yourself. Some people do lots of good things-for the wrong reasons.

Prof: (SLIGHTLY AGGRESSIVE) Is fighting for freedom a wrong reason?

Cop: I didn't mean you, although of course you did buy arms, and guns kill, they kill people with freedom

Prof: (INCREASINGLY AGGRESSIVE) I told you, some things you have to fight for.

Cop: That's what Batista said.

Prof: Batista didn't give a damn about people.

Cop: Yeah, but who decides who cares about people and who doesn't?

Prof: (ANGRY) What do you mean who? Everyone, you, me, each of us makes up his own mind and acts accordingly. But there are certain objective standards!

Cop: Like what?

Prof: Many of them! Like, ah, like the old cliché of means and ends. He who uses man as a means is amoral.

Cop: Isn't that what you did when you bought arms? Aren't the poor slobs who get mowed down by your guns being used? What about them?

Prof: I've told you already, damn it, that there's a difference. When one man sets up an apparatus to dominate other men, and those others take up arms, even kill, to destroy that apparatus, well, you can't say they're both equally guilty.

Cop: I didn't. You did. You talked about there never being a reason for killing. All I said was what my father told me, that "those who are guilty ...

Prof: are afraid of death" – and that's why you're afraid, isn't it?

Cop: That's right! And so are you.

Prof: I have nothing to be guilty about. My hands are clean.

Cop: Are they?

Prof: (BEGINNING TO LOSE CONTROL) They are, I tell you.

Cop: (CALM) And you feel no guilt?

Prof: Why should I?

Cop: Because you are trying to justify your crimes.

Prof: What crimes! I have committed no crimes.

Cop: You said killing is a crime.

Prof: Well, that certainly doesn't seem to bother you!

Cop: Frankly, I don't know if killing is always a crime. I don't think so, but I'm not really worried about that-or about what others think of me either.

Prof: And I am, is that it?

Cop: Aren't you? Isn't that why you really want to put up a good show for them?

Prof: No, damn it, no! Don't you understand anything! I ... (SUDDENLY HE STOPS, CALMS DOWN) I ... I am right ... I know I am ...

Cop: Are you? Are you really? Do you really care about other people? Do you really give a damn what happens to this stupid miserable world after you die?

Prof: (PAUSE, STARTS TO PACE AGAIN) But ... then ... if you're right ... all acts are equivalent.

Cop: I don't know about that. All I know is that you live in a world of make – believe.

Prof: (SHOCKED BY THE REMARK, VIOLENTLY) I suppose yours is a better one?

Cop: It's simpler.

Prof: Killing children?

Cop: (HEATING UP) That was an accident! I told you that before, an accident!

Prof: (SUDDENLY CRUEL) You burned her with a cigarette! That was no accident!

Cop: (SHOUTING, TAKING A COUPLE OF STEPS TOWARD THE PROF) Cigarettes don't kill!

Prof: (SAME) But she died, didn't she? You're responsible for her death! You killed her!

Cop: I didn't, I tell you, I didn't! All I did was burn her a little!

Prof: In her sex?

Cop: Yes, damn it, yes! But I didn't kill her! She must have had a bad heart or something! She just died!

Prof: (HORRIFIED) So it was you, not your men! You did kill her! You filthy beast! You inhuman coward! You ... you (PROF BURIES HIS FACE IN HIS HANDS, SILENCE)

Cop: (SUDDENLY CALM AGAIN, DROPS HIS HANDS, WHICH WERE BELLIGERENTLY WAVING ABOUT, TO HIS SIDE.) Yes. Yes. I did ... Does that make you feel better? Does that make your hands cleaner? Yes, I'm a child killer, and I try to lie about it. I lied to them (POINTING) to you and I even tried to lie to me. But it didn't work. I think maybe you have the same problem.

Prof: (VIOLENTLY) You filthy scum, how dare you compare me to you! You child killing, inhuman (HE CHARGES UP TOWARDS THE COP), torturing (GRABS HIS COLLAR) bastard! (THE COP, STRONGER BY FAR, BREAKS HIS HOLD AND THROWS HIM BACK. THE PROF STAGGERS, SLIPS AND FALLS TO THE FLOOR. HE STARTS TO RISE BUT STOPS AND LETS HIMSELF SINK TO A REST)

Cop: You're right, absolutely right, and that is why I must die. I know it now. I am guilty and I am afraid to die. And you know what makes it worse? I'll tell you. It's that I'm more jealous than I'm sorry. I'm jealous of all those other cops that got away and are now living it up in Miami in nice villas by the seashore, plenty of money in the bank and the Miami police to protect them. That's what really makes me mad. And I've got an account in a Miami bank too. That's right, I've got $200,000 stashed away there, just waiting for me. And here I am! What a joke! Pretty funny, isn't it? That's what I killed for. (PAUSE, PROF MAKES NO EFFORT TO RISE) And what about you, my friend, what did you kill for?

Prof: (RISING, VIOLENTLY) For Cuba! For Cuba, do you hear me! I'm no scum like you. I wasn't afraid of death. I was proud to die for a better Cuba!

Cop: (HIS TONE OF VOICE IS KIND) You intellectuals are all alike. You call it freedom, justice, morality, and somehow you get yourselves to believe it. I've never met anyone who's willing to die for them though. For their honor, yes, but not for all that talk. You know why the Fidelistas won? Because of their ideals? Hope for a better Cuba? Freedom? Justice? No! They won because they suffered. That's right, suffered! Each one of them fought and sacrificed his life because he suffered too much in the world as it was. That's what makes revolutionaries! Not books, not speeches, not ideals. Men! Men make revolutionaries. And what did you suffer about? Your stomach? Your tortures? Your wife getting raped? Your property getting stolen? Your friends getting shot? No my friend, you only suffered in your dreams, in your books, in your honor.

Prof: (SAD, WEARY) But I fought, I risked my life, I ...

Cop: You didn't even do that. You glorified your daring, that's all. You never thought you'd get executed. You never gave a damn about Cuba. Hungry peasants didn't affect you. Even Batista's tortures didn't trouble you. You slept at night, just as soundly as I did. The only thing you cared about was your right to go around saying hunger and rape and torture are wrong. It was your way of having power. In your lecture rooms, in your dreams, in your self-respect. Revolutionaries don't die for self-respect. They die because they hate, and they hate because they suffer, physically, not in books. And you wanted self-respect because your life was empty inside – not because you believed in justice. My life was empty and I filled it with killing in return for money and the hope of a good life. Your life was empty and you filled it with killing, killing from a distance that is, in return for self-respect and power (PROF SINKS ONTO THE SAME STOOL WHERE THE COP SAT EARLIER) That's why you wanted to die so damn bravely, wasn't it? You wanted to make it look good to the others but more importantly to you. It's a way of having power, power over your executioners. Isn't it?

Prof: (BURIES HIS FACE IN HIS HANDS) You're mad! You can't understand a thing! Why do I even listen to you (BEGINS TO SOB), you're nothing but a child-killer! I was a patriot! You don't realize how much I risked. I believed in what I was doing! I swear it!

Cop: Of course, you did. You believed all your talk of morality and progress. You had to, otherwise your life had no meaning.

Prof: (IT'S ALMOST LIGHT NOW) It does have meaning, it does (HE SOBS MORE HEAVILY), it does, it does, it has to.(THE CELL DOOR IS UNLATCHED, THEN OPENED, THE GUARD STANDS IN THE DOORWAY) What I did I did for others not for me! I swear it! Oh, God, God, there must be justice, there must be … oh, God, God …

Guard: (SOFTLY) It is time.

Cop: (FIRMLY BUT NOT OVERLY PROUD) I'm ready.

Prof: (HYSTERICALLY) No! No! Please! Call Fidel, Please! Let me talk to him, he will understand, I know him, we went to school together, he will understand. Oh please, oh God, someone, please tell me it wasn't in vain …

Cop: (TRIES TO HELP HIM RISE, GENTLY) Courage, my friend, courage … you must try to take yourself in hand … come my friend, come.

(CURTAIN)

CHAPTER NINETEEN

WHITMAN AND SPECK AGAINST SOCIETY

At the time of this writing the American economy was imploding. The machinations of Wall Street's avarice and the government's complicity in it stood bare. Given these circumstances, Tito's injunction at the end of this piece—which appeared in May of 1967 – that society breeds the mad men it deserves resounds. "What's happening now is that the vast majority of American tax payers are being royally screwed by the system," notes Gerassi, "We have to pay for the greed and manipulation of the Wall Street barons who should be completely expropriated and not have any golden parachutes. They are as much criminals in our society as Whitman and Speck."

WHITMAN AND SPECK AGAINST SOCIETY

One hot day last August, Charles Joseph Whitman, an "All-American boy" and Marine veteran, calmly climbed atop the University of Texas' 28-story limestone tower and, with a .30 caliber semiautomatic carbine, fired more than 100 bullets in all directions below, killing 14 people and wounding 31 others. His random act of violence followed only 18 days after the systematic murder of eight student nurses in a Chicago nursing school dormitory, for which a young seaman, Richard B. Speck, is now on trial (at time of writing).

The crimes were widely publicized; the nation responded with horror and fear - and with a puzzled sense of guilt. What had society done to Whitman and Speck to engender this terrifying revenge?

We can never know precisely "why they did it." We cannot, responsibly, re-create the inner storm that consumes an individual before and during such acts. But whatever private evils these men suffered inescapably reflected their outer world: the society we share with them and which they attacked. The forces that worked on them are at work on all of us, and they are forces that we set in motion.

In Viet Nam, we kill children. In Guatemala, we shoot peasants. In the Congo, we destroy tribes. All over the world, we are engaged in corruption, destruction, and murder. At home, we flee from cities. Women carry needles, sprays, even shock rods to walk the streets. Ghettos are crammed with dynamite. Peaceniks are called nutniks or even traitors. We have the highest standard of living in history yet we are obsessed with crime and death. The Great Society is a violent society-and a fearful society.

To civic leaders and politicians, the cause of our fear is simple enough: Crime is on the rise at home, rebellions are increasing abroad. Our safety, therefore, is at stake. Our way of life is threatened. But why this is so is not. so easy to explain. To some, like President Johnson, agitation all over the world is the result of nothing more than envy. And so, when the President visited Korea late last year, he told American G.I.'s at Camp Stanley:

"Don't forget, there are only 200 million of us in a world of three billion. They want what we've got and we're not going to give it to them." To KKK warlords at home, the argument is the same. "The niggers want what we white folks got," they say, "and we sure as hell ain't gonna give it to them."

But what is it that they do want? A better life? More televisions and refrigerators? Freedom? Self-respect and the respect of others? Or all of these things? And contrarily, is our freedom dependent on the denial of the freedom of others? Ho Chi Minh, North Viet Nam's president, has said that "nothing" is more precious than our independence and freedom." And Stokely Carmichael, head of the Student Nonviolent Coordinating Committee (SNCC), has often translated such a thought into an American Negro context by championing Black Power-the right for Negroes to make their own decisions in matters concerning their life and death, well-being, and self-respect.

Our politicians and statisticians insist that's not what they mean by violence. They mean the increase in crime, in disorder for disorder's sake. They mean Hollywood teenagers smashing up Sunset Strip for the hell of it. They mean Oakland's Hell's Angels on the rampage, boozing, drugging, frightening, and all of it in ecstatic admiration of the swastika. They mean middle-class youngsters who trade a solid education for a sordid combination of pot, LSD, loveless sex, and far-left clichés. In sum, what they mean is meaningless violence. But is there really such an increase in violence? The FBI says yes. Homicide deaths went up from 4.7 per 100,000 in 1960 to 5.3 in 1965, and violent crimes in general rose another 10 percent from 1965 to 1966. On the other hand, Lloyd E. Ohlin, an associate director of the National Crime Commission and one of America's top authorities on delinquency and corrections, says that the crime rate is fairly stable. In truth, nobody knows for sure. Most courts don't keep good records. The best guess is that about 700,000 people are charged with crimes each year (not including speeders, drunks, prostitutes, gamblers. and shoplifters), and that more than half are juveniles. The FBI's Uniform Crime Reports calculate that from 1960 to 1965 "police arrests of persons under 18 years of age jumped 54 percent."

Suicide is also on the increase. *Time* magazine estimates that "more than one in every 100 Americans now living have tried to kill themselves at one time or another." Statistics vary here too, and they can't be very accurate anyway since many families tend to conceal suicides because of the stigma attached to such deaths by society (even Ernest Hemingway's suicide was denied by his family for a few years). But one thing is certain: The more intelligent and/or educated an individual, the more he is apt to take his own life. Thus artists, professional men, and top executives commit suicide more than other people; doctors (two out of 100) and psychiatrists are most likely self-victims; and twice as many college students kill themselves as non-college youths of the same age.

Yet none of this is characteristic of America. Again according to FBI figures, which coincide approximately with U.N. figures, many European countries have a higher crime rate than we do. England's crime rate, for example, is up 55 percent in the last six years, while the U.S.'s is up only 40 percent. In suicides, according to U.N. figures, Hungary (28.6 per 100,000), Austria (22.8), Czechoslovakia (21.3), Finland (19.8), West Germany (41.7), Denmark (19.1), Sweden (18.5), Switzerland (16.8), Japan (19.3), and France (14.9) all top the official U.S. rate (1 per 100,000). On the other hand Italy has a low of 5.3, Ireland 2.0, Egypt 0.1, and Fidel's Cuba so few suicides that the percentage varies officially from zero to 1.0 (in 1963). However, according to R. Edwin S. Shneidman, chief of the Center for Studies of Suicide Prevention of the National Institute of Mental Health, while published statistics place American suicides at about 22,000 a year, the real figures may be two or three times that number.

Whatever the number of crimes (or suicides) committed in America or by Americans – it is not the quantity which has frightened us into an obsessive concern for our safety. Even if the crime rate were higher, ordinary people would not worry, so long as the crimes and the criminals were explainable by some fairly reliable, logically acceptable patterns. But they are not. In fact, a great many of our acts of violence seem totally devoid of reasonable motives, and in recent years some of them have been so sensational that they captured headlines all. over the world.

The first of these took place on September 6, 1949, when a quiet, Bible-reading, World War II veteran named Howard Unruh walked down a street in Camden, New Jersey, and fired his Luger at friends and neighbors, killing 13. "They had been talking about me for some time and making derogatory remarks," he told the police when he surrendered. He was declared insane and is now in a mental hospital.

Since then, there have been many acts of wanton killing, including the 11 people shot down in Nebraska and Wyoming, in 1958, by Charles Starkweather, a 19-year-old, myopic youth; who was electrocuted. But none has so shocked the nation as those that took place in 1966. First there was Thomas Lee Penn who claimed that he killed six people between February and May but "wanted them all to live, so they would turn me in, so I could get help." The murder of the student nurses followed in July. Chicago police called it "the crime of the century," until Whitman's rampage overshadowed it less than three weeks later. Next there was Arthur J. Davis who went on a shooting spree in Connecticut and killed six persons. Three months later, a quiet, pretty, girl-shy, 18-year-old, Robert Benjamin Smith, strutted into the Rose-Mar College of Beauty in Mesa, Arizona, told five women and two children to lie face down on the floor, spreading their bodies as spokes in a wheel, and calmly shot them repeatedly, reloading his .22 caliber target pistol as he went along. And finally, one Saturday last December, Gustave D. Williams purchased a .30-caliber rifle from a dealer at 319 West 42nd Street in Manhattan, walked a couple of blocks' east to Bryant Park behind the Public Library, sat on a bench for a while, then started shooting, killing two people before police bullets brought him down.

What terrifies Americans about these acts is that they happen any place, any time, and anyone can be a victim. There are no guarantees, no safe exits. A couple of years ago, an 85-year-old woman was raped by a young man in a Brooklyn subway. Last year, an old, highly respected Columbia University professor, Frank

Tannenbaum, was knifed in his own elevator. Three times in the last three years, the apartment below mine has been robbed, while mine, which is identical, has so far gone unmolested. Not long ago, a secretary was stripped and raped in her midtown New York office in midday.

While the single act of violence is horrible, the generalized fear it creates has even greater implications for our society. As one English woman wrote after living four months in Washington: "Crime is on the increase everywhere, but I cannot believe that it is in proportion to the fear which the American woman is now experiencing. I resent being turned into a 'hysterical female,' having to size up men as possible attackers, fearing to walk in the park alone or on the streets at night. ... At the local playground, the latest rapes, attempted rapes, muggings, and indecent exposures are compared. Someone leaves dirty notes in the laundry, and when I advertised in the newspaper for a job I was besieged by obscene telephone calls. I have never lived before in an apartment with a security chain and am forever embarrassed and disconcerted at having to eye people through the peep hole before opening the door. It violates all principles of politeness."

In fact, much more is violated, such as a sense of respect for one's fellow human beings and, therefore, respect for society as a whole. What can be great about a society where all women live in fear and all men must be careful not to talk to children or wander the parks admiring the birds less they be taken for molesters, queers, or nuts? What is so great about a society where such books as *Protecting Yourself and Your Family*, on sale for 25 cents in local drugstores, becomes required reading? The book advises readers on how to gouge out an attacker's eye with an index finger. "Don't remove your finger to jab again," it says, "instead keep twisting it." And if possible bring up a knee into his groin-and keep screaming all the time.

Fear is the most communicable of all diseases. Once it begins to spread, it reaches out with amazing rapidity to the most isolated corners of the country, and strikes with vicious effects. Thus one woman, Patty Johnson, living in the small (population: 50,000), peaceful town of Waterloo, Iowa, was infected by a single microbe: a dynamite blast at a local construction site. "I've had it," she wrote in her local paper, *The Sunday Courier*. "I'm fed up with a people who have concluded that the only way to settle a quarrel is with a gun, that the only way to get a 'kick' is to destroy." She had no idea what or who set off the charge, whether it was part of a labor feud or a prankster's nighttime escapade, but she concluded that today's violence was different from yesterday's, when yesterday it was caused only by the "culturally deprived." She wrote: "Violence is no longer the act of maniacs, but of those who are sane as you and I. The horror of their act is that they feel justified because they have a demand to be met, and society - that's us - hasn't fulfilled it. Violence has become the natural result of any grievance, brutality the logical conclusion for any injustice." To her question: "Have we become a nation of hoods?" she replied, "I believe the answer, sadly, is yes."

The answer, of course, is no-at least if by saying hood one means an aberration, an outcast, a mutation -for most of our crimes, curiously, are committed by our average citizen. Each person reflects society's values, and in our society it seems normal to kill. Most experts believe that violence in any society is not inbred, it is taught. It is the product of values, not their causes. And what are our values? It seems, our true values lie not in books or speeches or classroom pep talks, but in deeds. In the last six decades, more than 100 million people have been killed by military action alone. Can society digest such violence and then claim that killing is evil? According to Konrad Lorenz, Austria's brilliant naturalist and author of *King Solomon's Ring* and *Man Meets Dog*, violence in man is a tool of the intellect, as opposed to the instinctual use of violence for survival in the animal. In his latest book, *On Aggression*, Lorenz explains that violence has been around since the beginning of life. The animal relies on it to defend its flock, attack its prey, win its mate. But never does the animal resort to violence to conquer for the sake of conquering. To the animal, violence is limited to necessity. Thus, though two animals of different species may fight to a fatal finish, rarely do members of the same species go that far. A gesture of defeat by one is enough for the victor to control his anger. But not so for man. Having begun as a docile creature, man has developed violence as a weapon of conquest, as an art, gradually perfecting it to absurd dimensions. In animals, observes Lorenz, violence and love elicit the same intensity and, significantly, are interchangeable. Cats or dogs can battle each other energetically and passionately, but they can also love each other equally passionately. In both cases, the drive is motored by instinctual energy. But man, teaching himself hate and violence, sacrificing his amorous energy for a perfection in the art of destruction—and with it, sacrifices his respect for the docile, the peaceful, the gentle.

Thus man's heroes have become increasingly more violent. For Americans, first he was just a he-man, the tough but honest frontiersman or cowboy, then the good gangster who reforms at the end. Finally he became a cynical, callous, cold, automated, unprincipled brute at the service of "our" side. No matter what he did, being on our side made him "good." James Bond is the perfect example· of such servants and his manhood is characterized by his lack of commitment to anything but his job; love is an instrument, to be enjoyed, yes, but to be used. But would our lady from Waterloo, Iowa, call Bond a hood?

And what about Batman and Superman: extra-tall, extra-tough, extra-human – and extra-white? Are not our kids, in admiring these men, developing racial prejudice? Are not Hell's Angels a group of would-be Batmen? They don't fight against crime, true, but their search for superiority, for distinction goes beyond the "normal" man, beyond the poor slobs who live and work and play in Anytown, U.S.A.-that is, in Gotham City.

Violence is our way of life because we have made it our way. Our cigarette smokers would "rather fight than switch." Today, our government, it seems, would rather; kill than lose face. Our automobile companies would rather build death traps than safe cars. And our car buyers ,would rather zoom along at 100 m.p.h. in sleek, chrome-plated, tin coffins, than creep along at 60 m.p.h. in ugly but functional transportation vehicles. Is there really a difference between the punks who soaked the clothes of sleeping "bums" and set them afire in New York's Lower East Side and the gentleman who accidentally smashes his 350 horsepower wagon into a bunch of pedestrians? The kids' admitted they were getting "kicks," but may not the gentleman also be getting kicks from his jackrabbit acceleration?

White Americans are also upset about Negro violence. And indeed, there is much violence coming out of the ghettos – Watts, Harlem, Cleveland, Chicago. Why not? What have the Negroes learned in our society? Enslaved, beaten, subjugated, lynched, insulted, the American Negro has seen white man's justice applied mostly to the white man. Whatever progress he has made -and in real terms, not just legally, such progress is almost nil- he has won as a result of violence, or the threat thereof. First to be suspected of wrongdoing, last to be hired, the American Negro has had few rights and almost no privileges. Yet he is quickly drafted whenever "American Democracy" is at stake. In Viet Nam today, twice as many Negroes are killed in battle, proportionately, than whites, because twice as many Negroes are sent into the front lines. The Negro has been born and bred in violence-but it is not his violence or his society, it is the white man's.

This, too, has been the society of our youth. Taught to respect their elders, lectured to adopt America's values, they have learned instead that money talks, that cops are crooked, that governments lie. For example, in my magazine-article writing class at N.Y.U. last term, one of my students asked if he could write an article about the customs bureau and the import trade. What was interesting about it, I asked. "It's all corrupt," he answered. "You can import anything you want as long as you bribe." How do you know, I asked. "My father is an importer, he does it all the time."

This corruption is not an exception. Everything has to have its price in a society based on the Horatio Alger myth. Cigarettes kill but are good business. Run-proof stockings are manufacturable but are lousy business. Packages are phony. Life insurances are expensive. Newspapermen lie. Judges are manipulated. Are not all these acts acts of violence? Of course, they are not overt, but then, as Georges Sorel wrote in his masterful 1906 *Reflexions sur la violence*, the reduction of overt acts of violence in social relations is correlated with an increase in fraud and corruption, and fraud comes to replace overt violence as the road to success and privilege. In his classic work on political theory *The Machiavellians*, James Burnham added that those more adept at fraud than at force tend to cling to humanitarian ideals in an attempt to fool themselves about their own actions. Americans tend to fool themselves in just this way. And it is becoming increasingly evident that our youth is not fooled. Thus, youth may simply be reacting to this fraud-and chucking away all our humanitarian jargon by resorting to open violence.

As a result, modern youth has no respect for its elder's values. Whether our press admits it or not, whether the Warren Report says so or not, whether our schools and leaders and preachers realize it or not, today's youth knows that it is these old values which led to American planes dropping napalm on ordinary people in Viet Nam, to Bobby Baker's shenanigans, to American banker's business deals with the apartheid South African government, to the lies about U-2's, coups in Guatemala and Brazil, sugar plantation bombings in Cuba, and to President Kennedy's assassination. (Dismayed by the old values of violence in our society in relationship to the President's death, a Center for the Study of Violence has been recently established at Brandeis University to seek understanding and solution of the problem.)

Rejecting these values, some youngsters become self-isolated and seek their escape in pot or LSD. Others become rebels. They want to change society altogether. If they don't know quite how to do it, it is because they suspect and reject the values and methods of their rebellious elders, and substitute values have not yet been found. Hence the New Left has no respect for the Old Left. Still others become willing outcasts. It is not because they admire Hitler that the Hell's Angels adorn themselves with swastikas, but precisely because it shocks the rest of us. For that reason, also, non-homosexual male Angels kiss each other languishingly on the mouth - in public only. They despise all our values and value-makers, including the psychiatrists who would claim them to be homosexual. Whether rebels, outcasts, or escapists, they naturally neither respect nor-significantly-fear our police. They know about their shakedowns, their briberies, and the rest. Why should they respect cops who have always been on the wrong side of the billy club in any protest, any demonstration, any march, who rarely pay for services, who rarely ticket the rich or the important, who spend much of their time and most of their energy pursuing drunks, gamblers, addicts, and prostitutes, few of whom hurt anyone but themselves?

You and I may not be the violent types. We may not even be rebels or critics. We continue to pretend, to spout our humanitarian ideals, but we too have withdrawn our commitment from this society of inbred violence. That's why we don't like cops. The lady from Waterloo complains that the good Samaritan is dead. "The good American," she writes, "is now a member of a minority group. He must remain silent, pull his shades, and keep his own counsel." Perhaps it's too bad he hadn't done that in the first place. Instead he helped create society in his image. He profited well, but in so doing let his offspring grow up as monsters. Now the monsters are devouring his society-and the good Americans with it.

Despite our seeming horror, some of the monster-offspring are still presented as mythical heroes. Clint Eastwood in the movie A *Fistful of Dollars*, for example, is a widescreen, Technicolor sadist who kills for the sheer joy of it, although each time his six-shooter goes off he earns a good fistful- and goes home at the end both rich and admired. But other monster-offspring are very real. New York's Channel 13 showed a few last year; there were American pilots who, like characters from *Dr. Strangelove*, exulted when they saw burning victims running out from napalmed Viet Nam jungles. There are others. Beverly Deepe of the then *New York Herald Tribune* reported how "two Viet Cong prisoners were interrogated on an airplane flying toward Saigon. The first refused to answer questions and was thrown out of the airplane at 3,000 feet. The second immediately answered all the questions. But he, too, was thrown out." Jack Langguth wrote about still others in *The New York. Times*: "One American helicopter crewman returned to his base in the central highlands last week without a fierce young prisoner entrusted to him. He told friends that he had become infuriated by the youth and had pushed him out of the helicopter at about 1,000 feet." More monsters were found by John Wheeler who told *Tribune* readers how "A marine said several persons were burned seriously when one of the houses was touched off while its inhabitants were hiding in a bunker built into its floor. 'Kill them, I don't want anyone moving,' a marine said ..." What will satisfy the appetites of those Americans, give them pleasure, relieve their boredom after they get home-to Waterloo, Iowa?

The other monster-offspring, of course, are the Smiths and the Whitmans and the killer of the nurses in Chicago. Our press tells us they are nothing more than quirks, weirdos gone berserk. Are they? Or are they rather the products of our society, the manifestation of our greed and lust and obsessive admiration of the buck? Smith's father was a retired Air Force major working in an aerospace plant. The boy was brilliant in subjects he liked – English, literature, philosophy, and motivational research discussions. Friends said he "ridiculed love and compassion." He idolized Napoleon and Jesse James. He wanted success, headlines. He felt that the United States should use germ warfare "to wipe out the people of Southeast Asia – they're all animals and they're not important." In sum, Robert Smith was typical of thousands of kids all over America. A good boy, a quiet boy. A bit shy *yet* more honest than most about his feelings. As one of his teachers said, "I contend that as long as I live I would never pick Robert from my class as the one who would do something like this."

Whitman, too, was a good boy: an Eagle Scout at the age of 12, an altar boy, pitcher on the church-school baseball team, a newsboy with the biggest route in town. His father was a tough, ill-willed, quick-tempered man and Whitman reportedly hated him "with a mortal passion," blaming him for the separation of his parents. "It's true, I was strict," said the father, a former president of the local, Lake Worth, Florida, Chamber of Commerce. "With all three of my sons, it was 'yes, sir' and 'no, sir'. They minded me. But I gave them everything I could." Charles Joseph Whitman grew up tall and broad shouldered. He was a Marine, not a good one but a normal one, gambling, threatening his comrades, lending money at exorbitant interest. On a personal data form at the University of Texas mental-hygiene clinic, he listed his main interest as "how to make money." He married the "Queen of the Fair of Needville, Texas." In other words, he was an "average, red-blooded American." But he killed his wife, his mother, and, from his perch atop the U. of Texas observation tower, killed more than a dozen strangers. In his mother's house he left this note: "I have just killed my mother. If there's heaven she is going there. If there's not a heaven, she is out of her pain and misery. I love my mother with all my heart."

A week after he was gunned down by cops who finally broke into the observation tower, the press claimed he wasn't such a good boy after all. They quoted psychiatrists and pathologists who insisted that he simply "concealed his hostility." They recalled the fact that he had headaches, a tumor, and had once asked for psychiatric help. The tumor was found to be "incidental," his headaches unimportant. But he was "mean as hell" the *U.S. News and World Report* said. Then, too, it was not the fault of America's gun laws. Whitman had brought one of his weapons from Sears, Roebuck - on credit. But then so have all the other Texans, all the other Southerners, who used them on Negroes, on white integrationists, on President Kennedy. As for Whitman's hostilities, who doesn't have them? Who can look at our films, our TV commercials, who can read our press, who can listen to our politicians, who can go to war against a small nation halfway around the globe, who can learn of our big business dealings, who can try to cope with traffic without developing hostilities? Were Whitman or Smith or the nurse killer insane? Or were they a reflection of our own insanity? A society deserves the madmen it breeds.

AN OPEN LETTER TO EUROPEANS

The Bush Administration is itching to invade a country. Any country. Iraq.

Yemen. Perhaps Cuba, which has just been accused of aiding terrorists [NY Times, 18-09-02] because it gave tips to US intelligence services on how to catch them. Colombia may survive since it does US bidding. It has now even authorized its police to arrest anyone without a warrant, just like in the US [NYT: 12-09-02]. But Venezuela? To get rid of President Chavez, whose supporters, the NY Times admits, "are mainly among the 80 percent of Venezuelans who live in poverty, most of them, like Mr. Chavez, of mixed-race heritage" [22-09-02], Washington will surely organize a better coup than last time. After all, as the Times continued, our friends there are "the predominantly white middle and upper classes." Iran, against which US sanctions are causing scores of innocent deaths [NYT 11-09-902], is also on the list. So are the Philippines. And then who?

Europe? Why can't Europeans understand that the US is bent on dominating the world, yes including Europe. Not necessarily with troops. Certainly not in Europe. But as Europe should have understood by now as a result of the steel confrontation, and France even more so as a result of the banana fiasco, the US wants the world, certainly including Europe, to adhere to its standard of trade. It wants it to privatize its public schools, its retirement system, its unemployment benefits, well, every-thing, and junk its social contract. Whatever it costs, the US will demand total obedience to its criteria for doing business. The American empire is not like the old ones. It may want to control every country's political/ideological/religious/cultural way of life but its main drive is to control world trade – and it will kill or ruin those who try to stop it from doing so.

Of the rich and for the rich, the American government has established a corpora-tive state dedicated to making the rich richer, knowing full well that it means the poor will get poorer. If you accept US terms you survive, as a puppet, like England. (NY Times [22-09-02]: "Britain will never unambiguously choose Europe against America.") If not, and you are a rich powerful country, the US will get its flunkies to use the World Trade Organization rules it itself instituted to make you cry uncle. If you're poor, underdeveloped, trying to gain enough capital accumulation to build your infrastructure so as to help your people achieve a better life, the US will impose sanctions on you (Cuba, Iran) or will bomb you (Iraq), or invade you (Grenada, Panama, Nicaragua, Afghanistan) until you become a US puppet totally dependent on American largesse or until your economy is totally ruined.

Because the US is so rich and powerful, it can get proxies to do its dirty work.

Money does buy lots of allies. Like the Russians. Not so long ago, the CIA and Bin Laden's Al Qaeda were bosom buddies fighting the mean old Russians in Chechnya (after driving them out of Afghanistan) so US oil companies could take over the oil pipeline snaking its way from Baku (on the oil-rich Caspian Sea) past the Chechen capital of Grozny to the Black Sea (and on to the Mediterranean). Then Prime Minister Putin got smart and offered the US a deal [NYT, 19-10-01}. Chechnya could get 16 percent, the US and Russia 23, and the oil companies the rest. If Chechnya remained Russian, the former KGB leaders would collect a nifty 39 percent. So suddenly Russia and the CIA became loyal pals, and the CIA turned against AI Qaeda and the Chechen rebels. (As a corollary, Exxon-Mobil got the contract to develop the huge oil and gas fields in Eastern Russia [NYT, 30-10-02]) .

Of course this is typical of US operations. Back in June 2001, not long before 9/11, the US gave Taliban $44 million and invited its top leaders to visit the US. The CIA had decided that only Taliban could control Afghanistan, so the US should help it do so. Unocal could then outbid Bridas, the Argentine oil company, which was there first, to build a pipeline through the Khyber Pass and on to Pakistan and ocean transport. (Of course to achieve this, the US needed a friendly government in Pakistan, so a coup by General Musharraff seemed a very democratic thing to do.). But Taliban balked, so Unocal's president concluded a war was necessary. Mr. Bin Laden gave Mr. Bush the excuse he needed to put in a friendly government in Afghanistan – and get himself and his republicans reelected.

It also gave Bush the excuse to "talk" the various countries surrounding Afghanistan to "cooperate" with America's "anti-terrorist" campaign. US bases were quickly set up (a total of 60,000 US troops) in the former Soviet Muslim states of Kazakhstan, Uzbekistan, Turkmenistan, Kyrgyzstan, Tajikistan, (and Azerbaijan to the north of Iran and south of Chechnya). Run more or less viciously by ex-communist dictators who torture and murder their dissenters [New Yorker, 14-01-02], these "democratizing" strongmen, as our media now dubs them, get CIA and US military help to crush their independence movements – because all of these countries are rich in oil (Azerbaijan is ideally situated for a pipeline from Baku to Turkey), which the US covets. It's a great "way for Bush," said the Village Voice, "to prosecute a war for oil in the name of God." [11/17-09-02]

Furthermore, 9/11 gave Bush the gumption to demand, and Congress to quickly pass, the "Authorization for Use of U.S. Military Force" resolution, which gives him carte blanche to wage war on anyone or any country he alone holds responsible for hijackings. A month later, with almost no debate (indeed few had even read the 342-page document), Congress gave Attorney General Ashcroft permission to wipe out most of our civil liberties; the absurdly jingoistic "Uniting and Strengthening America by Providing Appropriate Tools Required to Intercept and Obstruct Terrorism (or USA Patriot) Act" let him deny attorney-client privilege and remove restraints on the FBI, allowing its agents to spy on community meetings, religious activities, the internet, every citizen's emails, and plant listening devices in any home, even in bathrooms, on the simple hunch that something illegal may be afoot over the toilet or in a shower. Since then, the Pentagon has set up a bureau, under the convicted (but pardoned by papa Bush) Iran-gate liar Admiral Poindexter, to monitor all, yes all, not just Moslem, students in US universities. And Ashcroft has tuned up a Patriot's Act II, which will allow the FBI to arrest anyone it deems a "supporter of terrorism" without a warrant, try him or her secretly, and send the hapless individual to a secret jail (or hand him or her to the military for secret military justice, including execution).

As it is, Bush has already decreed that any American he or Ashcroft deems an "enemy combatant" can be secretly arrested, secretly tried without a lawyer, secretly convicted, secretly condemned to death, and without judicial review, secretly executed, all by the military. This is a country where 121 prisoners condemned to death for rape and/or murder – all but one non-white – have been proven to be totally innocent after research by pre-law students. God knows how many more innocents have already been executed.

In one such case, the Boston office of the FBI has been found guilty [NYT, 17-09-02] of knowingly allowing its informants to commit scores of murders [repeatedly documented on CBS' "Sixty Minutes", and of deliberately framing an innocent man for them. (He was finally released this summer after spending 30 years in jail.) When Republican Representative Burton, a Bush conservative, asked that all the FBI papers on the Boston office be released to his investigating committee, Bush refused on "executive privilege" grounds and issued an executive order forbidding the release of any government documents.

Most Americans love it. "There's too much freedom in America," they shout.

Over 60 percent of Americans think we should get rid of the first, fourth, fifth and any other amendment which stops their government from jailing (if not killing) blacks, browns, yellows, reds and any other color save whites. And dissenters of any color. And defense attorneys. (As it is, US jails are over-filled; 60 percent of the more than two million inmates are black; there are more young blacks in jail than in school). "If you're not with me, you're against me," Bush says over and over again, and most Americans, and our mainstream media, cheer.

Bush can't jail German Prime Minister Schroder, no matter how much he would like to. But he can jail any American who calls him a power-mad fascist. On what grounds? Read the "USA Patriots Act," passed almost unanimously by Congress. Anyone supporting terrorism is defined as an enemy of the state. To criticize Bush, says the FBI, is to help terrorists, hence to be an enemy of the state who has no right to a lawyer and can be executed on Ashcroft's whim. The Bill of Rights? Says Martin Garbus, one of America's foremost constitutional lawyers in his new book, "Courting Disaster": basically, just plain dead!

For the time being Ashcroft's whim is limited mostly to Middle Easterners (and a few Latinos) who are arrested on mere looks, and immediately judged guilty by the press and people. The American Civil Liberties Union has been able to document that 1600 have been arrested, jailed secretly somewhere, and held incommunicado. My old colleagues at Time and Newsweek where I was an editor for almost ten years, tell me the figure is really 6000, but "shush, don't say it out loud, or we'll be in trouble." Meanwhile every yokel interprets the Patriot Act as his right to denounce his Muslim neighbors as "pro-terrorist," causing them to lose their jobs, be driven from their homes, have their stores burned or looted, and their kids so ostracized in school that they refuse to continue to attend.

In Georgia, that bastion of jingoistic hypocrisy, the "denouncer" who smeared three Muslim medical students driving to their Florida hospital internships, probably because their car was nicer or newer than hers, was hailed as a hero, and the media congratulated her civic responsibility. The three students were fired from their hospitals. Most officials applauded. New York authorities asked all citizens to do the same. And advertised the number to call if you see a suspicious Muslim: 1-800-SAFE-NYS – on television [Evening News, Channel 7, 1709-02]. Even the NYTimes now worries that we may have become "a nation of informers." [22-09-02]

Ok, you Europeans don't care. It's our internal affairs, you say. It doesn't affect you. Ah, but it does. Why do you think the US wants to overthrow Saddam Hussein? He may be a despicable human being, but far less so than the ruling family in Saudi Arabia or Kuwait. At least Saddam allows women to wear the clothes they wish, to get an education, to drive, to talk to men, to get jobs, to become doctors, scientists, teachers. Do you really believe the lies that Washington has been spewing up about Iraq?

Take the claim that each time US planes "patrolling" the "no-fly" zone have dropped bombs on Iraqi citizens it was out of self-defense. No less than 90,000 sorties in six years by US and occasionally British planes! Always self-defense? When 120 academics asked the New York Times to explain how come no US or British plane has ever been shot down or even just scratched if Iraq always fires first, the Times dutifully ignored our question.

So why do you Europeans believe the Bush Administration? Because it has perfected its double-talk? Without blinking an eye-lid, Secretary of Defense Rumsfeld shamelessly gloats that he has ordered more bombs, on more targets, because "I don't like the idea that our planes go out and get shot at with impunity." Of course, the New York Times, which quoted him [17-09-02], did not mention that not one single US plane had ever been shot at over Iraq, nor that the US (and England) have dropped more bombs on Iraq in the last five years than they did during the whole Korean war, the equivalent of ten Hiroshima "big ones."

A few years ago, the UN documented, and LBJ's former press secretary Bill Moyers duly reported on public television, that no less than half a million children had been killed by the sanctions on Iraq, which of course did not hurt Saddam one bit. Why do you go along with such cruel sanctions? Oh yes, I know, your representatives speak out against them weakly and meekly in the Security Council now and then. But they never tell the world why that US wants to keep them in force.

Nor do your representatives condemn Israel for violating – repeatedly – UN orders to get its settlers out of Palestine. Why? Because the US is on the side of Israel and refuses to consider the hundreds of innocent, mostly children, which Israel's occupation forces kill as acts of terrorism?

Now Bush & Co. want to kill more Iraqis (then probably Yemenites) on the grounds that sanctions are not enough. They say that Saddam is building weapons of mass destruction, that he is a liar, a thief, a murderer.

Perhaps. But only one country has ever used weapons of mass destruction: the United States.

Bush repeats endlessly that "I don't trust Saddam Hussein." Ok. But you certainly should not trust Bush, a consummate liar who demands inspection without conditions and when he gets it says, no, no, we said disarmament. Bush has campaigned for more money for his party by claiming he wants US capitalists to be transparent, to tell all about their business machinations to the American people. Yet he and his vice-president Cheney (who ran ENRON for years) have stead-fastly refused to reveal the outcome of the investigation of their own business shenanigans. And it was Cheney who ordered his Halliburton oil company to rebuild Kuwait's oil production system and even today is one of five US companies which buy Iraq's oil cheap via the spot market. What gets me, and should shock you, is that most Americans don't give a damn if their president and vice-president are crooks.

Congressional investigations have now revealed that both the FBI and the CIA, America's two biggest organized crime syndicates, knew a hell of a lot about 9/11 before it happened; no surprise. What Americans are not told but all my contacts at Time and Newsweek tell me is that they are convinced that Bush too knew (not the date, but the manner) and kept it secret so as to use it to crush his opponents. It's easy for him to conceal his crooked deals: just cry about those who died on 9/11 and demand vengeance by bombing innocent children.

You cried for the 3000 innocent folks who died at the World Trade Center.

Did you cry for the million the US pulverized at Hiroshima and Nagasaki? Or the thousands that the US and England snuffed out at Dresden, for no military reason. Do you ever whisper to your friends that the US twice seriously considered using nuclear bombs in Vietnam.

Remember the millions who died in Cambodia? The murderer was Pol Pot, right? Yes, but who gave him the arms and the intelligence because he was a US ally fighting America's enemy, the Vietnamese – who, by the way, never got credit for putting an end to the killing fields. And what about Indonesia where the CIA helped Gen. Suharto, who had collaborated with the Japanese during World War II, murder at least a million followers of Sukarno, who had fought the Japanese with us. In 1990 the CIA finally admitted its complicity in that mass extermination (NYT, 12-07-90); did you demand retribution? When Suharto decided to wipe out East Timor independence fighters, who gave him the arms?

And who created, trained, armed and financed Latin America's death squads? The men who murdered Bishop Romero in El Salvador were trained and indoctri-nated at America's infamous School of the Americas. So were those who murdered the Jesuits in Nicaragua or raped and murdered the nuns in Salvador or murdered almost a thousand old men, women and children in the horrendous El Mozote massacre, actually supervised from helicopters by two US colonels. In 1999, the Truth Commission concluded that Guatemala's 36-year civil war, which killed more than 200,000 people, was planned, started, financed, armed, and led by the CIA, contradicting "years of official denials of torture, kidnapping and executions" (NYT, 26-02-99). Did you demand UN sanctions against the US?

During "Operation Just Cause" – what a euphemism! – US soldiers killed between four and seven thousand innocent dwellers of Panama's El Chorrillo neighborhood on the excuse that General Noriega (a CIA agent for 17 years who would not give asylum to Nicaragua's torturing "contra" scum bags) was hiding behind it when, we now know, the US had the precise information that Noriega was in refuge at the Papal Nuncio's home. Did you ignore those deaths because the US was justified in slaughtering these poor folk because they were against US domination of Panama (and were all black to boot).

Did you cry when the US found a gangster named Savimbi to do its bidding in Angola, armed and paid him, got the apartheid army of South Africa to wage war with him against his own people, murdering at least two million and maiming an estimated five million more? When Congress investigated and asked CIA chief Colby why we supported Savimbi, he answered honestly: because the Russians support the MPLA government. What if Russia supported Savimbi, a Senator asked him. Then we would support the MPLA he said. "Our goal is to suck the Russians into spending men and money," Colby replied (the Nation, 20-05-96, 10-10-97). That openness cost him his life. Colby was assassinated. The US government ruled it a suicide.

True, the 30,000 tortured and murdered by Gen Pinochet in Chile, on orders, in effect, from Secretary of State Kissinger who told the world that no country so "irresponsible" to freely vote socialist had a right to survive, did arouse a few complaints in Europe. In fact, today he faces indictments in Spain and France, hence cannot risk to dilly-dally in Torremolinos or in Juan les Pins. But he can go lecture in Oxford as the personal guest of his friend British Foreign Secretary Jack Straw.

Bush may say out loud that if you are not with us you are against us and we will destroy you. But he merely says it louder. Every American leader said the same thing, at least under his breath. And used the cold war as an excuse to fight the poor who rebelled. We Americans don't allow real dissent. After all, we are the chosen of the chosen. We're the best. And if you don't agree, it means you are an idiot, or sick. That was how the Puritans justified killing Native Americans. They were "hostiles" – the Puritans' actual word – which means not quite human, so it was ok in god's eyes to kill them all. Facts have nothing to do with what we Americans have: a god-given right to remake the world in our image (and benefit, of course). And we will do it, whether you like it or not, because god is on our side, not yours. That's why Americans repeat ad nauseum: "God Bless America."

What are those facts, concerning Iraq? To begin with, Saddam was set up to invade Kuwait which was stealing Iraq's oil by drilling at an angle. Read US Ambassador April Glaspie's interview with Saddam when he made that complaint. It was published, probably by mistake, in the New York Times' fat "Gulf War Reader." She says very clearly that the US does not take sides in Arab country disputes (after the US helped Saddam massacre thousand of Iranian and Kurdish kids by giving Saddam arms and poison gas). Then read Scott Ritter, the team leader of UNSCOM weapon inspectors in Iraq; in 1993 the NYTimes did run [23-02-93] his statement that the CIA had completely infiltrated the Iraq weapons inspection teams and in 1998, when the US ordered him out (the inspectors were never kicked out by Iraq, another lie), it did make him a hero. But now it won't run his interviews, because he says: "By 1998, we were disarming Iraq. This, of course, was the last thing the United States wanted, because if you disarm Iraq you have to lift economic sanctions."[Extra! July/August 2002])

Why does the US want to clobber Saddam? For the same reason it went after Argentina's Peron, Brazil's Vargas, Quadros and Goulart, Guatemala's Arbenz, Ecuador's Arosemena, Guyana's Cheddi Jagan, Egypt's Nasser, Iraq's Kassem, Libya's Kaddafi, Kurdistan's Barzani and Ocalan, Haiti's Aristide, Jamaica's Manley, Indonesia's Sukarno, and on and on. Whatever their politics, whatever their ideology, whatever their narcissistic motivations, they hoped to better the lot of their people by buying from the cheapest seller and selling to the highest bidder. They wanted their country to be independent. If they followed the dictates of the US they knew it would make their own oligarchy richer and their poor poorer.

Saddam may be a bastard, but he wants the same for Iraqis. That's why he sold oil to independent bidders, never the US. Even the Washington Post admits that when it said [14-09-02]:

A U.S.-led ouster of Iraqi President Saddam Hussein could open a bonanza for U.S. oil companies long banished from Iraq, scuttling oil deals between Baghdad and Russia, France and other countries and reshuffling world petroleum markets.

Oil and the bases to guarantee US access to it, that's what causes all the murders. The US even went after the president of the tiny Pacific island of Palau, ordering the president's murder because he did not want to change the country's constitution making the atoll nuclear-free. The US wanted the island because it had a potential deep-water harbor (assuming its protecting coral reef was destroyed, as it was). It doesn't matter where, today US power is unchallenged and it has upped its ante: obey, buy and sell by our criteria - or die.

And Americans are perfectly willing to kill (as long as their own don't die) The favorite slogan in America is "kick ass." Americans have never been for the underdog. That's propaganda. We hate losers. When we wanted Saddam Hussein to destroy the Iranian Revolution, and gave him the "weapons of mass destruction" (anthrax and gas), which Bush & Co. now cite as a reason to kill Iraq's children (he did not, see NYTimes 31-01-03), we covered the bumpers of our cars with signs that read "Nuke Iran." Now our bumper stickers say Nuke Iraq. And people wear an American flag lapel insignia with the same belligerent pride that Nazis wore the swastika.

Prime Minister Schroder's Justice Minister Daubler-Gmelin was perfectly correct: the Bush Administration is full of Nazis. Certainly, US Secretary of Defense Rumsfeld and his top aide, Deputy Paul Wolfowitz, and of course, Attorney General Ashcroft are modern-day Nazis. Unfortunately (but understandably), Schroder had to fire her for voicing her perspicaciousness.

Most Americans don't know what really goes on. They never heard that the US violated every single treaty it has signed, beginning with land for Native Americans up to the World Court. When that court ruled that mining Nicaragua's harbors, which caused the death of four Dutch sailors when their ship was blown up, was an act of terrorism, and fined the US a mere $400,000, President Reagan said go to hell. When our cowboy pilots flying barely a few feet off the ground to have fun, killed 20 Italians on a ski gondola and President Clinton promised compensation, Congress said go to hell (If Italy had any honor it would have closed all US bases then and there and ordered all US soldiers out of the country). When Costa Rica, which has an extradition treaty with the US indicted John Hull, a CIA contract flunky, for murder and demanded his extradition, the US said go to hell.

When US servicemen rape and kill local young women in Okinawa, or Serbia or Afghanistan, and local governments demand justice, the US says go to hell. On the contrary, the US is now demanding and, it looks, will get total immunity for American soldiers and politicians or else no help and no money. What about the World Court treaty, signed by the US, which the CIA used as an excuse to over-throw the legally elected government of Milosevic in Yugoslavia? Does that mean the US now recognizes the Court? Go to hell!

Our Congress, which by all definitions except those of our media, is made up of whores, sold out to the corporations which can guarantee their re-election by giving then enough money to buy up the airwaves for their slogans at election time ($150 million just for the gubernatorial election in New York, reported the Times on 29-09-02), is too intimidated to vote no to any of Bush's repressive measures. So they go along, and hope to get quietly reelected. And the media repeats the lies that this is a democracy where all measures are heatedly debated. They even claim that the secretive, unelected WTO organization is democratic, and those opposed to it who agitate precisely to force it to be more open are not. Example from Newsweek [3004-01]:

> In Quebec, historically left-wing forces have joined hands to oppose the strengthening of democracy in the Western Hemisphere ... the anti-globalization crowd is antidemocratic ... trying to achieve, through intimida-tion and scare tactics, what it has not been able to get through legislation ...

Since when is the WTO open to legislation? These flagrant lies by the media would be laughable, if only the American public knew what really happens in their country and in the world. Every reporter, every editor knows that there are no elections at the WTO. That all is secret. That there is no democracy in the organization. But no one in mainstream America dares to call Newsweek a liar.

So come on Europe, force Americans to learn and save the world by saying to Bush & Co.: NO!

If you don't, your way of life, your character and your well-being will change. Once the US wins total economic domination at home and abroad, you will have to privatize everything, beginning with your schools. The pride of Europe now is that its best schools are public. In the US they're the worst. Here public schools are financed by local property taxes, so they're not bad in white, rich Westchester, where each student is allotted $17,630 per year. But they are dismal in black, impoverished Bayou, Mississippi, where the total amount available per student is $60 a year. No public school there has been able to buy a science book since 1963, or a computer.

All utilities, transportation, nursing homes, health centers will have to be private, and run at a profit. The US has not yet privatized its unemployment benefit system, but it will. Its statistics are one of America's most outlandish lies. Every country of the world counts its unemployed as people looking for a job.

In the US only those who receive unemployment stipends are counted. And they get it only for 26 weeks. If you are unemployed 27 weeks, you don't count. Nor if you are a college grad looking for a job. Or a mother who has not worked for years but now must go back into the labor market. America claims around 6/7 percent unemployed. Triple it, if you want to be accurate.

And no unions, please. If you make demands, American businesses simply close down and move to Indonesia or Honduras, where the governments will kill any organizer trying to get workers a minimum wage. Or China too. As a result only about 11 percent of US workers are unionized. Most get lousy pay and no benefits. That's why US products are cheaper than European.

And that's not all. Your own representatives to the World Trade Organization, where no minutes are taken and everything is secret, have agreed to destroy the Maastricht treaty. Their most evil decision: to privatize social security. Everything must run at a profit, like in the US, the only country in the world where there is no form of national health. No less than 40 percent of Americans have no health benefits at all. The private companies that run them in the US are called Health Management Organizations, better known as HMOs. They charge huge sums to belong and give their top brass millions and millions of dollars in salaries, benefits and bonuses. But if too many old folks require their services, they simply dump them from membership rolls. No one corporate system is more evil, no HMO officers greedier, no so-called "service" more vicious. But that's what you'll get when the US wins. And since Signa or Blue Cross/Shield or Oxford health organizations will buy up yours "mutuels" once you are privatized, you'll suffer like we suffer: 60 percent of Americans cannot afford preventive medicine or cancer check-ups or prescription drugs.

That's only the beginning. No more vacations guaranteed by law: the US doesn't have any (although for the time being most companies allow employees two weeks off after a year of work). No more paid pregnancy leave. No more free dental care or free eye exams or glasses. No more free child care. The poor are just plain lazy; they deserve to be poor, said Reagan. Republicans believe that too. So do many democrats. Bush certainly believes it.

Do you really want to be like America? A fundamentalist country where doctors who perform abortions are murdered on the grounds that they are murderers! And the murderers get away with it because Bush, Ashcroft & Co are all against abortions, despite the fact that abortion is legal in America.

Is America the most alienated country in the world? Some 70 percent are armed, and they will shoot you if you make a mistake, like the hapless Japanese student going to a Halloween party in Texas, killed by a red-neck because the kid stepped

on the yokel's property. Absolutely justified, ruled the court. No wonder that every year more than 20,000 Americans are shot dead.

So Europeans, save the world all from American domination: kick the US out of NATO. Close all US bases. (Remember de Gaulle: "No country is free if it has a foreign base on its soil"). The US wants to dominate NATO as another way of dominating trade, what you buy and what you sell. De Gaulle knew that. He did not trust the US or England ("You are an air-craft carrier for American goods," he told Prime Minister McMillan in February 1963). That's why he did not want England in the common market. He was double-crossed by Pompidou. When General Il Gallois, head of the Force de Frappe, came to have lunch with top editors at Newsweek, I asked him in French which way the missiles were pointing. He laughed and made a gesture with his hands, indicating both ways. De Gaulle knew what the US was all about.

For every Euro or dollar European employers pay a worker, they pay 48 cents to the government for its social services, and the vast majority do not complain because those service are good. In America, US employers pay 7 cents (and the services are terrible). So tax every American product, its cars, its wheat, its movies, its McDonalds, everything, 41 cents on the dollar. If the US retaliates by taxing your goods, retaliate even more, go ahead, tax US products 100, 200, 500 percent. The only area of the world where the US has a positive balance of trade is Europe. You don't need America. America needs you.

For the sake of humanity, please resist US adventures. You want to "democratize" Iraq? Trade with Iraq, don't help the US murder its innocent people – just so the US can get its oil and gas, and control the whole region. You may be next.

CHAPTER TWENTY-ONE

THE END OF OUR CONSTITUTION?

Rule of Law no longer exists in the US. It was totally destroyed on September 8, 1974. Since then, every American has known that punishment for an illegal deed depends on one's contacts. "It's who you know stupid."

Let us hope that President Barack Obama will change that, and bring us back into ethical civilization. To do so, however, he would have to indict the whole administration of George W. Bush, and certainly Vice President Cheney and former Attorney General Alberto Gonzalez and their staff, for crimes against humanity. But Congress and especially the US Supreme Court, by its usual 5–4 decisions, will not permit him from doing so. Hence, our chances of regaining our coveted Rule of Law is extremely meek.

Of course, the rich gangsters, whether CEOs of Bechtel, Enron, Halliburton, AIG, or any other major corporation, or the country's top bureaucrats, may act so outrageously that they may eventually spend time in jail, maybe, though certainly not presidents, vice-presidents or CIA heads who lie, cheat and violate so many laws that thousands, perhaps millions, of innocents are murdered all over the world every year. The disgusting corporate owners who give themselves millions in bail-out parachutes, enjoy very legally the good life, made from the pensions of hundreds of thousands of their retirees, who, after 30 years of loyal work, have to beg to survive.

But as we saw so vividly on television when Hurricane Katrina's devastating torrents wiped out New Orleans' shabby ghettos, the poor surviving black who lived there because they could not afford the white-owned high ground and who then had to steal food because their families were hungry, or more shocking to the white middleclass which escaped in their fancy cars, dared to steal a TV set – oh my god, property! – risked being killed by a vicious order issued to both local and military policemen: "shoot to kill." That's rule of law today, as re-defined by a bastardized Constitution.

Former Washington Post reporter Carl Bernstein said that "Watergate" was "not about a break-in. It was about a criminal conspiracy to undermine the Constitution by the President of the United States." But the Constitution has been undermined, crumpled, literally for centuries. And by and large, the US Supreme Court has either approved or remained silent. Some such cases are classics, such as when the court approved President Lincoln's order to blockade Southern ports *before* the declaration of war, or when it okayed the constitutionality under the War Powers Act of prohibiting liquor as detrimental to the nation's goal of raising enlistment for World War I – in 1919, *after* the war had ended (and that great ruling was pushed by famed liberal Justice Louis Brandeis).

More seriously, the court did not object to President Truman's "police action" invasion of Korea, or President Kennedy's "advisers" invasion of Vietnam or President Johnson's 1965 invasion of the Dominican Republic or President Reagan's similar act in Grenada, both on the grounds, totally fabricated, of saving US lives. The Supreme Court had three chances to rule on the validity of the War on Vietnam, and refused to issue an opinion. Nor, of course, will this court ever consider the possibility that "preventive war," as advocated today by the power-madmen in Washington, is totally in violation of the spirit of the constitution even if Congress gave and continues to give those madmen the legal tools with which to wage it.

More recently, the court has even destroyed a basic right of capitalist America, or rather the rights of small capitalists: it ruled that under the law of "eminent domain," passed by Congress to facilitate states wanting to build highways or bridges, a big corporation had the right to seize the property of small land or building owners if the result might create more jobs and/or more tax revenue. So now no home is safe in America from capitalist predators.

The most outrageous violation of the Constitution, so far, was carried out by a 5 to 4 decision of the Supreme Court in the 2000 election. True, Democratic Party candidate Al Gore's lawyers were stupid; instead of demanding a recall of all of the state of Florida, which we now know had elected him by over 50,000, he knit-picked a few counties, giving the Republicans a chance to say, yeah, but what about that other county. Still, in that case, the court validated a coup-d'etat, and no one moved. For the blacks, the poor, the exploited and the young, it just didn't matter any more; they knew there was no rule of law in America.

Aided by a "convenient" 9/11, the Bush clique claimed that national security demanded a continuous effort against terrorism, and used that demand to crush meaningful dissent in America. The Supreme Court under its new chief, John Roberts, approved, allowing the US to edge ever closer to a vicious fascist dictatorship.

Academia also approved. American best-selling historians, such as David McCullough, Joseph J. Ellis, Richard Brookhiser, Ron Chernow and Walter Isaacson, have long been extremely adept at re-writing US history so as to make it fit with what the average American has been taught since kindergarten. As Daniel Lazare meticulously documented in his *The Velvet Coup: The Constitution, the Supreme Court, and the Decline of American Democracy*, the US Constitution is used to put dissenters in jail or, as in the case of the Rosenbergs, to execute them, not to curtail the power or programs of presidents. It has been used to tell each child, that America's forefathers were noble, gentle and magnanimous.

It has been done *ad infinitum*. Every schoolboy believes, for example, that the American Revolution was waged by folks fed-up with exorbitant taxes imposed by nasty England. Fact is, as New York Times Book Review editor Barry Gewen wrote recently: "It was the English who were shouldering the real burden, paying taxes on everything from property to beer, from soap to candles, tobacco, paper, leather and beeswax." Even the infamous tea-tax, which we were all told started the revolution, was paid mostly by the British at home. As for America's heroes, they were mostly despicable, selfish, entrepreneurs. John Hancock, for example, was a millionaire smuggler and a thief, who with other "great founding fathers," such as the Adams, organized and paid an army of destitutes to toss the tea-crates overboard. Suffice to mention here just one "hero or heroes": George Washington. He refused to give blacks their freedom if they fought against England because he planned to sell off a few of his own. His own records indicate, as Henry Wiencek carefully documented in his *An Imperfect God: George Washington, His Slaves, and the Creation of America*, that Washington's slaves were miserably clothed, threatened with whippings, and pursued by dogs. But then most landowners, the backbone of the new Republic, were just as vicious – against blacks or whites, which explains why poor or middle farmers fought with England, not the colonists.

History must be used, say those historians heralded by both academia and the media, to praise America, and encourage its citizens to follow their leader – to hell if need be. As McCullough himself unashamedly said recently at a conference at Hillsdale College, an ultra-right-wing private school in Michigan: "We have to value what our forebears – and not just in the eighteenth century, but our own parents and grandparents – did for us, or we're not going to take it very seriously, and it can slip away." In other words, the task of history is to convince Americans that invading Vietnam and slaughtering 2,000,000 innocents or invading Iraq and killing 200,000 in two years (a hundred times more than Saddam Hussein managed to do in 30), or invading Afghanistan to crush Taliban after helping them come to power, or creating military death squads to murder US critics in Haiti, El Salvador, Guatemala, Chile, Argentina, Peru, Ecuador, Brazil, Uruguay, Paraguay, indeed wherever local folks managed to establish a fledging yes but start-up, democracy, is the real goal. It is, as one US official put it after every native on the island of Diego Garcia had been deported to misery and death in strange lands so the US could set up a base there, an "indispensable platform for policing the world."

So the US Constitution has become a farce, but the historians who control our value system, and the media which follows their lead, know how to praise it and fool most ordinary folks who are too exploited to read for themselves. But neither the government nor the historians nor the media can fool the people of America into believing that they are governed by rule of law. Not just because they saw the racist fabric of their government during Katrina's aftermath. Not just because they have learned that the rebuilding of New Orleans is planned as one huge swindle by developers, oil corporations, and the major banks. Not just because they notice, little by little, that it is always the same Washington insiders who make profits out of war or disasters, like Vice-President Cheney's Halliburton company getting all those no-bid contracts in Iraq and Louisiana.

The average American expects all that. He and she got the insight on September 8, 1974, a month after Nixon resigned as president. That's when un-elected president, Gerald Ford, pardoned Nixon not just for what we all knew he did as a gangster during his time in the White House but also for what we don't know he did. Could he have stolen $3 billion and filtered them into Swiss bank accounts in the name of an international murderer named Henry Kissinger? Could he have murdered a mistress, cut her up in tiny pieces and flushed her down the toilet? Whatever. Ford pardoned him for it all. To the near-unanimous approval of Congress, most judges, historians, criminologists, media editors, and probably every corporate

CEO whose goal is stability so as to make more money, Ford proclaimed (decree #4311) that he had granted " ... pursuant to the pardon power conferred upon me by Article II, Section 2, of the Constitution, ... a full, free, and absolute pardon unto Richard Nixon for all offenses against the United States which he, Richard Nixon, has committed or may have committed or taken part ..."

"May have committed or taken part!"

Imagine the respect the world would have had for the US if it had sent "I am not a crook" Nixon to jail? Imagine how every petty thief might have reacted?

After the stifling Fifties, America's youth already knew just what a closed society their country had become. At first it was their schools which bugged them, institutions, they quickly realized, which aimed at turning them into dehumanizing cogs in the system. Where was truth, where was justice, where was respect for one's fellow human being in what they were being taught in High School or College?

Thus, by the end of the Nineteen Fifties, a few High School seniors and College students began to say out loud what a great many felt: that America was a closed society based on only one value–money. They resented that their future was to be geared to getting it, and that to do so they would have to compete not only in the business world, but in universities, and against each other.

To "make it" in America, complained the new generation, we will have to become "experts," segregated, pigeon-holed, divorced from one another, unable to relate except through established institutions, totally dehumanized. For how else could a sociologist deal "objectively" with types? A political scientist predict behavior? A psychologist concoct stimuli for desired responses? Only if people are coerced or conditioned into living with their peer-group in their peer-places, accumulating peer-things on their peer-salaries, influenced by peer-produced television peer-programs, can pollsters predict their voting pattern, can admen channel their lust, can presidents appeal to their "patriotism" to spend 60 percent of the country's budget to defend us against non-existent enemies while increasing the power and benefits, as President Eisenhower warned the world on his departure from the White House, of the military-industrial complex – which in turn finances the elections, including that of the president.

In 1959, some of these young folk decided to try to stop their dehumanization and converged to Ann Arbor, Michigan, where they launched, in 1960, Students for a Democratic Society (SDS), adopting, two years later, the Port Huron Statement, written mostly by a 22-year-old former student named Tom Hayden. The Statement not only eloquently condemned America's political system for fostering racism, materialism, militarism and poverty, but also demanded the establishment of a new kind of "participatory democracy" wherein every citizen would share in the social decisions that directly affected his or her life.

At first, SDS focused on voter registration drives and civil rights in the South and in the ghettos of the North. But during the 1964 Free Speech Movement (FSM) launched by a philosophy junior at the University of California at Berkeley named Mario Savio, the new generation took on the bastion of corporativism in America's educational institutions, especially at its elite schools. "There is a time when the operation of the machine becomes so odious, makes you so sick," Savio told hundreds of Berkeley students, "that you've got to put your bodies upon the gears and upon the wheels, upon the levers, upon all the apparatus, and you've got to make it stop." The university reacted by arresting over 500 FSM peaceful demonstrators, causing a strike by more than 70 percent of the student body. Without access to the media, the new movement spread like wild-fire thanks mostly to its music (by Country Joe and the Fish, MC5, the Loving Spoonful, Bob Dylan, and especially The Doors and Jimi Hendrix) and the widening war in Vietnam. By the end of 1965, that war, as seen on TV, became repugnant to more and more of the youth. Scenes of US planes napalming poor peasants, beating and shooting suspected Viet Congs, who, every student knew, contrary to the propaganda spewed by the media, were fighting for a free independent nation.

Then, in January 1966, President Johnson announced an end of student deferments from the draft. Now, the movement's moral and political revulsion at the American ruling elite's crass materialism became personal as well: the students did not want to go fight and die in Vietnam. Thanks to the wide availability of birth-control pills, to the San Francisco's "diggers" whose "store" offered free everything, to the massive repressions carried out by every police force in America, to Martin Luther King Jr.'s linking racist subjugation in America with the war in Vietnam, and to the tremendous organizational skills of the Black Panthers in Oakland, California, resistance to the war, to racism and now to sexism and the characterization of women as second class citizens, to the established racial codes and hypocrisies, spread nation-wide. By the Fall of 1967, SDS listed over half a million members, anti-draft calls elicited huge rallies in no less than 200 cities, and over a million marched on the UN and on the Pentagon.

Then, tragedy struck. On April 4, 1968, while talking to aides on the balcony of the Lorraine Motel in Memphis, Mississippi, where he had gone to help the striking sanitation workers, who labored for incredibly low wages and disgusting conditions, Martin Luther King Jr. was shot and killed. By nightfall, more than 100 US cities were on fire and every black community vented its rage. But the white movement stayed home, watching on TV. The black-white alliance, created at Oakland stop-the-draft week in October 1967 and at the seizure of San Francisco State College on December 6th by students opposed to the war and racism, was destroyed.

More important, the possibility of a genuine humanizing revolution was also lost. For, is it possible that had the whites joined the blacks in those 100 cities, the National Guardsmen, many of them poor students trying to earn a few bucks, might, just might, have refused to fire on the black-white militants controlling their cities? After all, six days before the Shah of Iran fell because his army refused to fire on a massive demonstration in Tehran, the CIA had insisted that the Shah was much too popular and his army much too well organized for any possible over-throw. Could this be true in the new Babylon as well?

Had it succeeded in America, what would it have accomplished? Genuine participatory democracy? An end to exploitation? Free health care for all? Peace in the world? We'll never know. Some SDSers, black organizers and anti-war or counter-culture militants tried to continue the momentum. Abbie Hoffman and Jerry Rubin's Yippies (Youth International Party) sponsored various events, and joined forces with other radicals and the Black Panthers to demonstrate against the Democratic Party's convention in Chicago in 1968. Police repression, denounced as a gestapo by Massachusetts governor Abraham Ribicoff from the Convention podium, led to the "days of rage" and the militant Weather Organization to go underground.

But America's extreme right-wingers, neo-cons and neo-fascists slowly regained the streets, the schools, and all the board rooms. The FBI and the Oakland police decimated the Panthers, killing 28. Chicago Mayor Richard Daley's police drugged then murdered the city's brilliant (and beloved by all militants) young Panther leaders Fred Hampton and Mark Clark. Finally, in May 1970 four white students peacefully demonstrating against complicity in the war by their university, Kent State, were shot and killed by Ohio's National Guard. One week later, police fired into a woman's dorm at Jackson State University in Mississippi, killing two black students.

Fear prevailed. A few weeks later, at dinner in a Greenwich Village outdoor cafe, Jerry Rubin told this author, who had been a very close friend, "I'm going to quit. They've always been able to kill blacks. But now, Kent State shows they're willing to kill whites to keep their power. I don't want to die." Convinced that America is ordained by providence to rule the world, those Christian fundamentalists and their neo-fascist allies who gave the orders to kill, whether in Vietnam, Latin America, Kent State, Oakland, Jackson State, Grenada, and now Afghanistan and Iraq, have no compulsion to stop. Their goal is the whole world. To do that they have to stop dissent at home. America is already an armed camp. Cops and soldiers sporting machine guns guard every station of travel. To enter even a three-story ear-and-throat hospital in Manhattan, one must produce a "picture ID," as if a real terrorist wouldn't have one. By law (rule of law?) to criticize US foreign policy is now "tantamount to aiding and abetting terrorism," and, as CBS documented two years ago in its Sixty Minutes program, the FBI stated categorically that to criticize US policy towards Israel is to advocate treason. Armed with a so-called "Patriots Act" the fundamentalists have already shredded America's Bill of Rights. Now they are in the process of exterminating anyone all over the globe who does not recognize them as masters.

For those who had hoped to change America by chanting "Make Love, Not War," or "Burn Cards, Not People," for those who were beaten, jailed, framed by police but still had faith in the system, there seemed to be no hope left by 1974. The movement felt defeated. Most of its stalwarts gave up. They adapted, became, as we used to say of petty collaborationists during World War II, "good germans." Can the first black man elected to live in a white house built completely by black slaves change that? (New York, December 2008).

NOTES

1   Jean-Paul Sartre (1905–1980): French existentialist philosopher, novelist, playwright, refused the 1964 Nobel Prize for Literature.
2   Sephardic Jews are members of the Jewish Diaspora with roots in the Iberian Peninsula (Spain and Portugal).
3   Simone de Beauvoir (1908–1986): French author and philosopher whose works include 1949's *The Second Sex*, an important document in the Feminist Movement.
4   Diego Rodríguez de Silva y Velázquez (1599–1660): Spanish painter in the court of King Philip IV.
5   Opened in 1819, the Museo del Prado is located in Madrid, Spain.
6   And is today, Tito tells me, a venereal disease clinic.
7   Andre Breton (1896–1966): French author and considered main founder of surrealism; Marc Chagall (1887–1985): Russian-Belarusian-French painter whose paintings of a violinist perched atop a peaked roof inspired the title of the musical *Fiddler on the Roof*; Giacometti (1901–1966): Swiss sculptor and painter.
8   Alban Maria Johannes Berg (1885–1935): Austrian composer.
9   Ernst Cassirer (1874–1945): German Jewish philosopher; Edmund Gustav Albrecht Husserl (1859–1938): philosopher considered father of phenomenology.
10 Hélène de Beauvoir (1910–2001): French painter.
11 Andre Malraux (1901–1976): French writer who fought for the Republican cause in the Spanish Civil War.
12 Albert Camus (1913–1960): French author and philosopher.
13 Olga Kosakiewicz was one of de Beuvoir's students who wound up marrying Jacques-Laurent Bost, one of de Beuvoir's former lovers.
14 Born in 1927, as a young woman Greco fought in the French Resistance against the Nazi occupation and grew up to be a singer.
15 The pied-noirs, or "black-feet," were the French colonists in Algeria.
16 The Jewish-American communists Ethel and Julius Rosenberg are the only citizens of the United States to be executed for espionage, meeting their end in the electric chair in 1953.
17 Rafael Trujillo (1891–1961) was dictator of the Dominican Republic from 1930 until he was assassinated.
18 The Office of Strategic Services was the forerunner of the American CIA.
19 William Joseph Donovan (1883–1959) headed the OSS during World War 2 and is considered the father of the CIA.
20 Abraham Fortas (1910–1982) went on to be a US Supreme Court Associate Justice until the revelation that he had agreed to accept $20,000 annually from a Wall Street financier's foundation led to his resignation.
21 *Time, Fortune, Sports Illustrated*, and *Life* are some of the publications which anti-communist Henry Luce (1898–1967) founded.
22 Though he was trained as a medical doctor, Ernesto 'Che' Guevara (1928–1967) is best known for his role in the Cuban Revolution. Incidentally, Che was in Guatemala in 1954 when the United States overthrew the democratically-elected Arbenz government at the behest of United Fruit, an event that hardened his revolutionary anti-imperialistic commitment.
23 Born in 1934, Ralph Nader first rose to prominence as a consumer safety activist and as of late as a presidential candidate.
24 The Church Committee, or United States Senate Select Committee to Study Governmental Operations with Respect to Intelligence Activities, chaired by Senator Frank Church in 1975, helped bring to light for the American public their government's attempts to assassinate foreign leaders.
25 John "Handsome Johnny" Roselli (1905–1976) was a Chicago gangster who worked with the CIA in the 1960s to try and kill Fidel Castro.
26 The crafty Sisyphus was condemned by the Greek gods to roll an enormous stone up a hill, only to always have it roll back down and have to resume his task.

27 During the Cold War, Americans suspected of being sympathetic to the ideas of communism or the Soviet Union found it impossible to work because they were black-listed.

28 Tens of thousands of protestors took to the streets of Seattle, Washington in 1999 to protest the World Trade Organization Ministerial Conference.

29 Abbot Howard Hoffman (1936–1989) was a political activist who helped to start the Youth International Party (the "Yippies"). He was one of the Chicago Seven tried for their actions at the 1968 Democratic National Convention, represented by Leonard Weinglass and William Kunstler.

30 Born in 1948, Levy is a French journalist and public intellectual.

31 Daniel Pearl (1963–2002) was an American journalist working for the Wall Street Journal when he was captured and beheaded in Pakistan.

32 Born in the early 1870s, Rosa Luxemburg was executed on order of the commander of the right-wing Freikorps Garde-Kavallerie-Schützendivision in 1919, which though created by the socialist prime minister turned out to become the Nazi Gestapo with the rise of Hitler.

33 When Soviet sailors, soldiers and civilians, who had started the Russian revolution, rose up against the totalitarian Russian Soviet Federative Socialist Republic in 1921 the Red Army suppressed the rebellion.

34 Anarchist collectives in the Aragon and Catalonia regions of Spain were crushed by the Communists during the Civil War.

35 Huey Newton (1942–1989) was one of the founders of the Black Panther Party for Self Defense.

36 Born in 1936, Bobby Seale co-founded the Black Panther Party with Huey Newton. Seale was one of the original Chicago 8 arrested and tried for their role in protests at the 1968 Democratic National Convention in Chicago. Following his outbursts in court, Seale's case was separated from that of his fellow co-defendants and the Chicago Eight became the Chicago Seven.

37 New York University is a private university located in Manhattan. In 2008, a year's undergraduate tuition at NYU was $37,372.

38 Queens College is a university in the City University of New York's system and widely considered the "jewel of the CUNY system." Yearly tuition for New York State residents is $4,000.

39 Born and raised in Wales, Bertrand Arthur William Russell (1872–1970) was a British philosopher, mathematician, and pacifist.

40 The United States' Armed Forces' Reserve Officers' Training Corps (ROTC) is a college-based officer-commissioning program offered as a college elective in the United States.

41 From 1962 through 1975, the American political and literary magazine Ramparts was published.

42 Earning her lawyer's degree from Brooklyn Law School, Beverly Axelrod represented activists throughout the 1960s and 70s. She died in 2002.

43 Charles Garry was a civil rights attorney who died in 1991.

44 The Haight, a district in San Francisco, California, was a center of hippie culture.

45 Eldridge Cleaver (1935–1998) was a member of the Black Panther Party who later renounced the organization. Charged with attempted murder of a police officer, Cleaver fled the United States for Algeria where he placed Timothy Leary under revolutionary arrest for being a counter-revolutionary.

46 Norman Mailer (1923–2007), two-time Pulitzer Prize winner, was an American writer and one of the founders of *The Village Voice*, an alternative newspaper in New York City.

47 Herbert Marcuse (1898–1979) was a German philosopher and member of the Frankfurt School.

48 Ralph Milliband (1924–1994), Marxist political theorist, fathered two sons who have gone on to serve in the British government.

49 America's Hells Angels were hired to provide security by the Rolling Stones in 1969 at the Altamont Speedway Free Festival in California. Four deaths ensued during the show, including one young man who pulled a gun on the Hells Angels and was stabbed to death.

50 Gilles Deleuze (1925–1995) and Pierre-Felix Guatarri (1930–1992) were French philosophers.

51 French philosopher Michel Foucault was born in 1926 and died of an AIDS-related illness in 1994.

52 Edward Said (1935–2003) was an outspoken advocate of Palestinian rights.

53 One of Franz Fanon's (1925–1961) best known works is *The Wretched of the Earth*.

54 Born in 1917, Eric John Ernest Hobsbawm was a Marxist historian.

55 Christopher Hill (1912–2003) was an English Marxist historian.

56 Since 1983 Stanley Aronowitz has taught at the City University of New York's Graduate Center.

57 Guggenheim Fellowships are monetary grants that awardees (fellows) are allowed to spend as they see fit.

58 The Victoria Cross is the highest military decoration for valor awarded by the British crown.

[59] The Quakers (Religious Society of Friends) is a Christian sect started in the United Kingdom in the 17th century.

[60] The May Day holiday is International Workers' Day, a celebration of the labor movement's historic achievements. May Day is not celebrated in the United States, where its working class roots have been largely forgotten by a public that associates it with a pagan celebration.

[61] In American high school and college sports, the varsity team is the athletic team that represents the school in competition against other athletic teams. Members of the varsity team are awarded "varsity letters" that are usually sewn on letterman jackets.

[62] Dorothy Day's (1887–1980) social activism was fueled by her Christianity and anarchism. She co-founded the Catholic Worker Movement in 1933.

[63] A missionary movement founded in the 1930s, Friendship House relied on public education programs to fight for social justice.

[64] One of American socialist Michael Harrington's (1928–1989) best known books is *The Other America: Poverty in the United States*.

[65] Invented by Napoleon I in 1808, the French baccalaureate is the diploma necessary to pursue university studies at the end of lycee (high school).

[66] Leaving the Republican Party to join the American Labor Party, Vito Marcantonio (1902–1954) was sympathetic to labor unions and the socialist and communist parties.

[67] The second American Labor Party was founded in New York in 1936 by labor leaders and members of the Socialist Party; defunct since 1956.

[68] A co-ed, college preparatory high school, the Putney School is nestled in the foothills of Vermont's Green Mountains. The school offers its 225 students a progressive education focusing on the whole child and not just academics.

[69] Though New York city's mass transit system is known for its subways, Gerassi is referring to the former elevated line traversing the boroughs of Manhattan and Queens via the Queensboro Bridge.

[70] Officially known as the "Joint Legislative Committee to Investigate the Educational System of the State of New York", the Rapp-Coudert Committee was the New York State legislature's anti-Communist organization.

[71] In the context of the Cold War era, a fellow traveler was someone who sympathized with the Soviet Union and/or communism.

[72] When American composer Leon Botstein became president of Franconia College at age 23, he was the youngest president of a university ever. Since 1975, Botstein has been president of Bard.

[73] The liquor Tito is referring to is Sherry, made in and around the town of Jerez, Spain.

[74] Former Israeli Prime Minister and military leader, Ariel Sharon was born in 1928 and was forced to retire from politics after a stroke in 2006 left him in what is described as a vegetative state.

[75] One proposed answer to the Israeli-Palestinian conflict, the two state solution would erect a Jewish state and an Arab state in Palestine.

[76] When five Arab countries attacked Israel shortly after its founding in 1948, over 700,000 Palestinians were forced to abandon their land by a victorious Israel.

[77] The "Israeli lobby book" Tito is referring to is John Mearsheimer and Stephen Walt's The Israel Lobby and US Foreign Policy (Farrar, Straus, & Giroux, 2007).

[78] A key figure in the Scientific Revolution, Frenchman Rene Descartes argued in favor of mind-body dualism. *Tabula rasa* refers to his belief that human beings were born "blank slates" with no innate mental intelligence.

[79] Canadian journalist and anchorman of ABC's World News Tonight, Peter Jennings (1938–2005) was the youngest-ever US news anchor when ABC hired him in 1956.

[80] Following World War II, Berlin was partitioned into four military occupation zones administered by the Americans, French, British, and Soviets.

[81] One of the largest ecological disasters in human history, the Exxon Valdez oil spill in 1989 dumped nearly 11 million gallons of crude oil into Prince William Sound in Alaska.

[82] Single-payer universal health insurance does not mean that the patient herself bears responsibility for all payment. Often attacked by ideological opponents as a form of socialism, single-payer systems are run by the government and usually provide cradle to grave coverage for patients.

[83] The Columbia Spectator is Columbia University's undergraduate daily student newspaper, founded in 1877.

[84] Scabs is the derogatory term for workers brought in to replace striking union labor.

85 Pulitzer Prize winner Max Frankel (born 1930) was executive editor at the New York Times and worked for that publication for fifty years.

86 A stringer is a freelance journalist who makes ongoing contributions to a publication but is paid for each piece rather than receiving a salary.

87 Liberation Magazine was founded by A.J. Muste.

88 Naturalized American citizen, socialist Abraham Johannes Muste (1885–1967) was active in the civil rights, labor and pacifist movements.

89 The US Special Forces wear green berets.

90 An independent weekly newspaper, Army Times traces its current ownership to Gannett Company, the largest US newspaper publisher.

91 An autobiography of Richard Wright, *Black Boy* discusses Wright's youth in the American south.

92 24th president of Harvard, Nathan Pusey's (1907–2001) fight against McCarthyism began with Pusey's tenure as president of Lawrence College, located in Senator Joseph McCarthy's hometown of Appleton, Wisconsin.

93 Edward Murrow's (1908–1965) 1950s television show, See It Now, criticized Joseph McCarthy. Parent-network CBS refused to allow its logo on the show and also refused to provide any funds for the episode's publicity.

94 The Panoras Gallery is located in New York City.

95 When Alexander Eliot (born 1919) told his dad he did not want to go to Harvard, his father (who'd attended Harvard and started the Socialist Club while there) replied, "I wouldn't want you to attend a university whose President Lowell helped to condemn Sacco and Vanzetti." Art editor at *Time Magazine* for fifteen years, Eliot's fifteen books include 1957's *Three Hundred Years of American Painting*.

96 Often referred to as the "painter of the people," Andrew Wyeth was born in 1917. A major figure in the abstract expressionist movement, artist Jackson Pollock (1912–1956) earned his nickname "Jack the Dripper" from Time Magazine for his technique of placing his canvas on the floor and pouring paint on it.

97 When Fidel Castro came to power in Cuba, members of dictator Batista's government were put on public trial and executed.

98 Henry Luce's father and brother were both missionaries; Henry himself was born in China.

99 Herbert Matthews (1900–1977), *New York Times* reporter and editorialist, interviewed Fidel Castro in the Sierra Maestra Mountains during the Cuban Revolution.

100 Salvador Allende (1908–1973) was president of Chile until his death during a coup.

101 Argentine investigative journalist Rodolfo Walsch was "disappeared" in 1977. Born in 1927, Columbian Gabriel Garcia Marques is best known for his novels. Mexican writer Carlos Fuentes Macias was born in 1928.

102 Trained by Fidel Castro, Columbian Fabio Vasquez was one of the founders of the revolutionary ELN. Manuel Marulanda (1930–2008), nicknamed "Sure shot" (Tiro Fijo) by his comrades, was a Columbian revolutionary and founder of the Columbian revolutionary organization FARC.

103 Born in New York City in 1913, Lincoln Gordon was a United States Ambassador to Brazil and wrote 2001's *Brazil's Second Chance: En Route Toward the First World*.

104 The University of Washington Press Reissued Gerassi's 1965 *The Boys of Boise* in 2001.

105 In film and law, a seller options her work when she signs a contract that allows–but does not obligate–a potential buyer to purchase an item, such as a film, within a certain amount of time.

106 Famed US Civil Rights attorney Leonard Weinglass's clients have included Kathy Boudin, the Chicago Seven, Jane Fonda, and Mumia Abu Jamal, among others.

107 Co-owner of an apple orchard in east Kentucky, Frank Browning has authored or co-authored six books and was a staff reporter for National Public Radio.

108 Gerassi is referring to the French television version of the French literary magazine, Lire, founded by Bernard Pivot and Jean-Louis Servan-Schreiber in 1975.

109 Francesco ("Costello") Castiglia (1891–1973) was one of the most powerful Mafia bosses in the United States, leading the Luciano crime family. Bettors in the illegal numbers game wager money on the outcomes of three and four digit lottery drawings.

110 In May, 1970, National Guardsmen opened fire on Vietnam war protestors, killing four students at Kent State University.

111 A social activist in his early life, Jerry Rubin (1938–1994) went on to become a successful businessman.

INDEX

Breinigsville, PA USA
23 August 2009
222744BV00001B/2/P